A Journal of the American Civil War

Managing Editor:
Mark A. Snell

Director, George Tyler Moore Center for the Study of the Civil War
Shepherd College, Shepherdstown, West Virginia

VOLUME FIVE   NUMBER FOUR

Published quarterly by Savas Publishing Company

Subscription and General Information

Civil War Regiments is published quarterly by Savas Publishing Company, 1475 South Bascom Avenue, Suite 204, Campbell, CA 95008. Executive Editor/Publisher: Theodore P. Savas. Voice: 408.879.9073; Fax: 408.879.9327; E-mail: MHBooks@aol.com. Managing Editor: Mark A. Snell, George Tyler Moore Center for the Study of the Civil War, 136 W. German Street, Shepherdstown, WV 25443. Voice: 304.876.5429; Fax: 304.876.5079.

DISTRIBUTION: Trade distribution is handled by Peter Rossi at Stackpole Books, 5067 Ritter Road, Mechanicsburg, PA 17055-6921. Voice: 1-800-732-3669; Fax: 1-717-976-0412.

SUBSCRIPTIONS: $29.95/year, ppd (four books), individual and institutional. Back issues may be ordered from the publisher. Write to: Back Issues: CWR, 1475 South Bascom, Suite 204, Campbell, CA 95008, or call 1-800-848-6585, for pricing information, contents and availability. Please specify the volume and issue number when placing your order. Prepayment with check, money order, or MC/V is required. Two hundred and fifty signed and numbered four-issue Collector's Sets for the premier volume were printed. Cost is $40.00 ppd. Inquire as to availability. FOREIGN ORDERS: Subscriptions: $35.95/year, including surface delivery. Payment in United States currency only or MC/V. Allow eight to twelve weeks for delivery.

MANUSCRIPTS AND CORRESPONDENCE: We welcome manuscript inquiries. For author's guidelines, send a self-addressed, double-stamped business envelope to: Editor, *Civil War Regiments*, 136 W. German Street, Shepherdstown, WV 25443. Include a brief description of your proposed topic and the sources to be utilized. No unsolicited submissions will be returned without proper postage. Book review inquiries should be directed to Dr. Archie McDonald, Book Review Editor, Stephen F. Austin University, Department of History, P.O. Box 6223, SFA Station, Nacogdoches, Texas 75962-6223. (409) 468-2407. Enclose a SASE if requesting a reply.

Thanks to your support, *Civil War Regiments* has made a number of donations to Civil War-related preservation organizations. Some of the recipients of these donations are listed below:

ASSOCIATION FOR THE PRESERVATION OF CIVIL WAR SITES (LIFE MEMBER)

RICHARD B. GARNETT MEMORIAL, HOLLYWOOD CEMETERY

HERITAGEPAC / CIVIL WAR ROUND TABLE ASSOCIATES

SAVE HISTORIC ANTIETAM FOUNDATION / TURNER ASHBY HOUSE, PORT REPUBLIC, VA

THE COKER HOUSE RESTORATION PROJECT, JACKSON, MS CWRT

AMERICAN BLUE & GRAY ASSOCIATION

APCWS 1993 MALVERN HILL/GLENDALE CAMPAIGN

Cover art: "Jackson at Manassas,"
courtesy of Keith Rocco, Tradition Studios, Woodstock, VA

Civil War Regiments, Vol. 5, No. 4, Copyright 1997
by Savas Publishing Company
ISBN 1-882810-55-4

GEORGE TYLER MOORE
CENTER FOR THE STUDY OF THE
CIVIL WAR

CONTRIBUTORS:

Mark Bell is a longtime student of the Civil War and a full-time graduate student in the history program at Shippensburg (Pennsylvania) State University. He received his undergraduate degree in history from the same institution, and has served as a summer intern at Shepherd College's George Tyler Moore Center for the Study of the Civil War. This article is Mark's first published work.

Jeffrey Patrick is currently an interpretive specialist and historian at Wilson's Creek National Battlefield, in Republic, Missouri. His specialty is Missouri's role in the American Civil War.

Gregory D. Bova, a retired Air Force captain, has served in operations in Haiti, the Middle East and Bosnia. He is currently working for BDM Corporation at Fort Hachuca, Arizona, performing Command and Control test analysis. Greg's interest in Ship Island began when he was stationed at Keesler AFB in Biloxi, Mississippi, where he had an opportunity to study the actions along the gulf coast.

Brian C. Pohanka is a free-lance writer and the author of numerous Civil War publications. He has assisted as an historical consultant on several movie projects and is on the Board of Editorial Advisors for *Civil War Regiments*.

John Hennessey, who is associated with the Fredericksburg–Spotsylvania National Military Park, is the author of several books and articles on the Civil War. He is currently working on a command history of the Army of the Potomac.

Table of Contents

Introduction

Mark A. Snell

T his issue of *Civil War Regiments* focuses on some of the early battles and campaigns of our nation's costliest war. Unlike the campaigns that would follow, those waged in 1861 resulted in far fewer casualties and were usually conducted with smaller forces. Yet, because these engagements were the *first* of what would prove to be a long and bloody war, they were often remembered by their participants as intense and hard-fought affairs, the paucity of casualties notwithstanding.

Whether the conflict is the Civil War, World War I or Vietnam, early battles are often far different than subsequent engagements. Ill-trained troops, problems in command and control, preconceptions about war-making, political implications and preparedness issues (weapons technology, logistics and mobilization) are but some of the factors that differentiated fighting in 1861 from the bloodshed of 1863.[1] The essays in this book, together with the edited memoirs and letters contained herein, illuminate and underscore these differences.

We are proud to open this collection with an essay written by an historian who is, if he will pardon the expression, as "green" as the soldiers who participated in the Battle of Philippi. Mark Bell is a first-year graduate student in the history program at Shippensburg (Pennsylvania) State University. Between his junior and senior years at the same college he served as a summer intern at Shepherd College's George Tyler Moore Center for the Study of the Civil War. It was there that he developed a keen interest in the battles fought in what is now West Virginia. The fighting at Philippi is unique. It was the first "battle" fought in that state (which in June 1861 was still the Commonwealth of Virginia), and it was arguably the seminal land "battle" of the war. Mark's essay examines the formation of the First Virginia Infantry (U.S.), a three-month regiment raised in the western part of Virginia and trained in Wheeling, as well as the unit's role at Philippi. This small and relatively unknown engagement was fought on June 3,

1861, as part of Maj. Gen. George B. McClellan's campaign to secure the Baltimore and Ohio Railroad and control the western part of Virginia. Like the green soldiers who were fighting their first battles, Mark has now "seen the elephant." We are confident that his article, "A Day at the Races: The First Virginia (U.S.) at the Battle of Philippi," will be but the first of many such publications.

Although the campaign and battle of First Manassas has received more attention (both at the time it was fought and over the ensuing years), another large-scale campaign was unfolding at the same time hundreds of miles west of Washington and Richmond. This fighting west of the Mississippi River in Missouri had a tremendous impact on region and dictated the course of the war in the Trans-Mississippi Theater. Although Governor Claiborne Jackson had tried to pull his state into the Confederate fold, Federal forces prevented Missouri's secession at the point of the bayonet. Still, about 40,000 Missourians would serve in Confederate units before the end of the war (while more than 109,000 would serve in Union regiments). Jeff Patrick, an interpretive specialist/historian at Wilson's Creek National Battlefield in Republic, Missouri, shines some well-deserved light into this arena with the edited memoirs of one of Missouri's premier Confederate artillerists. In "Remembering the Missouri Campaign of 1861: The Memoirs of W. P. Barlow, Guibor's Battery, Missouri State Guard," we follow the exploits of 1st Lt. William P. Barlow, a Southern artilleryman who participated in and wrote about the battles of Carthage (July 5), Wilson's Creek (Aug 10), and the Siege of Lexington (Sept. 12-20). Barlow's memoirs describe in great detail the tactical and logistical problems encountered by Confederate forces operating in Missouri early in the war, and offer considerable information on what it was like to operate an artillery battery in the mid-nineteenth century.

A few hundred miles south of Missouri along the Mississippi Gulf Coast, another strategically significant—yet relatively bloodless campaign—was underway for the control of a tiny island. In "Ship Island: The Unwanted Key to the Confederacy," Gregory D. Bova (United States Air Force, retired), discusses the strategic significance of this sandy Gulf Coast island which sits just offshore from Biloxi, Mississippi, and the almost comical attempts by both the Confederate forces and United States Navy to seize and hold it. His contribution highlights the fact that there is still much to learn and read about the war's early months.

The final two articles in this volume are about the most well-known military event of 1861—the campaign and battle of First Manassas. *Civil War Regiments* advisory-board member and veteran contributor Brian Pohanka weighs in again, this time with the edited letters of Alfred O'Neil Alcock of the the 11th New York Fire Zouaves, one of the most famous of the early-war regiments. Captured during the battle and imprisoned for ten months, Alcock wrote a series of lengthy letters back to *The New York Atlas*, his former employer where he worked as the editor of the newspaper's "Fire and Military Department." It is Brian's hope that this article, and his forthcoming publication of Alcock's letters and memoirs, will serve to honor the memory of a sensitive and literate volunteer who soldiered in the ranks of the Federal zouaves.

We close this issue with a conversation with one of the finest military historians in the Civil War community and *the* expert on both battles fought on the plains and hills of Manassas. John Hennessy, who is currently associated with the Fredericksburg-Spotsylvania National Military Park, provides our readers with fascinating insights concerning his research on First Manassas, as well as some of the more interesting aspects of this famous engagement. According to Hennessy, "there are few battles of this war that have a larger body of material with which to work. Yet at the same time, there are few battles of this war that are harder to understand than what happened on the battlefield that Sunday afternoon." John Hennessy's research and writing has siginificantly helped us understand *what happened,* and we are proud to bring him to you.

In some respects it is almost amusing to read about the gross mistakes and naive expectations of the commanders and soldiers of the Civil War's early battles. Unlike those men, we enjoy the luxury of hindsight;: we know how the battles turned out and we have analyzed over and over again the mistakes that the combatants made. If we put ourselves, as far as possible, in the brogans and boots of the men who fought these engagements, however, our attitudes and understanding of these campaigns and battles changes. While enjoying these essays, memoirs and letters, keep in mind military historian John Shy's comments about the initial battles of any war:

> Both the peculiar quality of first battles and the difficulty caused by historical perspective in recapturing that quality are direct results of the roles ignorance and uncertainty play in first battles. All wars involve high levels of ignorance and uncertainty; if they did not, surprise, intelligence, and security would be far less important than what they are. But it is at the very beginning of a war when lack of knowledge or of confidence may dominate the situation, before commanders can assess the results of their first realistic test of estimates, assumptions, guesses, predictions, hopes, and fears.[2]

Indeed, a lack of knowledge, confidence, and experience did affect the outcomes of the Civil War's early battles, and in some cases the commanders, soldiers and political leaders learned a great deal from them. Perhaps even this far removed from that turbulent decade, we too can still learn.

Forward to Richmond!

Notes

1. John Shy, "First Battles in Retrospect," in Charles E. Heller and William A. Stofft, editors, *America's First Battles, 1776-1965* (Lawrence, KS, 1986), pp. 329-339.

2. Ibid., p. 328.

"We marched all night in a heavy rain, and Oh Lord, how I did think of General Washington's troops marching barefoot in the snow"

A Day at the Races
The First Virginia (U.S.) Infantry at the Battle of Philippi

Mark E. Bell

The first land engagement of the Civil War took place on June 3, 1861 at Philippi, (West) Virginia. Little remembered in light of later events, the action was hailed at the time as a great Union victory. For George B. McClellan it marked the beginning of a successful western Virginia campaign which would result in his promotion to the command of what would later become the Army of the Potomac. It was an inauspicious beginning to the war for Robert E. Lee, who made the rare mistake of failing to grasp the situation. For the men of the 1st Virginia (U.S.) Volunteer Infantry, a three-month regiment recruited from the northern panhandle counties of Brooke, Marshall, Ohio and Hancock in the weeks after the fall of Fort Sumter, the Battle of Philippi was their first, and in many cases, their only opportunity to "see the elephant."[1]

The 1st Virginia was a product of a divided state. While the sectional conflict in the years preceding the outbreak of civil war split the country into northern and southern spheres, it alienated the western counties of Virginia from those of the eastern part of the state. The divisive issue between the two sections was the institution of slavery. The eastern counties survived on large-scale production of labor-intensive crops such as tobacco and cotton, which lent themselves favorably to the use of slave labor. By contrast, small-scale, subsistence farming characterized the agricultural production in the western counties where both climate and terrain combined to produce an atmosphere which was not conducive to the use of the South's "peculiar institution." Furthermore, many of the inhabitants of these western areas were of German, Scottish and Irish descent. Having migrated south along the Ohio River from northern areas where they or their ancestors had originally settled, a majority of these residents were neither socially nor politically inclined to embrace the institution of slavery. Tied to the north by blood and economy, western Virginians in 1861 were certainly closer to their brethren in Ohio and Pennsylvania than to their eastern Virginian neighbors, a fact that would become all too clear to the Confederate government in the conflict to come.[2]

The first shots of the Civil War at Fort Sumter brought the opposing viewpoints between the two sections of Virginia irrevocably out into the open. On April 17, 1861, delegates to a special convention in Richmond met to discuss Virginia's path in the crisis and voted to secede from the United States. The delegates from the western counties, led by the Honorable John S. Carlile, returned to their homes to undertake the organization of Union resistance to secession. At a meeting in Harrison County, Carlile delivered his "Clarksburg Resolutions," which called for a special convention consisting of the five most able men from each of the western counties to meet at Wheeling. This convention led to the formation of the Loyal Government of Virginia of which Francis H. Pierpont was appointed governor.[3]

Even before Carlile called for the convention at Wheeling, indeed the day after Virginia seceded from the Union, meetings were held all across western Virginia for the purpose of expressing support for the United States. At one of these meetings, in Wheeling's Fourth Ward, 40 men enrolled in the "Rough and Ready Guards." James W. Bodley had the honor of being the first man to enlist in the new company. On April 26, the Rough and Ready Guards, under the leadership of Captain Andrew H. Britt, entered into the service of the United States and was officially designated as Company A, 1st Virginia Infantry. Soon thereafter the "Iron Guards," consisting chiefly of men from the La Belle Mill in Wheeling's Sixth Ward and commanded by Captain Edward W. Stephens, also tendered its service to the loyal government and was mustered in as Company B.[4]

In early May these two companies were placed into camp at the fairgrounds on Wheeling Island in the Ohio River. The men had neither armaments nor uniforms, but were provided with blankets by the loyal citizens of Wheeling. Major Oakes of the United States Army was assigned to organize what would eventually become known as Camp Carlile and to muster in the new companies as they arrived. Companies A and B were apparently adjusting well to camp life. Company B decided to take up residence in some of the stalls in one of the stables and busily set themselves to individualizing their quarters. The local newspaper, the Wheeling *Intelligencer*, reported that the troops were being drilled for three hours a day, leaving plenty of time for the men "to amuse themselves as their taste may suggest." The paper followed this statement with the hope that "a more rigid discipline will be enforced."[5]

By the middle of May, companies were arriving daily and were quickly mustered into service. On May 16, a company from Brooke County, under Mountford S. Stokely, arrived in Camp Carlile, but almost left before mustering because of a misunderstanding over the provision of equipment. The dispute apparently was settled and the group was mustered as Company D. The "Henry Clay Guards," also from Brooke County, came in that day as well. Their arrival must have caused a great amount of excitement throughout Camp Carlile due to the special cargo with which they arrived: 300 new muskets (the type of the armaments provided to the regiment is not known). The Federal Government, suspicious of the loyalties of Wheeling citizens, was wary of sending the arms directly to the troops in the city. However, through application to the Secretary of War, Simon P. Cameron, and through the services of Governor Andrews of Massachusetts, the muskets were sent to Wellsburg, Brooke County, under the care of Mr. W. H. Carothers and Mr. Campbell Tarr. They were then forwarded to Wheeling under the charge of the Henry Clay Guards, who were subsequently entered into the 1st Virginia as Company C.[6]

Other new arrivals at the camp during this period included George Trimble's "Washington Guards" followed by companies under Thomas Parke, James Kuhn and James Donnelly. These were mustered in as Companies E, F, G and H respectively. On May 21 the "Hancock Guards," a group consisting of the sons of well-to-do farmers, arrived from Hancock County under the command of Captain B. W. Chapman and entered the 1st Virginia as Company I. The final unit to enter the regiment was mustered in on May 23 under the leadership of Captain George W. Robinson and was designated as Company K, 1st Virginia Infantry.[7]

The regiment, as it was formed, numbered close to 800 men and consisted of a diverse group of individuals from all different backgrounds. The 1st Virginia's historian, C. J. Rawling, indicated as much when he wrote, "it became a task of magnitude requiring more than ordinary organizing ability to mould [sic] them into a unit." Captain Trimble's Company E, composed of 74 men, ages 18 to 37, provides a great illustration of this diversity. From this one company were natives of eight states: Virginia, Ohio, Pennsylvania, Maryland, New Jersey, Kentucky and New York; two foreign countries: Great Britain and Germany; and the Island of Jamaica. The company consisted almost entirely of blue collar workers, with a quarter of the men being iron workers. Other prominent occupations included seven coopers, six farmers, five papermakers and five nailcutters. The company also included two professionals: a druggist and a bookkeeper as well as eight men whose occupations were unknown.[8]

As more men entered the camp and Major Oakes had time to introduce some degree of organization, the discipline, which was apparently lacking early on, seemed to take effect among the men. Passes were now required to enter the encampment, and guards were posted at the entrances. Drill occupied the bulk of the 1st Virginia's day to the extent that one soldier reported he had, "drilled the heels off his boots." On May 20, companies A, B and C caused quite a stir in Wheeling when they marched into the city so that a flag could be presented to Company C by the ladies of Centre Wheeling. According to the accounts in the *Intelligencer*, "as they came down Main Street in a solid body, with the glittering bayonets, bright rifles and martial music, they presented a formidable and warlike appearance." There were also several dress parades during the regiment's stay in the camp, which always drew a large body of onlookers from the city.[9]

Life in camp, however, was not all drill and ceremony. The men of the 1st Virginia, it seems, had plenty of free time which they devoted to various amusements. Some spent the time perfecting their humble abodes. The more creative of the lot ascribed names to their homes such as "Pig's Misery," "Camp Hog Hole" and "Bogs of Bellhack." Others decided to name their bungalows in honor of Wheeling citizens who had been instrumental in aiding to the soldiers' comforts, and thus one could see names such as "Camp List" or "Camp Hubbard." Apparently music was also a popular diversion among the men in Camp Carlile. A reporter from the *Intelligencer* noted seeing groups of men clustered around banjo players, fiddlers and songsters. Still others used the time to practice drilling, pitching quoits, or wrestling. This activity came to a halt, however, upon the visit of ladies to the camp, which, "frequently operated as a check upon the sometimes too boisterous ebalitions of the soldiers."[10]

On May 23 the organization of the 1st Virginia was nearly completed with the appointment of Benjamin F. Kelley to the colonelcy of the regiment. Kelley, a 54 year-old railroad executive, was a native of New Hampton, New Hampshire and a graduate of the Partridge Military Academy in Vermont. (Partridge Military Academy later became Norwich Military Academy.) As a youth, probably during his teen years, he moved to West Liberty in Ohio County, Virginia. There he joined the Guards Military Company in Wheeling and eventually ascended to command of the Fourth Regiment of Virginia Uniformed Militia. Colonel Kelley was working as an agent for the Baltimore and Ohio Railroad in

Philadelphia at the time the war broke out and rushed back to take command of the 1st Virginia. On May 25, just two days after taking command of the regiment, Kelley was assigned to command all of the loyal forces then in western Virginia by Major General George B. McClellan, who was then in charge of the Department of Ohio. Henry B. Hubbard was appointed Lieutenant Colonel of the 1st Virginia, Isaac E. Duval, Major and Joseph Thoburn, Surgeon.[11]

Duval was a native of Virginia, but spent most of his life on the frontier before the war. After the discovery of gold in California in 1849, he led the first company to cross the plains from Texas to the gold

Colonel Benjamin Franklin Kelley
(as a major general)

fields. He also took part in the Lopez insurrection in Cuba where he apparently just barely escaped certain death by execution. Duval returned to the states at the outset of the war and, upon offering his services, was elected Major of the 1st Virginia.[12]

The arrival of Colonel Kelley in the camp was celebrated with a dress parade to which hundreds of spectators were invited. After drawing his men up in formation, Kelley took the opportunity to address the regiment and was reported to have said in part that, "the struggle which they were to be engaged was not a struggle of brother against brother, but it was for the maintenance of the Government; it was to ascertain whether we had a government or not." This was followed by an address by Mr. Carlile, who elaborated on Colonel Kelley's remarks by stating that the impending war, "was a struggle to determine the capacity of man for self-government—a struggle for life and liberty." Such fervent patriotic sentiments probably stirred deep feelings within the men of the 1st Virginia, emotions that the men would call upon in just a few days as they mustered the strength and courage to undertake their first campaign.[13]

While the 1st Virginia was forming at Wheeling, Confederate officials were busy organizing forces in the area as well. On April 29, Maj. Gen. Robert E. Lee, then commanding The Commonwealth of Virginia's Confederate forces, ordered Maj. Alonzo Loring, a Wheeling native, to muster into the army any volunteers who offered themselves. These troops were to be used to guard the terminus of the Baltimore and Ohio Railroad near the Ohio River, but were not to interfere with the peaceful operations of the line. Lee later modified his orders by confining Major Loring to recruiting troops from the counties of Tyler, Wetzel, Marshall, Ohio, Brooke and Hancock.[14]

The following day, Lee ordered Maj. Francis M. Boykin to collect troops in the vicinity of Grafton with the object of protecting the southern branch of the B&O to Parkersburg, also known as the Northwest Virginia Railroad. Additionally, Boykin was informed that two hundred flintlock muskets were to be sent, upon his order, from the recently captured arsenal at Harpers Ferry, then commanded by Colonel Thomas J. Jackson. Boykin was to report to Lee on the necessity of troops at Parkersburg and to communicate and cooperate, if necessary, with Major Loring.[15]

On May 4, Lee appointed Col. George A. Porterfield, a graduate of the Virginia Military Institute and veteran of the Mexican War, to command the troops Boykin and Loring then were collecting. Lee, who was obviously ignorant of the political situation in western Virginia, told Colonel Porterfield he could expect to raise at least five regiments for the protection of the region. On May 14, Porterfield arrived at Grafton where he mistakenly assumed he would find Majors Boykin and Loring with their troops. Years later, however, he described the scene he encountered:

> I had been informed that they [Boykin and Loring] would cooperate with me, and had expected to find them at their posts with some force already organized. On the contrary, upon my arrival I found myself alone in a county hostile to the South, without an officer of any experience to help me, then or afterwards; without money or supplies of any kind, or the means of getting anything to aid in organizing a military force.[16]

Colonel Porterfield proceeded to ride west, towards the village of Fetterman, where he was told some men had gathered with the intent to enlist in the Confederate Army. By May 16, he found several companies organizing in the vicinity, including groups from Pruntytown, Philippi and Clarksburg. This small force was unarmed, without uniforms and, according to Colonel Porterfield, would, "not for some months be more effective than undisciplined militia." That same day he informed General Lee of his dilemma, stating that he had not received the arms which were promised him from Harpers Ferry and that due to the popular Union sentiment in the area, recruiting was proceeding more slowly than he had anticipated. Lee further betrayed his ignorance of the situation by responding, "I cannot believe that any citizen of the State will betray its interests, and hope all will unite in supporting the policy she may adopt." Lee did concede to take issue with the provision of arms, however, sending 1,000 muskets and rifles from Staunton, in the Shenandoah Valley, and several hundred from Harpers Ferry. He also ordered several hundred reinforcements to be sent to Grafton from Staunton.[17]

On May 22, 1861, the first clash between the opposing forces took place when two small parties met near Fetterman. In the encounter one Union man, Thornberry Bailey Brown, whose company later became part of the 2nd Virginia (U.S.) Infantry, was killed and another was wounded. Two days later Porterfield marched his force into pro-Union Grafton where he was joined by four more companies of infantry and one of cavalry. In all, he had been able to collect a force of about 550 infantry and 175 cavalry with which to protect the railroad, but in Wheeling and across the Ohio River at Camp Dennison, Ohio, a Union force numbering in the thousands was gathering, ready to move into the heart of western Virginia at a moment's notice.[18]

On May 26, Porterfield learned that the Federal force was, in fact, ready to march. In order to slow down the expected advance, he ordered two bridges along the Baltimore and Ohio Railroad to be burned. Major General McClellan took this action as an act of war and ordered troops from camps Carlile and Dennison, including the 1st Virginia, to move on Grafton the next day. Other regiments joining the expedition included the 16th Ohio Infantry, commanded by Colonel James Irvine; the 9th Indiana Infantry Regiment, Colonel Robert H. Milroy commanding; the 14th and 18th Ohio Volunteer Regiments, under Colonel James B. Steedman; Colonel Thomas T. Crittenden's 6th Indiana; and the 7th Indiana, under Brigadier General Thomas A Morris. Morris assumed command of all the Indiana troops, and upon arriving in Grafton took command of the entire expedition. McClellan also sent Colonel Frederick Lander, one of his aides-de-camp, with two six-pound artillery pieces. In all, about 4,000 Union troops were converging on Grafton.[19]

The 1st Virginia received their orders to move just after midnight on May 27th and eagerly set about preparing for the march. Soon after, a storm broke, which according to one reporter from the *Intelligencer*, contained, "such [claps] of thunder, vivid flashes of lightning and sheets of rain. . .seldom heard or seen." During the storm, the regiment practiced drilling and firing, and at daylight, marched into the depot of the Baltimore and Ohio Railroad. Despite the early hour, hundreds of Wheeling residents turned out to see the regiment off, including many of the wives, mothers and girlfriends of the soldiers. The *Intelligencer* reported that once upon the train "some of them went to snoring in the cars; but the more boisterous amused themselves by singing the Star Spangled Banner, Dixey's [sic] Land, etc." During the movement a musician in Company G, Frederick Fowell, was killed by the accidental discharge of a gun, becoming the 1st Virginia's initial casualty in the war. In spite of this incident, the movement to Grafton was a complete success. General McClellan was so impressed that he recommended Colonel Kelley for promotion to brigadier general.[20]

Upon learning of the Federals' movement, Colonel Porterfield wisely decided to withdraw to Philippi, about 15 miles south of Grafton. The arrival of the Union force in Grafton was completed two days later, by which time Colonel Kelley already had devised a plan to capture Porterfield's force at Philippi. Kelley was ready to move on June 1, but when General Morris arrived to take command, he postponed the proposed movement for a day. Morris feared pro-Confederate spies in the area would betray the objectives of the plan and therefore hoped to throw the spies off the trail by delaying the march.[21]

Philippi, located along the eastern bank of the Tygarts Valley River on the Beverly–Fairmont Pike, was the product of the formation of Barbour County in 1843. To the north of town the Pike crosses Talbott's Hill at the present day location of Alderson–Broaddus College and descends to the river where a two-laned covered bridge crosses over into the town at which point the Beverly Pike becomes Main Street. The bridge was constructed in 1852 and remains today as the only such bridge on a Federal road. Near the bridge is the town commons, which served as the Confederate camp. At the center of the town stands the large, red brick courthouse, which is accented with white pillars. Other prominent buildings include the Barbour House and the Virginia House, the latter which Porterfield would use as his headquarters. As the Beverly Pike leaves the town to the south, it passes by a large natural landmark known as Big Rock. Both Kelley and Porterfield would use this prominent point as a key landmark in their respective plans.[22]

The Union tactical plan, as it finally evolved, called for Colonel Kelley to move with six companies of the 1st Virginia, nine companies of the 9th Indiana and six companies of the 16th Ohio, a total of about 1,600 troops, by way of the Baltimore and Ohio Railroad to Thorton, six miles east of Grafton. In order to enhance the ruse, Colonel Kelley had it advertised that he was moving to Harpers Ferry. From Thorton, the Federals were to march the 22 miles to Philippi under the cover or darkness. When close to town, Kelley's column would split into two wings with Kelley leading one wing and Colonel Milroy in charge of the other. While Kelley's force approached Philippi from the east, the column under Milroy was to march by way of the Morgantown Road and through the village of Cross Keys to a point on the Beverly Pike south of Philippi, and then march north to Big Rock. Set to arrive at 4:00 a.m., these two wings would be poised to cut off Porterfield's retreat.[23]

A second column, containing the 7th Indiana and commanded by Colonel Dumont, was to leave Grafton and move west along the railroad to Webster where he would join and take command of the 14th Ohio and 6th Indiana, as well as Lander's artillery. Once formed, the column of 1,400 men would move south along the Beverly Pike to Philippi, a distance of 12 miles, taking position on Talbott's Hill. Upon the arrival of both columns, Colonel Kelley was to signal the start of the attack by firing a single pistol shot, at which point Lander's artillery would open fire on the Confederate camp while Dumont's column moved to take the two-lane covered bridge on the Beverly Pike at the northern entrance to the town. This move was designed to dislodge the Confederate force in the hope that Kelley's column could then intercept it as Porterfield tried to retreat south.[24]

The plan seemed simple enough in theory, but for raw troops even the simplest task could be daunting. Adding to the complexity of the movement was the fact that it was to take place under the cover of darkness, a mission that would prove difficult for even the most seasoned veterans, much less new recruits. Just

The restored Philippi Bridge today

Courtesy of Steve Cunningham, Charleston, WV

when it seemed things could not get more difficult, it began to rain as the two columns left Grafton. The storm would last throughout the night, and at first it seemed that the precipitation might threaten the successful execution of the plan. As Kelley's column moved southward along unimproved roads and backwoods trails towards Philippi, his men became bogged down in a quagmire. A private in Company G, Thomas S. H. Carr, wrote,

> We marched all night in a heavy rain, and Oh Lord, how I did think of General Washington's troops marching barefoot in the snow. It would have been the same with us if it had been snow that night. Our fine shoes had pulled off in the mud. The only way we could keep our powder dry was to keep it in our guns, for one load was all we had when it began to rain.[25]

Dumont's column, while certainly not enjoying the rain, was not having nearly as difficult a time as Kelley. Their route to Philippi along the Beverly Pike was much shorter than Kelley's route. Adding to their advantage was the fact that the Pike was macadamized, making the road much more suitable for foul-weather marching. Still, it was quite a dreary night. To help guide his way through the darkness, Colonel Dumont ordered Lieutenant Ricketts from Co. B of his regiment to go out in front with a red lattern. The young lieutenant protested with the argument that, "I don't want a record as the first man killed." He conceded, however, and made it through the night without incident to himself or anyone else.[26]

Although the heavy rains slowed their progress, everything else seemed to be moving along according to plan. As far as Kelley and Dumont were concerned, their movements had been shrouded in secrecy. This was far from the case. Soon after their march began on June 2, Mrs. George Whitescarver, whose husband was with Porterfield at Philippi, learned of Kelley's plans from her neighbors in Pruntytown, just west of Grafton. She immediately set out for Philippi where she met with Colonel Porterfield and told him of the Federal force's objectives. Later that day two more women, misses Abbie Kerr and Mollie McCleod, brought Porterfield further information which confirmed that which Mrs. Whitescarver had provided. With this information in hand, Porterfield met with his officers and resolved to retreat further south towards Beverly, a march of 24 miles. There was some confusion among the officers as to when this retreat was to take place. It seems that some believed the movement was to occur at first light, while others were under the assumption that it was only to take place upon the appearance of the Northerners. Whichever the case, Porterfield did not seem to be too concerned, in large part because of the terrible

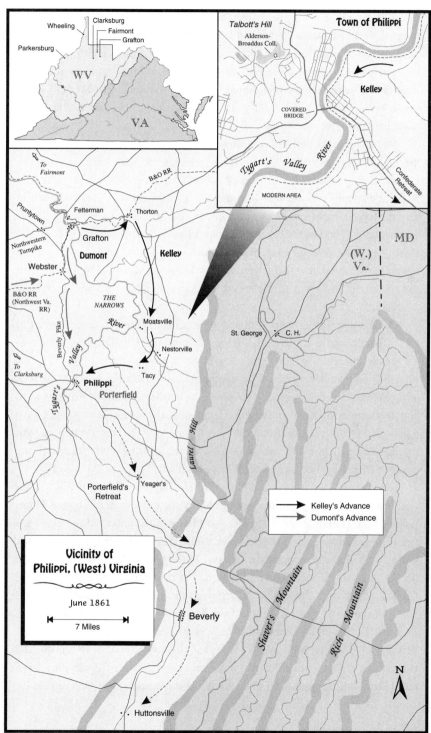

Town of Philippi

Talbott's Hill
Alderson-
Broaddus Coll.

Kelley

COVERED
BRIDGE

Tygart's Valley River

Confederate Retreat

MODERN AREA

To
Fairmont

B&O RR

Thorton

Pruntytown

Fetterman

Grafton

Dumont

Kelley

Northwestern
Turnpike

Webster

B&O RR
(Northwest Va.
RR)

THE
NARROWS

River

Moatsville

St. George

C. H.

MD

(W.)
Va.

Beverly Pike

Valley

Nestorville

To
Clarksburg

Tacy

Philippi
Porterfield

Tygart's

Laurel Hill

Porterfield's
Retreat

Yeager's

Kelley's Advance
Dumont's Advance

**Vicinity of
Philippi, (West) Virginia**

June 1861

7 Miles

Shaver's Mountain

Rich Mountain

Beverly

N

Huttonsville

Mark A. Moore

storm. Believing that "any army marching tonight must be made up of a set of damned fools," Colonel Porterfield ordered his pickets, the men who would warn of Kelley and Dumont's approach, to come in at midnight to rest for the next day's march. Thus, while Porterfield was warned of the attack well before-hand, he chose to play the odds, quite reasonably assuming that his foe's green troops would not be able to carry out their plan under conditions that would make hardened veterans wince.[27]

So far, however, Kelley and Dumont had been doing a good job of defying the odds. In order to help find his way through the dark, wet, forest trails, Colonel Kelley secured the services of a local man, Jacob Baker, as a guide. But Baker apparently became confused under the circumstances, and managed to lead the force astray from its intended line of march. Kelley later charged Baker got lost on purpose, but was never able to prove it. Whether on purpose or not, Baker seriously delayed the column. More importantly, however, it put the column on a road that would lead to the northeastern side of Philippi rather than the southeast. Unknown to Kelley at the time, his plan was now in serious jeopardy.[28]

As the designated hour of attack approached, Colonel Dumont began to worry that he would fail to get his force into postion. He ordered his column to the double-quick and, exhorting his men onward, covered the last five miles in a little over an hour. He arrived at his appointed postion just before 4:00 a.m. and, with Colonel Lander, proceded to place the artillery. Without being able to communicate with Kelley's column, Dumont had no idea of the misfortune which had befallen his comrade. If the fog of war had not created enough problems already, a most unusual event occurred which entirely threw off any possible chance of success that might have been left.[29]

As Dumont's men moved up the northern slopes of Talbott's Hill to their positions overlooking Philippi, they passed by the farmhouse of Thomas Hum-phreys. Mrs. Humphreys did not take too kindly to the arrival of her uninvited guests, especially since her eldest son, Newton, had enlisted in the Barbour Grays, a Confederate company encamped in the town below. She tried to seat her 12-year-old son on a horse so he could to ride into Philippi and warn the Confederate troops. Union soldiers removed the young boy, an act which was met by a shower of rocks and sticks from Mrs. Humphreys. She boosted her son on the horse again, and once more he was yanked off by the Union soldiers. Mrs. Humphreys retreated to the house, but quickly returned with a pistol and fired at two of Dumont's soldiers. Fortunately her aim was poor and she missed the soldiers but Dumont, who did not witness the incident, was able to hear the errant shots. Assuming that it was Kelley's signal, he ordered the artillerymen to sight their guns and fire at a row of white tents in Philippi. The tents belonged to the men of the "Upshur Grays," commanded by John C. Higgenbotham.[30]

The presence of the Union force was now known to the Confederates in Philippi. Without any further instructions from Porterfield, the company officers assumed the time for retreat had come. The *Intelligencer* reported that the Confederates, "scattered like rats from a burning barn. . .they ran, fled most ingloriously. . .ran like sheep in every direction that promised safety." Later, witnesses to the battle ascribed to it the name "the Philippi Races." The Confederates, however, weren't exactly running like sheep. They were obeying the orders they had received the night before to fall back towards Beverly upon the appearance of the enemy. They were to meet and reform at Big Rock, ironically the same point Kelley had indicated as the spot for Milroy's wing to be posted. Owing to the excitement of the morning's events, however, Porterfield was not able to rally his men until they reached Huttonsville, about eight miles south of Big Rock on the Beverly Pike.[31]

Soon after Lander's guns opened, Kelley's column was spotted marching into town from the east, too late to be of service, for the last of the Confederates were moving through the southern end of town, some turning and firing random shots as they went. Kelley rushed into the town with companies B and C of the 1st Virginia right behind him. Lander, seeing the need to communicate with Kelley now that the plan had gone awry, immediately set out upon what *Leslie's Illustrated Weekly* newspaper later called, "A Daring Ride." He jumped on his horse and flew headlong down Talbott's Hill, across the covered bridge and into the streets of Philippi. Just as he came upon Kelley, the latter was struck in the breast by a shot from the pistol of a Confederate quartermaster, William Sims. Lander spurred on his horse in pursuit of Sims and successfully apprehended him. The men of the 1st Virginia immediately set upon the man fully with the intent to hang him. Colonel Lander designated the man a prisoner of war, to which Kelley reportedley agreed, telling his men that he had been legitimately shot in battle and that they had no right to hang Sims.[32]

Colonel Kelley was moved to the Ashenfelter House and laid on the porch, where, presumably, he was examined by a surgeon, quite probably Joseph Thoburn, the 1st Virginia's surgeon. At first the wound was thought to be fatal. General Morris, in a preliminary dispatch to General McClellan, wrote that he feared as much. McClellan, in turn, reported that Kelley was in fact dead, a report that was headlined in newspapers all across the North. Fortunately the wound was not as severe as first thought, leaving general Morris to write in his official report, "I am glad to know [the wound] will only deprive us of his valuable counsels and assistance for a few weeks."[33]

On the Confederate side, Colonel Porterfield had a close call himself. He noticed a group of blue-clad soldiers formed near the covered bridge. At first he

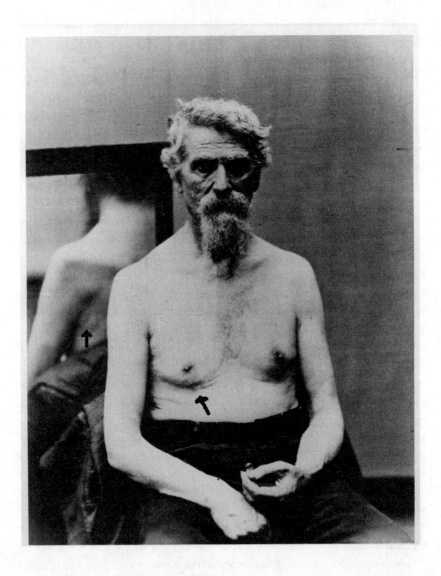

Benjamin F. Kelley posing for a photograph of his wound, showing entrance and exit points (arrows). Photograph taken in 1877 for the Army Medical Museum, Washington, D. C.

Armed Forces Institute of Pathology

believed that it was one of his companies, the Hardy Blues, so named for the color of their uniforms. As he approached the men, both he and one of his officers noticed they were carrying the flag of the old Union. Both officers turned their horses around nonchalantly and rode out of town, apparently the last of the Confederates to leave. For a short time the Union forces tried to pursue the fleeing Confederates, but owing to the exhaustion among the troops from the previous night's march, the pursuit was short-lived.[34]

The "Battle" of Philippi was over. In the engagement there were fewer than 20 casualties. In addition to the wounding of Colonel Kelley, four other men from the 1st Virginia, Privates Peter Fierrang and Alfred Work of Company C and Privates Michael Chancely and Theodore Marsh of Company D, were wounded. Work was wounded near the eastern edge of Philippi and afterwards was carried to the house of William K. Hall where his wound was examined and dressed. As for the Confederates, the number of casualties has never been accurately ascertained. General Morris' report estimated the loss at between 15 and 40 killed with an untold number wounded. This was certainly not the case. Confederate casualties almost certainly numbered less than ten. One of the Confederate wounded was 18-year-old Private James E. Hangar, of the Churchville Cavalry. He had been hit in the leg by a six-pound solid shot as it ricocheted off the ground. Hangar was taken to the surgeon of the 16th Ohio, James D. Robison, who examined the leg and amputated it seven inches below the hip, the first of tens of thousands of such amputations which would occur in the four years that followed. While recovering from the operation, Hangar designed an artificial limb for himself. After his recovery, he was contracted by the Confederate government to produce similar prosthetic devices for other amputees. After the war, Hangar became a prominent international businessman, producing his "Hangar Limbs" for world-wide distribution.[35]

While the plan to capture the Confedeate force at Philippi failed, the battle was hailed as a great Northern success. After the attack, General Morris, who was in Grafton during the battle, reported to General McClellan that the Union force had "captured a large amount of arms, horses, ammunition, provisions, and camp equipage." Years later Colonel Porterfield disputed this claim, saying, "I had no provisions, wagons, horses (except the cavalry not captured), nor medical stores. If these were captured they were taken from citizens and not from my command." One fact that cannot be disputed is that the Union forces did take three Confederate flags that day. One was the "Palmetto" flag which flew over the Babour County Courthouse. Another belonged to Hangar's Churchville Cavalry. The third was Porterfield's headquarters flag, which was taken by First Lieutenant Charles E. Griffin of the 1st Virginia's Company B. Griffin carried the flag with him back to Wheeling where he presented it to a group of ladies from the neighborhood of the La Belle works, where the company had originated.[36]

For a while after the battle, the 1st Virginia remained in Philippi and took up quarters in some of the houses and a church. The regiment later was split into smaller battallions. One battallion was sent to Rowlesburg and another to Grafton, while Company G was left to guard Philippi. In July a battallion of five companies of the 1st Virginia was sent to Laurel Hill where it took part in some minor skirmishing. The balance of the 1st Virginia's service was limited to guard duty and other such details, with the companies being scattered throughout western Virginia to cover the line of the Baltimore and Ohio Railroad. During this relatively peaceful period, the regiment did not suffer any substantial losses either to disease, wounds or accidents, though the regiment was not totally immune to such privations of war. For example, Private Thomas W. Morgan of Company C was discharged by reason of an unstated disability. On July 4, 1861, Samuel Troup of Company I was wounded by the accidental discharge of a weapon. Less than a week later, Henry Hale of Company G died of Typhoid Fever in the hospital at Grafton. John Dean of Company H also perished, presumably of disease, although the exact cause, date and place of death are not stated. The final casualty of the 1st Virginia was Alexander H. Vance, who was injured in a railroad accident.[37]

The 1st Virginia completed its term of service and was mustered out on August 27, 1861, at Camp Carlile. The Surgeon Joseph Thoburn was commissioned Colonel of a newly reorganized three-year regiment which was to also carry the designation as the 1st Virginia. The reorganized 1st Virginia—later to be called the 1st West Virginia—took part in all of the campaigns of the Shenandoah Valley, as well as venturing east to participate in the campaign of Second Manassas. Colonel Thoburn, while never receiving a star, rose to command a division of what would be called the Army of West Virginia. He was killed at the Battle of Cedar Creek on October 19, 1864.[38]

Sixty days after receiving his wound at Philippi, Colonel Kelley was promoted to Brigadier General and placed in command of the Railroad Division with the chief responsibility of protecting the Baltimore and Ohio Railroad. In 1864, he rose to command of the Department of West Virginia and was given a brevet rank of major general. After the war Kelley married Mary Clare Bruce, who was the daughter of Colonel Robert Bruce of the 2nd Potomac Home Brigade. His family also included six children from a previous marriage to Isabel Goshorn, who had died in 1858. Kelley served for a time as superintendent of Hot Springs in Arkansas before retiring to Washington D.C. and a summer home at Swan Meadows, Maryland. He died in July, 1892 and was buried in Arlington National Cemetery.[39]

Major Isaac Duval was absent for the action at Philippi, as was Lieutenant Colonel Henry Hubbard. After the regiment was mustered out, Duval was given the command of the Ninth Virginia Volunteers. While serving in the Department of West Virginia, he was promoted to the rank of Brigadier General. He ended the war commanding the "Hancock Veteran Corps." After the war, he served in the West Virginia State Legislature as well as the United States Congress.[40]

The men of the 1st Virginia did not win for themselves a glorious name on the nearly bloodless field at Philippi. Events in the East, specifically the Battle of First Bull Run soon overshadowed the Battle of Philippi. However, the results of this small affair had very important political and military ramifications. First, by pushing Confederate troops initially from Grafton, and then from Philippi, Federal forces were able to take control of the Baltimore and Ohio Railroad. This railway provided a vital transportation link between East and West which both sides could have used to their advantage. Losing this line seriously damaged the Confederates' ability to move troops in and out of the western counties and thus severly limited their ability to control that section of Virginia. Also, the loss of the western counties to Union forces jeopardized Confederate abilities to protect the Shenandoah Valley, a region they needed to safeguard because of its rich, fertile fields. Capture of the Shenandoah Valley meant not only the loss of these farmlands, but also the opening of another route that Federal forces could use to march on Richmond. Politically, the entrance of Union troops into Virginia, and their willingness to push the Confederates, boosted pro-Union morale and allowed for the peaceful election of delegates to a second Wheeling Convention which led to the formation of the state of West Virginia. It is doubtful that the men of the 1st Virginia (U.S.) fully realized the impact their actions had on the future of their state.[41]

Notes

1. C. J. Rawling, *History of the First Regiment Virginia Infantry* (Philadelphia, 1887), p. 19. The 1st Virginia is more commonly known as the 1st West Virginia Infantry. However, because the western counties of Virginia did not become a state until 1863, West Virginia units were initially designated as Virginia units. For the sake of historic accuracy, the Virginia designation will be used here.

2. Clayton R. Newell, *Lee vs. McClellan: The First Campaign* (Washington D.C., 1996), pp. 11-14.

3. Ibid, pp. 16-17, 104. West Virginia did not come into being, however, until June 20, 1863.

4. Rawling, *History*, pp. 17-18; Adjutant General's Report, 1st Virginia Infantry, George Tyler Moore Center for the Study of the Civil War, Shepherdstown, West Virginia, microfilm reel 2.

5. Wheeling *Intelligencer*, May 16, 1861.

6. Ibid, May 17, 1861; Theodore Lang, *Loyal West Virginia 1861-1865* (Baltimore, 1895), pp. 234-235.

7. Rawling, *History*, pp. 20-21; Lang, *Loyal West Virginia*, p. 233. Refer to Appendix A for a complete list of the commissioned officers of the regiment.

8. Rawling, *History*, p. 11; Adjutant General's Report, 2.

9. Wheeling *Intelligencer*, May 17, 1861; May 20, 1861.

10. Ibid, May 17, 1861; May 22, 1861.

11. Ibid, May 23, 1861; Lang, *Loyal West Virginia*, p. 320.

12. Ibid, p. 351.

13. Wheeling *Intelligencer*, May 23, 1861.

14. U.S. War Department, *The War of the Rebellion: A Compilation of the Official Records of the Union and Confederate Armies*, 128 vols. (Washington D.C., 1890-1901), series I, vol. 2, pp. 788, 802. Hereinafter cited as *OR*. All references are to series I unless otherwise noted.

15. Ibid, pp. 790-791.

16. Richard L. Armstrong, *25th and 9th Battallions Virginia Infantry* (Lynchburg, 1990), p. 1; *OR* 2, p. 802; Colonel George A. Porterfield, "A Narrative of the Service of Colonel Geo. A. Porterfield in Northwestern Virginia in 1861-'2," *Southern Historical Society Papers*, vol. 16 (1888), p. 83.

17. *OR* 2, pp. 885-857, 873-874.

18. Armstrong, *25th and 9th Battallions*, pp. 1-2; Eva Margaret Carnes, *The Tygarts Valley Line: June-July 1861* (Philippi, 1961), pp. 30-31.

19. Jack Waugh, "Long Distance Victory: McClellan's First Battles," *Civil War Times Illustrated*, vol. 12 (November, 1983), p. 10; Carnes, *Tygarts*, pp. 32-33; Armstrong, *25th and 9th Battallions*, p. 4; Newell, *Lee vs. McClellan*, p. 86.

20. Wheeling *Intelligencer*, May 28, 1861; Rawling, *History*, p. 23; Adjutant General's Report, 2; Carnes, *Tygarts*, p. 32.

21. Armstrong, *25th and 9th Battallions*, p. 2; *OR* 2, p. 66.

22. Carnes, *Tygarts*, pp. 21-22, 47.

23. *OR* 2, pp. 66-67; Carnes, *Tygarts*, pp. 36-38; Newell, *Lee vs. McClellan,* pp. 91-92. Four of the six companies from the 1st Virginia which took part in the Battle of Philippi include Companies B, C, D and G. It is not known which other two companies from the regiment took part.

24. Ibid.

25. Newell, *Lee vs. McClellan*, pp. 91-94; "Rebel's Hell: The Civil War Journal of Thomas Sutton Hayden Carr," (unpublished memoir) George Tyler Moore Center for the Study of the Civil War, Shepherdstown, West Virginia.

26. Newell, *Lee vs. McClellan*, p. 94; Carnes, *Tygarts*, p. 44.

27. Newell, *Lee vs. McClellan*, pp. 92-95; Waugh, "Long Distance Victory," p. 12; Carnes, *Tygarts*, pp. 40-41.

28. Carnes, *Tygarts*, p. 45; Newell, *Lee vs. McClellan*, pp. 94-95. 29. Waugh, "Long Distance Victory," p. 12.

29. Ibid; Carnes, *Tygarts*, p. 46; Armstrong, *25th and 9th Battallions*, p. 5.

30. Ibid; Carnes, *Tygarts*, p. 46; Armstrong, *25th and 9th Battallions*, p. 5.

31. Armstrong, *25th and 9th Battallions*, p. 5; Wheeling *Intelligencer*, June 6, 1861.

32. Rawling, *History*, pp. 26-27; *Frank Leslie's Illustrated Weekly*, June 29, 1861; Carnes, *Tygarts*, pp. 51-53.

33. Carnes, *Tygarts*, pp. 52-53; *OR* 2, pp. 66-68.

34. Newell, *Lee vs. McClellan*, p. 97; Carnes, *Tygarts*, p. 49.

35. Adjutant General's Report, 2; *OR* 2, pp. 67-68; Hu Maxwell, *History of Barbour County: From the Earliest Exploration and Settlement to the Present Time* (Morgantown, 1899), p. 257; Newell, *Lee vs. McClellan*, p. 98; Carnes, *Tygarts*, pp. 55-56; It is not known what captured cavalry Porterfield is referring. Union reports do not make any references to capturing cavalry.

36. *OR* 2, p. 64; Porterfield, "Narrative," p. 87; Carnes, *Tygarts*, pp. 50-51.

37. Rawling, *History*, pp. 28-29; Adjutant General's Report, 2.

38. Lang, *Loyal West Virginia*, pp. 238-240.

39. Ibid, pp. 241, 321.

40. Ibid, pp. 242, 252.

41. Newell, *Lee vs. McClellan*, pp. 100-101; David L. Philipps, *War Diaries: The 1861 Kanawha Valley Campaign* (Leesburg, 1990), p. 49.

"No one. . .could believe how quickly those raw country boys picked up the intricate artillery drill."

REMEMBERING THE MISSOURI CAMPAIGN OF 1861

The Memoirs of Lieutenant William P. Barlow, Guibor's Battery, Missouri State Guard

edited by Jeffrey L. Patrick

Although scarcely remembered today because of its location in the neglected Trans-Mississippi Theater and the fact that it occurred in the early months of the war, the Missouri Campaign of 1861 was one of the most significant events of the American Civil War. Missouri's location between the Union and Confederate states, its manpower and resources, and its river systems and trails, made the state an important target for both sides.

By the end of the first year of the conflict, pro-Confederate forces operating in Missouri had handed three costly defeats to Union field armies at the battles of Carthage, Wilson's Creek and Lexington, but had failed to seize and occupy large amounts of territory or the important cities of St. Louis, Jefferson City and Kansas City. They also had been unsuccessful in holding the initiative and driving Union forces from the state. Ironically, all three Federal defeats eventually helped secure Missouri for the Union by calling the attention of military strategists in Washington to the crisis in the Trans-Mississippi.

Nonetheless, pro-Southern units such as the Missouri State Guard gained recruits and valuable combat experience during their service in the war's opening months, many taking their training with them into Confederate service. The mere presence of the State Guard and their Confederate allies in Missouri de-

manded the attention of thousands of Federal troops west of the Mississippi
River.

Arguably, the Missouri Campaign formally began in February 1861, in St.
Louis. There, Congressman Francis P. Blair, Jr. became worried about pro-
Southern sympathizers in the area and their possible seizure of the city's U. S.
Arsenal. Blair pressured Washington into sending a company of Regulars from
Fort Riley, Kansas to help protect the Arsenal's 60,000 muskets and other
military stores. These troops arrived in St. Louis on February 7, 1861, under the
command of Capt. Nathaniel Lyon, whose fanaticism for the Union cause and
determination to defend U. S. government property guaranteed few concessions
to the Missouri secessionists.

Shortly after Lyon's arrival in St. Louis, it began to appear as though his
presence was unnecessary. On March 4, a convention met in St. Louis to consider Missouri's political alternatives. Its members voted overwhelmingly
against secession, stating that there was no adequate cause for Missouri to
secede. But Missouri Governor Claiborne Fox Jackson was not to be deterred in
his mission to pull the state into the Confederacy. When President Abraham
Lincoln called on Missouri in April 1861 to furnish troops to put down the
rebellion, Jackson refused, calling Lincoln's request "illegal, unconstitutional
and revolutionary in its object, [and] inhuman and diabolical. . . ."[1]

On May 6, Governor Jackson called out the Missouri State Militia for a
training period at Lindell Grove, on the western edge of St. Louis, in an encampment christened "Camp Jackson." Jackson also received word that four
bronze cannon were to be shipped from Baton Rouge to St. Louis for use by the
militia in seizing the arsenal. Lyon decided to act swiftly. On May 10, after his
superior, Department of the West commander Gen. William S. Harney had gone
to Washington, Lyon mustered about 8,000 Regulars and home guardsmen and
surrounded Camp Jackson. The militia men quickly surrendered, and Lyon organized his 700 captives for the march back to the arsenal where the prisoners
would be paroled.[2] On the way, a hostile crowd gathered. Rocks were thrown,
shots were fired, and more than two dozen civilians and soldiers were killed in
the melee.

General Harney's return to the city helped restore order. He met on May 20
with Sterling Price, a former congressman, governor and Mexican War general
acting as Jackson's representative, and together they drafted a formal agreement
in which the state authorities would maintain order in Missouri—if Harney
agreed to take no further military action. The "Price-Harney Agreement"
seemed to be the mechanism to end the strife in St. Louis. By the end of the

month, however, Frank Blair had seen to it that Harney was relieved and Lyon promoted to brigadier general in his stead.

Despite the temporary peace forged by Harney and Price, Lyon had several reasons to be concerned about the situation in Missouri. Between May 9 and 15, the Missouri legislature passed a series of bills giving sweeping powers to Governor Jackson, and authorizing him to form a "State Guard" to defend Missouri against "invaders." Nine military districts were organized, each containing a division of troops led by a brigadier general. Many residents of the state were shocked by the Camp Jackson bloodshed and, driven from their previously neutral stance, were only awaiting a mobilization order to take the field with the Missouri State Guard. Sterling Price was appointed a major general to head the entire State Guard organization.

Lyon soon decided to break the peace and take the offensive. On June 11, he met with Governor Jackson and General Price at the Planter's House Hotel in St. Louis, and after four hours of debate, the Southerners offered to disband the State Guard and prevent Confederate troops from entering Missouri. In return, Lyon was asked to demobilize the pro-Union home guard units that had already been organized and not occupy any other properties than those already held by Federal troops. Lyon did not trust either Jackson or Price, however, and would not surrender his ability to act at will to protect Federal interests. The meeting ended without agreement, and the Missouri Campaign formally began.

Price and Jackson hurried to Jefferson City and ordered the State Guard mobilized. Lyon was not far behind. He envisioned a two-pronged strategy to deal with his enemies. Part of his force of Regulars and volunteers under Capt. Thomas Sweeny would move to Springfield, in southwest Missouri, and there wait to form one arm of a giant pincer. Lyon would take the remainder of his army up the Missouri River, capture the state capital at Jefferson City, control the river traffic, then march overland toward Springfield to hopefully drive the still-mobilizing State Guard into a trap between his force and Sweeny's command. At the last minute, Sweeny was delayed in St. Louis, so Col. Franz Sigel assumed command.

The initial movements of Lyon's plan worked flawlessly. On June 15 he captured Jefferson City, then moved down the river to the village of Boonville, where Governor Jackson intended to make a stand with a few hundred of the State Guard. On June 17, the Union forces easily routed Jackson's ill-trained troops. Faced with an overland campaign across much of the state, Lyon was now forced to halt and assemble supplies and reinforcements at Boonville. He did not resume his pursuit until early July.

This critical delay gave Price and Jackson time to flee south, picking up recruits as they withdrew. Their objective was Cowskin Prairie in extreme southwestern Missouri, where the State Guard was ordered to concentrate. With Lyon delayed, the only force to worry them was Sigel's. The fiery German quickly headed west from Springfield to the town of Carthage to engage the State Guard. On the morning of July 5, in the fields north of the village, he brought the Southerners to battle. Heavily outnumbered, the Federals fought an all-day delaying action into the town itself before finally being forced to withdraw eastward. Jackson and his men reached Cowskin Prairie safely, but Sigel's raw volunteers had proved themselves equal to the task of combat. In the meantime, Lyon pressed south from Boonville. On July 13 he arrived in Springfield and soon united his forces with Sigel's men, forming the 7,000-man rmy of the West.

At Cowskin Prairie, Sterling Price labored to organize an effective army to oppose the Unionists. Uniforms were nearly non-existent, as most men were "entirely clad in the homespun butternut eans worn by every Missouri farmer," according to one eyewitness.[3] Arms were also varied. While a few were modern military weapons, most were arms brought from home. One veteran wrote that "[a]nything that could be construed into the semblance of a weapon was to be found there."[4]

Price's ill-trained, ill-armed, and ill-equipped force was not destined to face Lyon alone. By late July, the State Guard had been reinforced by 2,200 Arkansas State Troops under Gen. Nicholas Bartlett Pearce, along with 2,700 men led by Confederate Brig. Gen. Benjamin McCulloch, the latter relatively well-armed and equipped Confederates from Louisiana, Texas and Arkansas. Altogether, the Southern force, now under the leadership of McCulloch, numbered some 10,125 armed men. About 2-3,000 remained unarmed.

McCulloch's army began a movement up the Telegraph Road, the major artery in southwest Missouri, toward Lyon in Springfield. They went into camp on August 6 along both banks of Wilson's Creek, about 10 miles southwest of the city, close enough to mount a major assault. By August 9, both sides were convinced that a surprise attack was the preferred course of action. McCulloch reluctantly agreed to a night march that would enable him to strike Lyon at daybreak on the 10th. Lyon not only decided on an early morning attack on the 10th as well, but divided his outnumbered command: while Lyon struck the northern end of the Confederate camp, Colonel Sigel would march 1,200 men to attack the southern end of the camp and prevent any Confederates from escaping. The Federals left their camps in the early evening of August 9 and moved toward McCulloch's encampment.

Also on the evening of August 9, the Confederates prepared to march on Springfield. Soon a light rain became to fall. McCulloch feared that the pockets and cloth bags used by many of his men to hold their ammunition would become wet and render their gunpowder useless, so instead of departing he ordered the men to lay on their arms and prepare to move the next morning. The Confederate pickets had been withdrawn in preparation for the march, but after the move was canceled the sentinels were not replaced. Thus, McCulloch's army had no advance warning of the impending Union attack. As dawn approached, many of the Southerners still were sleeping and a few others were preparing breakfast. Shortly after 5:00 a.m. on Saturday, August 10, Lyon's approaching forces encountered the first Southern opposition, and the Battle of Wilson's Creek began.

After pushing aside some State Guard cavalrymen, Lyon's Federals moved onto the north slope of a high piece of land that both sides would soon call "Bloody Hill," cresting the rise around 6:00 a.m. Their advance was slowed, however, by artillery fire from the eastern side of Wilson's Creek. The shells were coming from Capt. William E. Woodruff's Arkansas Battery, which lobbed its ordnance into the advancing Union line, slowing it and allowing the State Guard units time to hastily form a battleline across the hill. By 6:30 a.m. the Federal advance was stopped.

At the southern edge of the Confederate encampment, Colonel Sigel enjoyed early success. Once the sounds of Lyon's initial contact were heard, four Union cannon emplaced on the heights above a Confederate cavalry camp roared to life and rapidly caused panic in the Southern ranks. The stampede cleared the fields in front of the Federals. Sigel's brigade finally took position astride the Telegraph Road to block any Southern escape from Bloody Hill.

This promising situation quickly unraveled for Sigel. The Confederates unlimbered two batteries to rake the Union position, and a Confederate force moved up the bluff in front of Sigel's men. Assuming they were the 1st Iowa Infantry (they were dressed in grey, the uniform color of the Iowans) Sigel's men held their fire. Unfortunately for the Federals, the approaching Confederates were the 3rd Louisiana Infantry. The Louisianans fired a volley and charged, scattering the startled Federals and capturing three 12-pounder howitzers and two 6-pounder guns. One arm of Lyon's bold pincer was broken, leaving the general and his outnumbered command was left to fight alone.

Back on Bloody Hill about 7:30 a.m., the Southerners launched their first major assault on Lyon's line. After fierce fighting that lasted about a half hour, the Rebels withdrew, and by 8:30 a.m. the hill fell silent again. At 9:00 a.m., Price launched a massive attack and the fighting became "almost inconceivably fierce," in the words of Union Maj. Samuel Sturgis.[5] At times the opposing lines closed to within thirty or forty yards, but neither side was able to gain a permanent advantage.

Although he had been wounded in the head and leg earlier that morning, Lyon placed himself at the forefront of the fresh 2nd Kansas Infantry. As Lyon and the Kansans moved toward a thicket of underbrush, a volley rang out. A musket ball penetrated Lyon's left side, and he became the first United States general officer to die in the war. Shortly after Lyon's death, Price disengaged his men and regrouped for yet another assault, the third and final of the battle.

Major Sturgis, the highest ranking Regular Army officer not killed or wounded, was now in command of the Federal army. He faced a number of grim prospects. His force still was vastly outnumbered by the Confederates, low on ammunition and Sigel's fate was unknown. In addition, Sturgis soon learned that he faced yet a another assault, the largest concentration of the enemy to advance against the Federals thus far during the battle. Three regiments of Arkansas State Troops and a Missouri State Guard regiment, which had remained idle throughout the morning, comprised the new attack force. Price himself led these 2,000 men toward Sturgis' position on the Southern left flank. The reinforced Southern column surged forward again about 10:30 a.m.

Despite a heavy pounding, the Union line held against the onslaught for thirty minutes, and Price once more withdrew his forces. During this lull, Sturgis was warned about the perilously low ammunition supply. By about 11:30 a.m. the Union commander gave the order to disengage, and his men began their slow withdrawal to Springfield, where they arrived around 5:00 p.m. Nearly a quarter of the Federal Army had become casualties, with 258 killed, 873 wounded and 186 missing.

The Confederates cautiously moved to the crest of Bloody Hill and watched the Federals retreat in the distance. Rapid pursuit was not an option, largely because their ammunition supply, like Sturgis', was low, and it was widely believed that Union reinforcements were on the way. In addition, the Southerners had likewise suffered heavily in the battle, losing 12% of their total force, at least 279 dead and 951 wounded.

The Union army began a retreat early the next morning to the town of Rolla, the nearest railhead about 110 miles northeast of Springfield. A few hours

William P. Barlow later in life

Missouri Historical Society

later the leading elements of the Southern army entered Springfield. Soon, however, the fragile alliance of Price, McCulloch and Pearce began to splinter. Price was in favor of an immediate advance to the Missouri River to sever the Union supply line, gather recruits and retake the state. McCulloch resisted this strategy, claiming that his supplies were nearly exhausted, an advance deep into Missouri would overextend his supply lines, and.his men still very undisciplined. In addition, his orders were to protect Arkansas and the Indian Territory, not seize Missouri. To make matters worse, Pearce's Arkansas troops had reached the end of their enlistments, and by late August had voted to return home. By that time, Price had started to march his State Guard north alone, intent on the capture of the Union garrison at Lexington on the Missouri River. McCulloch's men remained in southwest Missouri a few weeks, then finally fell back into northwest Arkansas for good.

Price succeeded in capturing Lexington on September 20 after a short siege, but was soon forced to retreat back to southwest Missouri. Western Department commander Gen. John C. Frémont led a large Union army to recapture Springfield on October 25, but he was relieved of command and his force withdrew, leaving the city once again in the hands of the Missouri State Guard. The Southerners remained in Springfield until February 1862, when a new force under the command of Maj. Gen. Samuel Curtis drove Price from Springfield to Arkansas. There, Curtis met the combined forces of the State Guard and McCulloch's troops under the overall command of Gen. Earl Van Dorn in the decisive battle of Pea Ridge on March 7-8. In this action the Confederates were soundly defeated and McCulloch killed. After Pea Ridge, Missouri was firmly in Union control, although the state was beset by vicious guerrilla warfare and periodic Confederate raids for the remainder of the war.[6]

Perhaps one of the most complete narratives of the service of a Missouri State Guard unit during the dramatic Missouri Campaign of 1861 was written by First Lieutenant William P. Barlow, of Henry Guibor's Battery.[7] Born on June 17, 1838 in New York City, Barlow apparently travelled to St. Louis with his parents in 1852, where he learned the printer's trade. He became active in a local militia company, the St. Louis Grays, and became a volunteer fireman. Just before the outbreak of the Civil War, Barlow saw active service with the militia in guarding the Missouri border from incursions by Kansas jayhawkers. Despite his Northern birth, Barlow became a staunch defender of Missouri and states' rights.[8]

Barlow's post-war recollections of his service with Guibor's Battery are an invaluable record of life in the State Guard. He describes in detail the formation of his battery, its role in the battles of Carthage, Wilson's Creek and Lexington, and his struggle to survive between actions. Barlow was an astute observer of men and events, and his pen offers a highly entertaining but factually sound account of the trials of forming a citizen army under the most adverse circumstances. His memoir highlights the difficulty of leading these men into combat without adequate training but with an abundance of nerve and spirit.

Barlow's narrative begins with his flight from St. Louis after the failed Planter's House conference.

When Guibor's battery left St. Louis "between two days," June 13, 1861, it numbered but two members—the now veteran captain and the writer.[9] We were Camp Jackson paroled prisoners and had served respectively as first and second lieutenants in the light battery of the Missouri state force kept in active service on the Kansas border during the preceding winter, known as Bowen's Southwest battalion.[10] Six months' service under [John S.] Bowen's West Point discipline and drill had made fair soldiers of us, and the federal authorities by an indirect tender of a colonel's commission to [Henry] Guibor and one of major to me, had ascertained, by our indignant refusals, how we stood upon the Union question. We did not believe that our paroles would protect us from arrest, and took precautions accordingly. Gov. Claib Jackson issued his proclamation calling the state to arms on the 12th of June, and the next day we were notified that warrants were issued for our arrest, almost before the ink was dry.[11] This caused the battery to muster itself into service three days sooner than was intended, and as Guibor and myself separated at the corner of Fourth and Pine streets, a few minutes after being warned, the sight of a United States marshal in charge of Overton Bassett—whose warrant had been issued with ours—proved that we had little time to lose.[12]

Keeping quiet until after dark we left the city on different roads for a previously selected rendezvous twenty-one miles out, and started to find satisfaction for Camp Jackson. Guibor told his family he was going to the country on a short trip. Four very long years passed before that short trip was completed. The "Battery" was well mounted, both men and horses hardened by active service, and we made a forced march for Jefferson City where we expected to get copies of army regulations and artillery tactics shipped by Capt. Martin Burke of the St. Louis Greys in a box of soap.[13] But Gen. Lyon reached

Jefferson [City] one day ahead, and we started for Boonville, but were again too late.[14]

At that time in city and country the one sovereign remedy for all political evils was to "arrest" somebody. On arriving at Versailles our inquires for the army arouse suspicion, and we were politely placed under surveillance during one night. But the next morning we so distinguished ourselves teaching two companies the mystery of wheeling by fours that suspicion was abated, and we pushed on, intercepting the retreating forces at Warsaw on or about the 22d of June.[15]

Our first experience after joining was a second arrest. While eating breakfast the next morning a pompous ruffian swaggered into the room and demanded, "Whose company do you belong to?" A contemptuous reply, which it were safer to have worded more civilly, drove him off, but in a few minutes a powerful man, bearded like a pirate rushed in, whisked out a rusty old dragoon sabre, and with one grand flourish of this blade proclaimed us his prisoners.

The indifferent manner in which we continued eating astonished our captor—the brave and worthy Capt. Sam Livingston of Versailles, whom I last saw a veteran in 1864 commanding his company in Cockrell's brigade in Alabama.[16] Much disappointed at not having a fight he finally rested the point of his sabre upon the floor and courteously waited until we finished breakfast.

Our not belonging to some company—regiments were then unknown—was ample proof that we were spies, and we were closely guarded a few hours, until Gov. Jackson could be found, by whom we were recognized and vouched for.

The governor introduced us to Gen. M. M. Parsons, who in turn introduced us to the "artillery wagons," as the battery was called, which were in his division in charge of the same Capt. Livingston who had captured us and who was very glad to get rid of them.[17]

The result of an inspection of the outfit was my disgusted query to Guibor: "Are you going to take charge of this thing?" Yes, he decidedly was, and we were installed as captain and first lieutenant respectively. No two men, raging with a desire to get even for the Camp Jackson massacre, ever had a more discouraging set of tools offered to work with.

There were three guns, four six-pounder caissons, battery wagon and forge, each drawn by a four-mule team, in plough or wagon harness, driven by a long, lean Missourian with a single checkline. Of ammunition there was about a half supply, and of equipments nothing but one sponge-staff. Not a friction primer could be found. The only way to discharge the guns was to build a fire of fence-rails and "touch them off" with burning splinters after priming from a powder-horn. A pint of water applied to the pocket of the man who carried the matches would have effectually silenced the battery until the next farmhouse could be reached. One old linstock—a relic of the ancient days—and a small supply of quick match were all the boys had thought necessary to take from the Liberty arsenal in the way of small equipments.[18]

The men, reasoning by analogy, could load a piece as they would a shotgun, and had a hazy notion of stopping vent with the bare thumb, and they knew that the call, "O yes, O yes, Capt. —'s company, parade here!" meant come out of the brush and bunch up in line if they felt like it.

Our past winter's experience in a battery well-equipped, uniformed and drilled, had given us high notions. The contrast was too great, and that night, when Guibor and myself lay down on our single half-blanket with only our hats to cover with, we went to sleep wondering how we should meet Totten's regular battery, whose rapid and precise drill we had admired in St. Louis.[19]

Then we went to work in earnest: Guibor's inventive ingenuity was equal to every necessity. Dry fence rails, hewn down with an axe and finished with a drawing knife, made good sponge-staffs, and sheepskins answered for sponge cover until we captured better ones, while cotton rope, saturated with turpentine, made a species of quick match as a substitute for friction primers, which was at least better than none.

Our first grand exhibition of artillery was in firing a salute at Camp Lamar (where Rains' division joined Parsons') to celebrate the arrival of "Kelly's men," under Col. Joe Kelly and Capts. Stephen Coleman and Rock Champion. Guibor stopped vent and I sponged and loaded, to the great admiration of hundreds who had never even seen a piece of artillery before.[20]

But we soon had the boys well enough instructed to do their own firing, rapidly and correctly. By constant work and drill, in the morning before, and at night after the day's march, in a week's time we gained an astonishing degree of efficiency. No one, who had not witnessed it, could believe how quickly those raw country boys picked up the intricate artillery drill. We only taught each man one particular duty, and did not "change numbers." And by forming regularly "in battery" or "action front" each night, in that week's time, the drivers of pieces and caissons learned to swing their four mule teams around with a vigor, if not with an accuracy worthy of veterans. If the mules were wild, and wouldn't stop when Guibor ordered, "Halt," and the drivers yelled, "Whoa-a," that was not the driver's fault, and a piece of "flying artillery" on a broad Missouri prairie could easily be wheeled around into its proper position.

We had relinquished our notions of style, and our sole aims in life were to kill Yanks and to get something to eat.

On our second or third day's march I witnessed a new way of giving orders. Our division had taken the wrong road, and Gen. Parsons sent his quartermaster, Col. Tom Monroe, to reverse the head of the column.[21] The colonel galloped to the front of the leading wagon, halted, drew a navy six, cocked and pointed it at the leading driver's head and yelled, "Turn around thar,' you, and go back!" Our teamsters were more independent than generals, but that one "turned around" with no back talk.

The battery also quickly acquired a peculiar way of its own. The next day Col. Bob McCulloch joined the column by an intersecting road, at the head of a long string of mounted men, just as our guns were passing.[22] Seeing the way blocked, the old gentleman bawled out, "Get out of the way with them artillery wagons!" It has always been a mystery why the brave but kindly old man did not resent my indignant reply of "Go to hell."

But this was the way everyone looked upon the artillery. Almost every day someone would take command and it took much ugly talking to convince those willing, but unmilitary people that the battery was disposed to consider itself an actual military organization. . . .

The affair at Carthage hardly rose to the dignity of a respectable skirmish, but it was impressive and grand to us then. I remember feeling the beauty of the scene as our mules maliciously wheeled the pieces into battery, and we looked down from our slight ridge and saw the bright guns of the federal battery and their finely uniformed infantry deploying on the green prairie, about 800 yards distant. Both sides formed in silence and stood looking at each other. As soon as we were ready Guibor galloped over to Gen. Parsons and asked permission to open the fight. It was given. I carefully pointed the right piece, Guibor nodded his head, bang she went, and the first shot we ever saw fired in earnest—the first gun for Missouri-went flying through the air. The enemy must have fired at sight of our smoke, for this shot had barely reached them when their answering shot came roaring by, carrying off [the] left and right arms of Hicks and Doyle—front and rear rank men—of Kelly's command, who were standing sturdily on our left.[23]

Weightman's—afterwards Bledsoe's—battery, formed a short distance to our right, also opened fire immediately.[24] For the next half hour I remember little. It was an almost continuous roar of whizzing shot and bursting shell; mules standing on end; one team stampeding with a limber toward the enemy, and getting well out in front before a mounted officer overtook and brought them back; men becoming exhausted by hard work and excitement in the hot sun; and I all the time praying that the enemy would run, and thus bring this horrid battle to an end. Yet, with all this fuss, we had but two men slightly wounded.

After twenty minutes to a half hour of this harmless artillery duel, Gen. Parsons ordered an advance, and when I returned from the field hospital, after some slight personal repairs, the enemy were retiring over Dry Fork creek, just in rear of their position, with Kelly's boys skirmishing in the timber to our left and practising their first "rebel yell."

I well remember that we all thought his contemptible little skirmish a great battle and a great victory, and when our last shot was sent rolling over the prairie, about a half mile beyond Carthage, after dark, and the pursuit ceased, we were very glad the awful battle was ended, and went into camp thoroughly tired out. Our reward was the following in Gen. Parsons' official report: ". . .and also Capt. Guibor and Lieut. Barlow of the artillery. I might recount several instances of personal valor of the two last mentioned officers which came under my own observation, but it is sufficient to say that by their prowess the artillery of my division won a position on the field."

After an experience of real fighting in real battles this high praise will sound ludicrous to the old soldier, but the general was in earnest, and we accepted the compliment as well earned, honestly feeling that we had participated in a decisive engagement, with perhaps, a mental reservation that we were heroes on a small scale.

After Carthage Guibor's ingenuity was exercised in establishing an "arsenal of construction." We had found a number of loose, round shot in the battery wagon. A turning-lathe in the town supplied sabots, and the owner of a tin shop contributed straps and canisters, iron rods donated by and cut up in the black-smith shop made good slugs for the canister and a bolt of flannel, needles and thread, freely given by some dry goods man, furnished material for cartridge bags. A bayonet made a good candlestick, and at night, after the day's march, the men went to work sewing cartridge bags, strapping shot to the sabots, filling the bags from a barrel of powder placed some distance from the candle, in the meantime watching each change of the wind and fearing it might blow a spark from the candle and blow us up.

My first cartridge resembled a turnip, rather than the trim cylinders from federal arsenals and would not enter a gun on any terms. But we soon learned the trick, and at the close range at which the next battle was fought our home-made ammunition proved as effective as the best.

While at Carthage our rascal, Jack Murphy, learned the boys an old regu-lar's trick.[25] The quartermaster had secured a lot of stores, including whiskey, in a store and placed a guard from Rain's division over them. Jack inspected the outfit, mounted his horse, galloped to camp, and soon Corporal Casey, with nine more of Kelly's boys, stole out, carrying their guns and accoutrements.[26] As they drew near the store these well-drilled soldiers formed in double rank, took the lock step, under Jack as sergeant and Casey as corporal of the guard, marched up to the guard—"halt, front, order arms," and the officer in charge was informed in pompous military style that "Your guard is relieved, sir!" Who could doubt it, when the only drilled and unformed soldiers in the army stood there, as rigid as statues, eyes to the front, at silent attention, and all this backed by Jack's sweeping military salute with his own dragoon sabre. Not a doubt entered the heads of the guard, and they quickly turned over their valuable stores to these choice plunderers. This store was on the southeast corner of the square, a small, one-story frame building, and within a short distance of "tall timber." Placing three men on post, the rest went inside, filled as many tin buckets as they could carry with whiskey, drank all they dared to, and when the coast was clear loaded up, hurried into the woods and came to camp. The speedy result, or course, was a large number of drunken men.

Our next movement was to Neosho and thence to the Arkansas border.

It is not pleasant to dwell on our march to Cowskin prairie or our tedious waiting and starving there. I remember few incidents outside of our incessant hard work.

One was, on our return march to Springfield, seeing the road marked with the blood of our barefooted men while crossing the rocky Osage range.

Of Archie McFarland, afterwards colonel of the Fourth Missouri, then adjutant of McBride's division, visiting our camp with three potatoes in his pocket and when we gave him some tough beef acknowledging that he was so weak from starvation as to be barely able to ride his horse.[27]

Of how, for dinner, we simply halted in the road by a corn field and roasted the green corn on a fire of fence rails, and once lived two days on this diet alone.

Of how freely the farmers gave one-half their crops and one-half their cattle, and how one good man grumbled when the next division came along and asked for the remaining half.

Of seeing one of our powder wagon drivers seated on a barrel of powder, light his pipe by striking a match against the side of the barrel, and plenty of loose powder in the bottom of the wagon, which, as the driver well knew, had shaken out of the barrels.

The strangest feature was that money was absolutely no use. I had a good supply of gold and silver, but could purchase nothing. What the people could spare they gave freely, and money would not be received.

We had got an old tent, labelled in large letters, "Catahoula Guerrillas," from Hebert's Louisiana regiment, and each night the same old exercise—a barrel of powder in one corner, a lighted candle in the other, with the boys between filling cartridges—was repeated.[28] It was very hard work.

In the mean time, we had been gradually replacing our mules with horses, and by the time we reached Oak hills, or Wilson's Creek, considered ourselves in good fighting trim again.

Our next battle—Oak Hills or Wilson's Creek—was to be a real battle. No long-range skirmishing, but a close, deadly and persistent struggle on both sides, often at forty to sixty yards, in the close underbrush.

As ordnance officer of Parsons' division I had, on the 9th of August, issued ammunition for battle, and we were under orders to march that night. Our ordnance stores consisted principally of powder in one-pound canisters, G. D. caps and bar lead. Most of the men carried hunting rifles and each of the men had his own bullet mould. Each company carried enough hand-melting ladles to mould their bullets. We had a few buck and ball cartridges for shot guns and minnies [sic] for Kelly's men, who alone carried rifled muskets.

On the morning of August 10 the battery was parked on the Cassville and Springfield road.[29] We were completely surprised, a six-pound shot waking us from a sound sleep. Instantly [we were] in commotion. This was our first alarm, and I well remember how all rushed for the horses and guns, rolling our pieces of blankets as we ran. Orders were unnecessary. Each knew his work, and the horses, standing all night ready harnessed, were quickly hitched up, and inside of five minutes we were following Kelly's noble fellows, advancing rapidly to the northwest to assist Rain's division, encamped on the higher ground in that direction.

In advancing from a quarter to a half mile, we were under fire from the first, and wounded men were already coming back, and probably within twenty minutes from the opening gun we were hotly engaged with Totten's battery, Kelly's boys supporting us. We were very close, and one of the enemy's guns was soon silenced, when we saw a man walk up on his knees and insert a cartridge in the muzzle of the gun. Rock Champion, seeing this, called out "My God, don't kill that fellow. He is too brave a man." And this within probably less than thirty minutes from the time when we were all in a sound sleep.

I thought that we were certain to be defeated, and when Sigel closed in our rear, also thought I would be hung if captured fighting under my parole.

Then for the next six hours, it was "pull Dick, pull devil," with the devil ahead nearly half the time. I know nothing about the battle, except what occurred immediately in front of our guns. In the many positions occupied by Parsons' division that day it was an almost constant give and take—repulsing the enemy and advancing and being ourselves repulsed in turn and falling back a short distance, or moving to the right or left, wherever the fire was hottest or Gen. Price sent for us.

We first discovered that we were surrounded, when in moving from our extreme left around by the rear towards the right, following a narrow ridge, we came out of the woods right under Sigel's guns formed in battery and pointed at us on the high ridge just south of the creek, about 250 yards distant. We were completely at their mercy, as on our first movement towards forming in battery they could have riddled us. As a feeler they fired one shell, but as we kept on at a slow walk they evidently mistook us for one of Lyon's batteries and allowed us to pass their front.

We were soon hotly engaged again, and from then till the close all is to me a confused medley of close fighting and rapid moving. Three different times—I think it was four—we formed in battery behind dense thickets, loaded with canister, and waited until the enemy advanced to within fifty yards before opening fire. Once we let them come up within fifty feet, and waited too long, for Corporal J. Foley, gunner of the left piece, was killed by a bayonet thrust forcing us to open fire. The man who killed him came out of the bushes right among the cannoneers, not knowing they were there, lunged out with his bayonet and got away. Twice during the day I drew my pistol to shoot federals within thirty of forty feet, and—it seems strange now to tell it—could not spare the time even to aim at one.

Gen. McCulloch rode into the battery several times, and once dropped a federal with his carbine but a few yards in our front.

This will give some idea of how close the battle was fought. I visited the ground fourteen years after and found that a half mile square would more than cover the real fighting and maneuvering of our battery in the battle.

Of the general course of the battle, as previously stated, I know nothing until the wind-up—a separate affair in itself—when having had a few minutes rest, and got cooled down, my recollection is clear. It is worthy of record, as I have never seen a correct account of the finish, and also to show a rare instance of bravery of a soldier, which, in older countries, would go on the historic page.

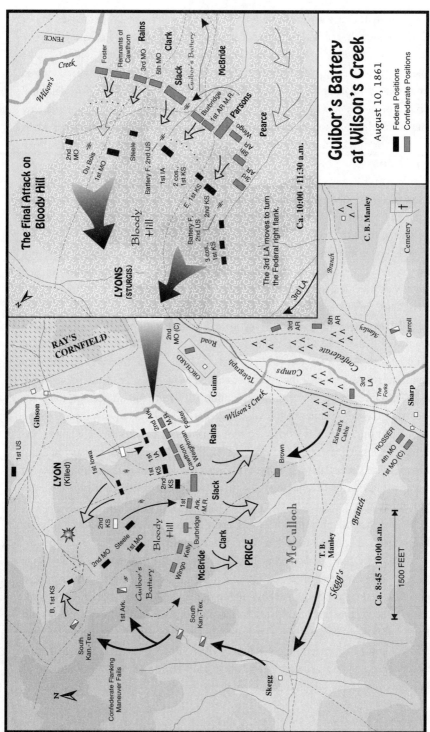

Mark A. Moore

Guibor's Battery at Wilson's Creek
August 10, 1861

Federal Positions

Confederate Positions

The Final Attack on Bloody Hill

Ca. 10:00 - 11:30 a.m.

The 3rd LA moves to turn the Federal right flank.

Ca. 8:45 - 10:00 a.m.

1500 FEET

The enemy had been repulsed all around the circle, front and rear, and firing had almost ceased. Our lines advanced, Churchill's Arkansas regiment on the left and Kelly's men on right on the battery, and formed facing what is now called "Bloody Hill," upon which, looking through the undergrowth, we could see the federals also deploying in a dense blue line, about 150 yards distant.[30] Our guns were loaded with canister, pointed, and the men sat down to await developments. Gen. Price rode up and said he believed the opposing line was a regiment he had sent around from our left. On being assured, very positively, to the contrary, he tried to send up some skirmishers from a regiment on our left, but the men ignorant of the art of skirmishing, did not go. So, to satisfy the general that we were in imminent danger, a private soldier in the battery was called for:

"Jack Murphy."

"Here, sir; here, sir."

"Jack, Gen. Price wants you to go up there and get killed for him. Find out if they're feds or not."

"I'll do't, sir; I'll do't."

Jack was an old regular—a recent deserter from the [s]econd [D]ragoons—an Irishman, and his eyes fairly danced at the thought of showing off before Gen. Price. Jack mounted his big gray stallion, drew an old single-barrelled horse-pistol and started to the front at a trot, his face covered with a huge grin as he heard the general say in a kindly tone:

"Tell him not to expose himself too much. We do not want to lose the lives of brave men."

This only made Jack the more daring, and he rode right up to them—how close I dare not say-but about half a company fired at him. He turned and came back at a run, obliquing to our right to clear the front of the battery, and so soon as he was out of the way every piece fired at once. Then commenced another of those strange silent advances of our infantry, without orders, on right and left with the discharge of our guns, our infantry fired a volley, advanced a few steps, loaded, fired, and in this manner slowly advanced down the slope and up the opposite side, disappearing in their own smoke amidst that terrible "long roll" of musketry, where one shot cannot be distinguished from another.

Gen. Price intently peered into the bank of smoke for a minute or two, then slowly followed, while we in the battery, being compelled to cease firing canister by the advance, threw a few round shot high, for moral effect, then ceased firing altogether, and listened in awe-stricken silence, marking by the sound that our line was slowly, but steadily advancing until suddenly the firing ceased, and there was silence all over the field.

The battle ended as abruptly as it commenced. The enemy let go all at once and scattered through the woods to the rear, one small battalion exciting the admiration of our men by going off in perfect order in columns of fours at the double quick with arms at right-shoulder shift.

It was some time before anyone could comprehend that the battle was really ended, so sudden was its cessation, but word soon came that Gen. Lyon was killed and his body identified, when we at last realized that our apparently certain defeat had changed into certain and complete victory.

I also realized that a beaten army is only a little worse off physically than the victorious one, for we were too badly cut up and too thoroughly exhausted to think of pursuing.

A final count showed less than ten rounds of ammunition and an average of three horses per gun, with a loss of fourteen men, out of about sixty engaged.

For the names of ten of the killed and wounded I am indebted to the wonderfully correct account of the battle by Capt. J.H. McNamara of St. Louis.[31] Both Guibor and myself had forgotten most of them, but how familiar their names sound now.

Killed—Corporal J. Foley, gunner of left piece, bayonet.

Corporal W. H. Douglas, gunner, right piece; cut in two by round shot.

Private W. N. Hicks, No. 4 second piece.

Wounded—First Sergt. J. J. (Johnny) Corkery (of the old "St. Louis Greys").[32]

Privates R. J. Brown, N. Dayton, M. O'Neil, F. G. Studdart, J. G. Shockley, C. D. Zumalt, Adam—(a German), and to the best of my recollection three others, whose names cannot be recalled.[33]

The most peculiar feature of this battle was the grim silence observed by all during the long hours. Old friends like Guibor and myself, and brothers, even, standing side by side at the same gun, set their teeth firmly, and only spoke when positively necessary. It was the same in the infantry on either side of us—no cheering and very few orders. They had not learned the "rebel yell." All fought in silence. Sometimes the line would simultaneously, without an order, advance as the enemy gave way, and again slowly fall back when too hard pressed, without an order from anyone, never confused, never in a hurry. I have been in many battles since, but have never seen anything like this.

"Old" Guibor, as a few friends called him, though a young man, sat his horse as solemnly as if going to church. When replying to any specially heavy fire, Gen. Parsons was certain to ride in between the guns, twisting his beard and seemed even more quiet and deliberate than usual.

Gen. Price often rode up, sometimes under the hottest fire, gazed earnestly into the smoke, often without uttering a word and twice without a single attendant. In this quiet coolness there was absolutely no difference between generals and men in the ranks.

I noticed several times how carefully old hunters loaded their heavy hunting rifles when dead and wounded were lying thick around them; they would place a piece of cotton or buckskin over the muzzle, press down the ball a little, pull an old knife from the pocket, cut off the patching, return the knife and ram the ball gently down, put on a cap, then gaze under the smoke and look for a shot. It did not appear to be courage, but all seemed to be dazed or horrified into an unconsciousness of danger; all seemed to feel that they must fight and that they could not possibly do anything else. I cannot describe it, but it was different from anything I saw afterwards.

I have since been much impressed, on looking back, with the willingness and promptness with which our green men in the battery handled the guns. We had received thirty men the day before, just from their homes, and these were the first pieces of artillery they had ever seen. But all the new men as readily as the old ones—jumped promptly at the first word and obeyed intelligently and unhesitatingly. It was never necessary to repeat an order. The men had, without the slightest pressure from officers, quietly resolved themselves into that condition called by martinets "strict discipline."

This was purely voluntary and could not have been maintained otherwise, as each felt at perfect liberty to go home when he pleased, and none had been regularly mustered into service. In fact, about his time one of our cannoneers "resigned" to take a situation at the Joplin lead mines, and left as a matter of course without opposition or remonstrance.[34]

I select one little incident of this battle as indicating the material these raw country boys were made of.

Our line had been forced from the crest of a ridge, and the battery had just reached the bottom when a wheel horse of a gun was killed. The battery was ordered to ascend the hill in rear and open fire, leaving the gun and its detachment alone under the enemy's fire. The men removed the dead wheel-horse and put a lead horse in its place, which was also shot down before starting. This left but two live horses, hitched tandem, and the brave fellows then removed the wheel harness from the first horse killed, harnessed the sergeants's horse, pulled the gun by hand away from the two dead animals, hitched up again and rejoined the battery, pulling up the hill with three horses, the men assisting at the wheels.

I doubt if this feat was excelled—I never heard of its being equalled—during the war.

Another incident will give some idea of the spirit of patriotism with which Missourians fought for their homes.

An old, white-haired gentleman—a Campbellite preacher—came to Rock Champion the night before battle, and said he considered it his duty to fight in the expected battle at Springfield, but did not know how to load a gun. I well remember how Rock drilled him by the camp-fire that night, showing him how to tear a cartridge with his teeth and impressing upon him the necessity of pouring in the powder first and of putting in the minie ball right end up. The worthy old man was killed next morning, almost at the first fire.

Gen. McCulloch so worded his official reports as to convey the impression that this battle was fought by his troops, assisted by Missourians. That it was essentially a Missouri fight is shown by the official reports of killed and wounded. . . .[35] McCulloch's troops, notably the Third Louisiana, Pearce's Arkansas brigade and Churchill's mounted rifles, the latter fighting as infantry, did splendid work, and without them we would certainly have been defeated, but it is not necessary for their well-earned fame that Gen. McCulloch's reports should go uncriticized and the credit withheld from Missouri of doing the major part of the heavy work.[36]

The next day after the battle we marched a short distance, and on the next, August 12, went into camp at Phelps' farm, two or three miles southwest from Springfield. As we were going into camp Capt. Guibor was informed by a citizen that Gen. Lyon's body was "lying back there by the side of the road, thrown over the fence." Knowing Mrs. John S. Phelps to be a prominent Union lady, Guibor sent this message to her, describing the place, and asking if she desired to take charge of the body.[37] The man who carried the message to Mrs. Phelps returned and reported that she had sent a wagon with a negro driver after the body. Soon afterwards it was reported that the wagon had returned with the body, and soon after this Mrs. Phelps sent a request to Guibor for some men to bury it, and he called for volunteers. A squad from the battery and Kelly's infantry immediately went over and buried the body. When the men returned and reported that they had completed their work, at Capt. Rock Champion's laughing suggestion, he, Col. Joe Kelly, Capt. Guibor, Lieut. Crow and myself, with perhaps a few others, went over through Mrs. Phelps' garden and, standing beside the grave, were so unchristianlike as to "exult" over having the hero of Camp Jackson safe under ground.[38] I believe now that Gen. Lyon regretted the Camp Jackson massacre as much as anyone, but at that time we had not recovered from the shock of seeing our men murdered when prisoners, and we felt morbidly revengeful.

For twenty-two years all concerned in this burial have believed that the flag-of-truce party, which received the body from Gen. Price on the evening of the battle, had stampeded in the hurried retreat of the federal army and thrown the body over the fence. This was the general belief in our camps, and was seemingly proven by the fact that when Guibor sent the message to Mrs. Phelps that the body was lying by the roadside, the man who carried the message did not bring back any contradiction, but simply the reply of "thanks," and when the wagon was sent and soon returned with the body, we thought, as a matter of course, that the general supposition was correct. But a series of articles, published in the [St. Louis *Missouri Daily*]*Republican*, throw an entirely different light upon the matter.

Dr. E. C. Franklin, surgeon Fifth Missouri (United States) volunteers, states that he took charge of the body at 10 p.m. at headquarters, on the night it arrived, in presence of Gens. Scofield and Sturgis, and left the body in charge of a Mr. Beal, undertaker, "who performed the last obsequies."[39] Dr. Franklin also states that he engaged Mr. Beal to make the coffin, paid him for it and has his receipt. He also believes that his assistant surgeon, Dr. Melcher, "had charge of the detail" that buried the body.[40]

Then Dr. Melcher, Fifth Missouri Volunteers, in anther communication, states that he in person received the body from Gen. Price on the battlefield and with five *Confederate* soldiers escorted the body to Springfield in a wagon driven by one of the *Confederates*, and met the flag-of-truce party about half way to Springfield; that he delivered the body to Maj. Schofield at the house used for headquarters, arriving at Springfield at "nearly 8 o'clock" (the night of the battle, August 10), and that between 1 and 2 p.m. the next day, August 11, the [C]onfederate troops came in and "took possession of the town and house where the body lay."

Dr. Melcher also says that on passing Totten's camp that officer relieved the ([C]onfederate) escort and sent them back to their command, and a new driver was furnished.

Maj. C. C. Rainwater of St. Louis states that he was one of the [C]onfederate escort accompanying the body from the battlefield to Springfield; that the body was carried in Gen. Price's ambulance, and that they met the flag of truce party, who returned to Springfield with them, where this flag of truce party placed the body in a house, took possession of the ambulance and departed with it towards Rolla.[41]

Mrs. Lula Kennedy, now living in Springfield, states that by 9 o'clock a.m. of the 11th she saw the body "at Maj. Dorn's house, in charge of Mrs. Phelps and Mrs. Beal," and that a servant of Mrs. Phelps drove the body to her (Mrs. Phelps') house that day.[42]

Capt. Guibor and myself know that the body was not buried until the second day after the battle—August 12—from its having been buried by our men on the day we camped on the Phelps' farm.

On comparing these later reports it is plain that our belief at the time, that "the flag of truce party stampeded and threw the body over the fence," should be modified by substituting "into a house" for the last three words, for they carried off Gen. Price's ambulance, which was returned a few days later.

It is also plain that the federal officials carefully evade the point of how their commander's body twice fell into our hands, and of its burial by our men.

No other course seems left to them in face of their official and personal assertions of victory on that field, which alone gives the subject any importance.

Our friends on the other side do not need this subterfuge to maintain their reputation for hard and gallant fighting at Oak Hills. Gen. Lyon must have been an officer of rare ability to bring his men persistently to the attack for six long hours, for on other fields the federals did not always continue their efforts after repeated repulses. They were defeated, and very badly, too, while we were nearly as badly used up. To paraphrase the Duke of Wellington's description of a battle, it was hard pounding and they got tired first. It was, in fact, as it proved by official reports, the hardest fighting done by either side during the first year of the war.

After such a smash-up as the battle of Oak Hills the battery imperatively needed refitting. After going into camp at Phelps' farm near Springfield, Mo., we first took a good rest, and—what was better—got enough to eat once more.

Siegel's battery was in our possession, parked in line with our guns. When the Third Louisiana captured this battery and brought guns and caissons pell-mell down the hill and across the creek by the road from Sharp's house, we happened to be moving across the field in that vicinity and the Louisiana boys turned their cumbersome trophies over to us, glad to be rid of them. I noticed an old blue [?] worm in the hooks under one piece which had a familiar look and then recognized the guns as our old pieces taken from us at Camp Jackson. There was the new gun carriage made by our artificers at Ball's Mills the preceding winter to replace the clumsy old "Gribeauvael" which Gen. Jas. A. Harding had found at Jefferson and sent to us on the border.[43] These were the guns on which Bowen, brightly remembering his cadet days—had carefully instructed us in the "school of the piece," and breathed harsh censure when drivers broke poles in turning too short on field days. We were glad to get our old friends into camp, and hoped to keep them. But alas, Gen. McCulloch refusing to advance with us, demanded the guns, and took them to Little Rock to remain on exhibition.

Only the bare guns, however, were given up. We simply stole everything else and denied having received it. How nicely that brass-mounted federal harness looked on those fat federal horses. And how welcome were the friction primers and small equipments.

Gen. Price told Capt. Guibor, when the latter made a vain attempt to retain Siegel's guns, that, as the captured small arms, then in the hands of the men, were simply indispensable he had in reply to McCulloch's demand for trophies of the battle, arranged to turn over the artillery and retain the small arms.

Our next move was to replenish empty ammunition chests. A foundry in Springfield was taken possession of, six-pound balls cast, cast iron rods cut into slugs for canister and in two or three weeks, well rested and equipped, we started north for the Missouri river.

The next day after the battle of Oak Hills, as I should have stated before, the federal prisoners were introduced to our army ration. Guibor, Rock Champion and myself visited the prisoners to look for friends from St. Louis. While talking with them, a wagon load of green corn was driven inside of the fence which surrounded the prisoners, whereupon one of them inquired: "What is that for? We have no horses."

Champion replied: "Those are your rations."

Col. John S. Cavender of St. Louis angrily replied: "Is that the way you feed prisoners?"[44]

Champion: "Yes, that's all we have, and we give you the best we've got."

And this was the truth. But as the corn ripened and every mill was set grinding for the army we soon had cornmeal and fresh beef, though often were out of salt. And we even had potatoes at times.

Soon we were on the march northward, and next met the enemy at Dry Wood, a few miles east of Fort Scott, on the 7th of September, 1861.[45] About noon, as we were quietly jogging along through the narrow belt of timber skirting Dry Wood creek, we were startled by a sharp rattle of rifles just ahead, instantly followed by the boom of Bledsoe's battery, which sounded startlingly close, and it was. We hurried on, one or two hundred yards, and came out upon the open prairie into a dense grass just the height of one's shoulders when mounted. Over this rank growth we could see the smoke of Bledsoe's guns, and close in front of them the heads of a few mounted federal officers, apparently urging their men on to the guns where Bledsoe was said to be lying wounded.

Capt. Guibor with the battery, and Rock Champion with our partners, Kelley's men, pitched right in without orders and soon drove the enemy back. Then seeing Gen. Price trotting up we waited an instant for a definite order and received a very indefinite one. The general had just emerged from the timber, and had no time to look or plan anything except to fight on general principles. Riding up and making a sweep with his hand from the northwest around to the northeast, he simply said:

"Take your battery up there and open on 'em."

And the whole military situation was summed up in this simple order. The narrow road through the timber was a gorge, through which our men must advance to deploy on the ground we then stood on. Our four guns and about 100 infantry must advance at once and attack an enemy of unknown force to gain and hold the ground necessary to form line of battle on, and this in a dense grass where men on foot could not be seen over fifty feet away.

We checked the enemy's head of column and advanced so quickly that some 300 yards space was gained before we, in turn, were checked, and found ourselves in a dangerous position. A number of our cannoneers were soon shot down, and in a few minutes but three men remained unhurt on the left gun. The federals were closing around that flank, and the piece was firing extreme left oblique, canister at point-blank range. I ran over to help them, when a shell burst in front and I saw the "fur fly" from the neck of Moulds, a tall cannoneer, who asked permission to go to the rear. This was refused, and we fired three rounds more, when Moulds' left arm dropped, helpless from his wound, leaving but two sound men. We then limbered up the gun and sent it to the rear, feeling that all the others would be lost. The next gun in line was then turned to sweep the flank; when Drake, a tall printer, who was sponging and loading, caught a minnie [sic] close up under his right collar bone, and asked me if he was dangerously hurt, fearing the disgrace of going to the rear with a slight wound.

I saw that the ball had made an ugly hole, but also noticed it was as high up that he could not see it and told him, "No, go to work!" Drake returned to his gun, loaded twice, when his entire shoulder seemed to let down and returned, saying mournfully, "Oh, lieutenant, you're fooling me; I'm badly hurt." "So you are, Drake. Go to the rear."

In the meantime Moulds, who had been forgotten, had gone to Capt. Guibor and complained that he was wounded and I would not let him go back.

These two incidents show of what material those splendid boys were made.

About this time I had lost all hope. But looking over to the right, there stood Kelly's men sturdily in line, loading and firing with beautiful deliberation. Rock Champion, six foot one and a half high, wearing long cavalry boots, was raging like a mad bull up and down the line of file closers yelling, "aim low." In the centre Guibor sat his horse, apparently cool and certainly solemn, and just then Gen. Parsons rode up, slowly twisting his beard, to see how we were getting on. O, how slow his men were forming line back there near the timber, and Guibor showing the general the enemy's heads through the tall grass, slowly but surely swinging around us. Gen. Parsons actually "hurried" back, his line advanced, when suddenly the enemy ceased firing, and our front was clear. The enemy broke at sight of the advancing line, which did not fire a shot. This was one instance where moments were precious. Fifteen minutes longer delay would have ensured our capture, and Lexington could not easily have been taken without artillery.

We then continued on toward Fort Scott until the cavalry reported Gen. Lane retreating toward Warrensburg, when our head of column was turned in that direction. At Warrensburg it appeared that Lane had gone westward toward Kansas, while some Home Guards had fallen back to Lexington, whither we followed, meeting Mulligan's command in line of battle about three miles from the town.[46] These people Gen. Price made one enormous "grab" for, going at them with a rush, but they prudently went back also with a rush, which continued until we were close under the fort. Three times we formed in battery and once loaded only to draw the charges and push on. Under the impression that we were to carry the fort by an instant assault we opened a hot fire at close range, which was hotly returned and a six-pound shot soon passed through one of our limber chests, cutting a bundle of port-fires to pieces and scattering them around when each piece ignited by the explosion commenced a frightful fizzing and sputtering. Rock Champion stood in their midst and, too proud to run in the presence of his men, drew himself up waiting to be blown to pieces, calling out "Hello, Guibor, what the d—-l kind of an infernal machine is this they're throwin' at you?"

Guibor simply laughed in reply, and Rock, much relieved, relaxed from his rigid attitude and tried to laugh, too, but it was a weak attempt.[47]

We then went into camp at the fair grounds and spent a week in manufacturing ammunition for the siege. Solid shot and grape were cast in a foundry in town, and we soon had a good supply.

At last we were gratified with the order for battle.[48] Early on the morning of September 18 Parsons' division was formed on the road to the left to attack from the up river side, the infantry carefully loaded their muskets, and all advanced.

On nearing the hill at the north end of the town we noticed a long column of our men in front opening to right and left and before any one understood the move, the battery and Kelly's men found themselves marching up this lane, the men on each side presenting arms. Gen. Price had selected us to carry this hill, which the enemy appeared to hold in force.

The street was lined with ladies, sobbing and waving their handkerchief and one old gentleman mounted a gate post and "exhorted" our marching column in true camp-meeting style. This fuss and preparation indicated a "forlorn hope" and I remember that, while feeling proud of the compliment, we feared the consequences. Our partners—Kelly's men—with arms at right shoulder shift, gripped their pieces with a painful tightness, and, like the cannoneers, took short, calculating steps, in place of their usual long, free stride.

But Gen. Price had shrewdly posted his brass band under cover at the foot of the hill, and as we approached they struck up a lively Irish battle tune—"Garryowen," Rock said it was—and the effect was magical. Up came the heads, the grip was relaxed, pieces resumed their proper slope, and these well-drilled soldiers instantly swung off into the regulation tramp.

Up the hill we went with two guns, the infantry charging on each side, all in a scramble and all together, meeting a tolerably hot fire, but not the murderous fusillade which was expected. Our infantry opened fire, our two guns were formed "action front;" a negro woman with a white baby went flying across the street under fire, and Jack Murphy sent a solid shot bang through a brick residence close on our left. Cursing him for not firing canister down the street, I jumped from my horse, ran to the gun, and while pointing it at the line in front caught a minie in my left leg; while stamping the ground to learn if the bone was broken, the men seemed to be gazing over my head, and looking around, there sat Gen. Price quietly in the saddle, intently looking at all in a kindly parental way. He had closely followed us up the hill. The enemy instantly gave way, not being in force, we quietly followed, invested the fort and opened a slow fire.[49]

Soon afterward Gen. Price ordered the battery to move rapidly to the river and bring in a steamboat then passing, and here occurred the last attempt of an outside to take command. Jimmy Edwards of Parsons' staff was sick that day, and his place was taken by a very worthy young man named Buchanan, who was new in the service.[50] Gen. Parsons, receiving the same order, sent this aide to repeat it. He did not know how to deliver an order, and seeing the battery moving at a trot, planted his horse across the road and ordered a halt, intending, in his innocence, to tell the boys where to go and what to do. Capt. Guibor was in a hurry, and was outraged beyond endurance by many repetitions of this offence. He ordered the young man out of the way, and not being obeyed, drew and fired at him, but as his pistol was brought down, with a vicious snap it fell into the hand of Sergt. Ed McBride and the ball went high over head.[51] The surprised look of the young man proved that he was innocent of intentional offence, an explanation followed and the affair was laughed at. But it put an effectual stop at last to the habit of irresponsible persons trying to order the "artillery wagons" around. We reached the river in time, and with two shots brought in the steamer "White Cloud" loaded with stores.[52]

The battery then took position on a hill about 400 yards to the northwest of the fort, and settled down to regular siege work.

The first day we tried to burn the college buildings inside the fort with hot shot, but a man was stationed in each room with a shovel and the rascals pitched our hot shot out of the windows as fast as we threw them in.

On the second day cannon-balls became scarce and valuable, and each side commenced hunting up those received and sending them back. Many shot were sent back and forth three or four times each, as we discovered by observing their polished sides, made by penetrating earth or brick walls.

As our lines cut off Mulligan's boys from the river, they soon suffered for water, and on the second day we were told that a woman came out of the fort to a spring midway between the lines and filled a number of canteens, correctly judging that our men would not fire upon her. On her next trip, as we were told, she brought a bucket, but some of our old hunters, with their heavy hair-trigger rifles, had crawled up within a hundred yards and splintered the bucket in her hands. They could stand canteens from the fair sex, but drew the line at buckets.

Some of our men foraged a basket of wine, and it looked strange to see a cannoneer, black with powder after his gun was fired, break the neck off a bottle by striking the wheel tire, take a drink, pass it around and load again.

As soon as the ladies of Lexington became somewhat accustomed to the fire a number of venturesome ones visited the battery with baskets of provisions, and during the three days' siege we fared well. We only permitted these fair caterers to approach the guns when we were resting and, the enemy's guns were spent, and then they would stand behind the brick houses and listen to the frequent whiz of the minnies [sic] in wonder.

I remember that one lady, after we had finished dinner and returned her empty basket, wished to remain and see the guns open fire, and we were compelled to almost drive her away, as the brick walls of a dwelling-house gave little protection from the enemy's shot at that close range.

One day a six-pound ball passed over so close to a gun which Parker Dunnica was sighting as to lift his cap from his head, and with a loud crash cut a leg off an infantry soldier who was leaning against a garden-fence looking on. The poor fellow did not know what was the matter, and stood several seconds dumbfounded, but finally looked down and saw that his leg was gone. It was only then that he knew what had occurred, and his wondering look changed to an expression of terror, but he still stood up, leaning on the fence, until two of our men carried him away. I seized a piece of cord from a limber and started to tie up the leg, but seeing a surgeon near by laughing at my excited manner stopped and yelled at him, "Why, the man will bleed to death." The cool doctor's reply was, "Nonsense, he'll be down there in the hospital and the surgeons 'll have him safe long before the blood starts," and on looking again at the crushed stump sure enough but two drops of blood could be seen. It was my first lesson in surgery. The doctor then told me that it would probably be five minutes before the blood would start, and as the field hospital was only a hundred or two feet back there was no use in getting excited about it. My greenhorn attempt to save the man would probably have killed him. In the meantime wagons were steadily bringing in hemp bales from the country, of which the infantry improvised sap rollers—portable breastworks, the men called them—and our lines were steadily advanced under a constant fire, closer and closer, until about 3 o'clock on the evening of the third day our men had in some places gained secure positions within about sixty yards of the enemy's lines.[53] Since noon the firing had been steadily growing heavier, and at this time the men seemed by a sudden inspiration to determine to end the affair by a general assault. The enemy's fire was principally concentrated upon Slack's and Harris' divisions on the river side and to the eastward, and was very heavy, when Guibor caught the inspiration and advanced from our position on the northeast, running the guns by hand down the slope and up to within canister range and opened a heavy enfilading fire, which partially silenced that of the enemy. Our infantry then commenced swarming over their hemp-bales, when a white hand-kerchief was raised inside the federal lines.[54] It was immediately pulled dow, but it had stopped our fire and numbers of our men stood there in the open space uncertain whether to advance or go back. Then another flag was raised and the official surrender soon followed.

Mulligan had held on a little too long and only the unauthorized action of some one who saw the emergency and threw up his white handkerchief, saved their lines from being carried by assault, when many of their brave fellows would have been uselessly shot down.

Gen. Parsons paid the battery and Kelly's men the neat compliment of sending us inside the works to assist in receiving the prisoners.[55]

Guibor's move in charging a fortified position with light artillery was novel and original, but it was done just at the right moment and succeeded. Gen. Parsons' compliment of marching the battery inside as though the guns might be gratified by a close view of their own work was as new an idea in war as was that of the men in improvising portable breastworks. But the entire army was "original" in every sense, and each man and boy was rapidly learning the art of war in his own way.

Many will remember the old farmer who came in each morning with his rifle and dinner-basket, put in a full day's work, and returned home at dark.

The capture of so many fine horses from Mulligan's cavalry caused a general horse-stealing mania to possess the command. Rock Champion's horse was stolen, and he borrowed Guibor's on which to pursue the thief. Recovering his own, on returning through Lexington he stopped at the quartermaster's office a few minutes, and on coming out found Guibor's horse gone. Rock returned to camp in despair, for the horse was a valuable one, and found the animal had arrived before, having been stolen by one of his own men, who returned to camp, learned the horse belonged to Guibor, and returned it to the battery.

Rock Champion was sent by Gen. Price to conduct the captured officers to Gen. Frémont's headquarters, at or near Jefferson City.[56] When he arrived there Frémont stepped from his tent and took a deliberate, impertinent stare at the stalwart rebel, and Rock, after coolly returning the stare, and seeing that Frémont, with excessive dignity, did not propose to recognize him, made an about face and gave the general his first and last view of a [C]onfederate's rear, standing in this position until Frémont entered his tent.

Champion, on his return, gave a minute account of the numbers, arms, discipline, etc., of the federals, ending with "and every wagon has a tar-bucket slung under it."

We soon commenced our retreat southward, and marched leisurely to Shoal creek, near Neosho. By this time the constant care and hard work had worn us out, and when, with failing health, we looked at our broken-down teams, and thought of the long marches in prospect, with the continued day and night work necessary to manufacture our ordnance supplies, our courage was not equal to the attempt and we resigned, to try our fortunes in the [C]onfederate army proper.

Rock Champion joined us, our resignations were accepted by Gen. Price and returned with the following letter:

HEADQUARTERS, M.S.G., CAMP AT NEOSHO, Oct. 28, 1861.—It affords me much pleasure to state to all friends of the South, that Capt. J.R. Champion, Henry Guibor and Lieut. W.P. Barlow deserve at their hands every facility which can be afforded them in their efforts mentioned to promote the success of our cause. They have each and all conducted themselves in camp with satisfaction to me and always shown gallantry on the field. All friends of the South will, therefore, receive them as men who are entitled to every respect and confidence at their hands.

STERLING PRICE,
Major-General Commanding M.S.G.

The battery was turned over to Capt. Gora [57] and we proceed to Memphis, Tenn., where Guibor's Confederate battery was organized from the Camp Jackson exchanged prisoners.[58]

In this manner ended Guibor's battery in '61.

W. P. BARLOW.

Both Lieutenant Barlow and Guibor's Battery went on to see extensive service during the remainder of the war. Barlow left Guibor to serve in the Watson Louisiana Battery and to command his own battery before the Confederacy's collapse. Guibor and his men moved east of the Mississippi River and saw action during the Vicksburg and Atlanta Campaigns, as well as the battles of Franklin and Nashville. They surrendered in the spring of 1865.[59]

William Barlow's post-war career was nearly as eventful as his service with the artillery. He became editor of the Mobile, Alabama *Register*, and later chief of police in that city. He married Mary Jane Walthal in 1873, and returned to St. Louis by 1877. There he worked as a printer until his death from pneumonia on December 27, 1896, at the age of 58.[60]

Doubtless other men like Barlow looked back fondly on the days of 1861, when the "best blood and the bravest men of Missouri" improvised an army and won some of the Confederacy's earliest and most dramatic victories.[61]

Notes

1. U.S. War Department, *The War of the Rebellion: The Official Records of the Union and Confederate Armies,* 128 vols. (Washington, D.C., 1880-1901), series III, vol. 1, pp. 82-83. Hereinafter cited as *OR*. All references are to series I unless otherwise noted.

2. Among the Camp Jackson captives was the artillery section of Major W. Clark Kennerly's Southwest Battalion, commanded by First Lieutenant Henry Guibor and Second Lieutenant W.P. Barlow. William C. Winter, *The Civil War in St. Louis: A Guided Tour* (St. Louis, 1994), p. 49.

3. Otto C. Lademann, "The Battle of Carthage, Mo.," in *War Papers Read Before the Commandery of the State of Wisconsin, Military Order of the Loyal Legion of the United States,* 4 vols. (Milwaukee, 1914), vol. 4, p. 134.

4. F. F. Weed, "In the Battle of Carthage, Mo.," *Confederate Veteran,* vol. 26 (1918), p. 392.

5. *OR* 3, p. 67.

6. Several major works detail the movements of the various forces during the Missouri Campaign of 1861. For further reading, see David C. Hinze and Karen Farnham, *The Battle of Carthage: Border War in Southwest Missouri, July 5, 1861* (Savas Publishing Co., 1997); John McElroy, *The Struggle for Missouri* (Washington, D.C., 1913); Christopher Phillips, *Damned Yankee: The Life of General Nathaniel Lyon* (Columbia, MO, 1990); Thomas L. Snead, *The Fight for Missouri* (New York, 1886); Jay Monaghan, *Civil War on the Western Border, 1854-1865* (Boston, 1955).

7. Barlow's narrative appeared in the St. Louis *Daily Missouri Republican* in three installments, entitled "Light Battery Service in 1861," published August 1, 1885, "Guibor's Battery in 1861," published August 8, 1885, and "More About Guibor's Battery," published August 22, 1885. Portions of the three articles have been rearranged from their original format by the editors in order to maintain the chronological order of the narrative.

8. St. Louis *Post-Dispatch,* December 28, 1896. Some disagreement exists as to Barlow's place of birth. The 1880 Missouri census lists his birthplace as Michigan, with both parents born in New York. *Tenth Census of the United States, 1880, Population Schedules for St. Louis, Missouri,* Ward 17, Micro T9, National Archives, Washington, D.C., reel 733.

9. Henry Guibor (1823-1899), a native of Alsace, France, served six months in the Missouri Volunteers in the Mexican War, and entered state service as a lieutenant of artillery on December 1, 1860. He led a battery in the Southwest Expedition of 1860-61 and at the capture of Camp Jackson. He was promoted to captain in the state service on June 28, 1861 and the same rank in the Confederate service on March 25, 1862. In civilian life he was a deputy marshal of the criminal court of St. Louis. Winter, *Civil War in St. Louis,* pp. 137-38; *Compiled Service Records of Confederate Soldiers Who Served in Organizations from the State of Missouri,* Record Group 109, Micro 322, National

Archives, Washington, D.C., reel 81. Hereinafter referred to as *Compiled Service Records*.

10. John S. Bowen (1830-1863), a graduate of West Point and a lieutenant colonel in the 1st Regiment, Missouri Volunteer Militia, served as an officer in the Southwest Expedition, in which Missouri militiamen were ordered by Governor R. M. Stewart to the Kansas border to defend the state against raids by "Jayhawkers" in November 1860. Winter, *Civil War in St. Louis*, p. 22. Although many militiamen soon returned home, a portion of the militia force, led by Bowen and including Barlow, remained on the "border" until the following April. Detailed accounts of the expedition's activities may be found in Brown and Company's *History of Vernon County, Missouri* (St. Louis, 1887), pp. 243-68, and in Phillip Thomas Tucker's *The Forgotten "Stonewall of the West": Major General John Stevens Bowen* (Macon, GA, 1997).

11. On June 12, Governor Jackson issued a proclamation calling for 50,000 militiamen to repel any invaders of the state and protect the lives, liberty and property of Missouri's citizens. The same day, General Orders No. 11 was also issued, ordering all commanders of Missouri State Guard districts to assemble any available troops for actual service. U.S. War Department, Record and Pension Office, *Organization and Status of Missouri Troops In Service During the Civil War* (Washington, D.C., 1902), pp. 263-65.

12. Probably Overton W. Barret, captain of Company B, 2nd Regiment Missouri Militia, captured at Camp Jackson and whose name appears on a list of men offered for exchange in October, 1861. Barlow's name appears on the same list. *OR* series II, vol. 1, pp. 555-56.

13. Captain Martin Burke commanded Company A, First Regiment, Missouri Volunteer Militia (St. Louis Grays), a unit that surrendered at Camp Jackson. James Peckham, *Gen. Nathaniel Lyon, and Missouri in 1861* (New York, 1866), pp. 132-33.

14. Lyon's troops captured Jefferson City on June 15, and two days later routed the State Guard forces led by Governor Jackson at the Battle of Boonville. Christopher Phillips, *Damned Yankee: The Life of General Nathaniel Lyon* (Columbia, MO, 1990), pp. 217-20.

15. Governor Jackson's forces retreated from Boonville toward Warsaw, where they arrived sometime after June 21. Arthur Roy Kirkpatrick, "The Admission of Missouri to the Confederacy," *Missouri Historical Review, vol.* 55 (1961), p. 366. One newspaper account claims June 25 as the date of Barlow's arrival in Warsaw. St. Louis *Republic,* April 21, 1895.

16. Probably Captain Samuel Livingstone of Company C, 1st Rifle Regiment, Sixth Division, Missouri State Guard, known as the Morgan (County) Rifles. Richard C. Peterson, James E. McGhee, Kip A. Lindberg and Keith I. Daleen, *Sterling Price's Lieutenants: A Guide to the Officers and Organization of the Missouri State Guard, 1861-1865* (Shawnee Mission, KS, 1995), p. 182.

17. Major General Mosby Monroe Parsons (1822-1865) commanded the Sixth Division, Missouri State Guard during the Missouri Campaign of 1861. He fought in

Arkansas in 1862 and 1863, and in the Red River Campaign and Price's Missouri Raid in 1864. Parsons was killed in Mexico by Republican forces the following year. Ezra J. Warner, *Generals in Gray: Lives of the Confederate Commanders* (Baton Rouge, 1959), pp. 228-29.

18. The "Missouri Depot," commonly called the Liberty Arsenal, was seized and held by prosecession forces from April 20-27, 1861. In addition to slow match, artillery ammunition and equipment, three bronze Model 1841 six-pounder field guns were taken as well, and provided to Guibor's Battery. Major Nathaniel Grant to Colonel H. K. Craig, 3 May 1861, *Records of the Chief of Ordnance, Letters Received (1861),* Record Group 156, National Archives, Washington, D.C.; Peterson et. al., *Sterling Price's Lieutenants,* p. 191.

19. A reference to Captain James Totten's Battery F, 2nd U.S. Artillery Regiment, which had surrendered the Little Rock Arsenal to the secessionists in February, 1861, but had then been allowed to withdraw to St. Louis. *OR* 1, pp. 646, 666.

20. Governor Jackson led the retreating State Guard forces to Warsaw, then to Lamar, Missouri after the Battle of Boonville. There they encamped and received reinforcements in the form of General James S. Rains' Eighth Division on July 3, then the combined force marched south toward Carthage on the morning of July 5. Colonel Thomas L. Snead, "The First Year of the War in Missouri," in Robert U. Johnson and Clarence C. Buel, eds., *Battles and Leaders of the Civil War,* 4 vols. (New York, 1884-89), vol. 1, p. 268. Kelly's Regiment also arrived from Lexington to bolster the State Guard forces for the Battle of Carthage. Captain Joseph M. Kelly began his State Guard career as commander of the Washington Blues Company, which was detailed to Jefferson City during the Camp Jackson capture. His company then became Company E, 1st Rifle Regiment, Sixth Division, and Kelly soon was appointed to command the regiment. In 1862 he became commander of the Sixth Division. Stephen O. Coleman served as a first lieutenant and as captain of Kelly's company before his death at Wilson's Creek on August 10, 1861. John Rockham Champion served as first lieutenant of the St. Louis City Company, which also avoided capture at Camp Jackson. He became captain of the company when it was also assigned to the 1st Rifle Regiment, Sixth Division. Peterson et. al., *Sterling Price's Lieutenants,* pp. 172, 181, 183, 291.

21. Lieutenant Colonel Thomas Monroe was appointed quartermaster-general of the Sixth Division, Missouri State Guard on May 20, 1861. Peterson et. al., *Sterling Price's Lieutenants,* p. 173.

22. Robert A. McCulloch, Sr., was appointed a lieutenant colonel with the 1st Cavalry Regiment, Sixth Division, in June, 1861. Ibid., p. 174.

23. Private William H. Hicks, a twenty-four year old Missouri bookkeeper in Kelly's Regiment, had his right arm amputated due to the cannon shot wound on July 5, 1861. He was sent to the General Hospital at Springfield, Missouri on August 10, 1861. A Private Thomas Doctor, almost surely the same man, is listed in the Hospital Register as a twenty-three year old Irish baker and resident of Missouri who was wounded by cannon shot and suffered an amputated left arm on July 5, but was diagnosed as "nearly

well," and was sent to the General Hospital on August 25, 1861. *Missouri State Guard Records, Hospital Register, 5 July 1861-25 December 1861,* Missouri Historical Society, St. Louis. Irishman Thomas Doyle, a St. Louis baker, served in Company A of Kelly's Regiment and lost his left arm above the elbow from the solid shot fired from Sigel's guns. One source claims he continued to serve throughout the war and surrendered in 1865. Douglas Harding, "Kelly's Boys," unpublished manuscript in Wilson's Creek National Battlefield Library, Republic, Missouri.

24. Hiram Miller Bledsoe served as captain of the 1st (Lexington) Light Artillery Battery that was formed in May, 1861. The battery served at the Rock Creek skirmish in June, the Battles of Carthage, Wilson's Creek and Pea Ridge, and the siege of Lexington. Peterson et. al., *Sterling Price's Lieutenants, p.* 287. Colonel Richard Hanson Weightman commanded the First Brigade, Eighth Division of the State Guard, to which Bledsoe's Battery was attached for the actions at Carthage and Wilson's Creek. *OR 3,* pp. 22, 128.

25. Private John Murphy, a member of Kelly's Regiment, Sixth Division, later joined Guibor's Battery. Douglas Harding, "Kelly's Boys," unpublished manuscript in Wilson's Creek National Battlefield Library, Republic, Missouri.

26. Dennis Casey, age 30, was born in Ireland but emigrated and became a farmer in Missouri. He served as a private in Company B, 1st Infantry Regiment, Sixth Division, and was wounded in the thigh during the Battle of Wilson's Creek. Admitted to the General Hospital at Springfield, he was listed as being on furlough as of October 4,1861. *Missouri State Guard Records, Hospital Register, 5 July 1861-25 December 1861,* Missouri Historical Society, St. Louis.

27. Captain Archibald MacFarlane was appointed adjutant of the 2nd Infantry Regiment, Seventh Division, Missouri State Guard on July 10, 1861, and served until September 4, 1861. He was then elected colonel of the regiment. Peterson et. al., *Sterling Price's Lieutenants,* pp. 202-203.

28. The "Catahoula Guerrillas" are identified in one source as Company D, Wheat's (1st Special) Battalion, Louisiana Infantry, which served in the Eastern Theater. The Third Louisiana Regiment, a different organization which fought entirely in the Western Theater, was led by Colonel Louis Hebert during the Missouri Campaign. Arthur W. Bergeron, Jr., *Guide to Louisiana Confederate Military Units* (Baton Rouge, 1989), pp. 76-79, 149-151. The Missourians probably did not "acquire" this tent legally. General McCulloch accused the Missourians of the theft of his tents left at Cassville, and another writer accused General Parsons of appropriating the camp equipage of the Louisianians for his own use. *OR 3,* p. 672; Victor M. Rose, *The Life and Services of Gen. Ben McCulloch* (Philadelphia, 1888), p. 191.

29. Also known as the Telegraph or "Wire" Road, leading from Springfield, Missouri to Fort Smith, Arkansas. For other accounts of the role of Guibor's Battery in the battle, see *OR 53,* pp. 431-34; Edwin C. Bearss, *The Battle of Wilson's Creek* (Springfield, MO, 1988), and further accounts by Barlow himself in the New York *Times,* September 2, 1861, and the *Springfield* (MO) *Patriot,* February 15, 1883.

30. Barlow is probably mistaken. Colonel DeRosey Carroll's 1st Arkansas (State) Cavalry took position on Guibor's left just before 9:00 a.m., forming the far left of the Confederate line of battle. Colonel Thomas J. Churchill commanded the First Arkansas Mounted Rifles at Wilson's Creek, which he led in support of the State Guard on Bloody Hill, but not near Guibor's Battery. *OR* 3, pp. 109-110; Bearss, *Battle of Wilson's Creek,* pp. 103-06.

31. One source lists Captain James H. McNamara as the Paymaster-General of the Sixth Division, Missouri State Guard. Another lists him as the orderly sergeant to Division Adjutant General Austin M. Standish at the headquarters of General Parsons, the division commander. Peterson et. al., *Sterling Price's Lieutenants, p.* 173; Col. John C. Moore, *Missouri,* in Gen. Clement A. Evans, ea., *Confederate Military History, Extended Edition,* 17 vols. (Wilmington, N.C., 1988), vol. 12, pp. 350-53.

32. Captain John J. Corkery is identified in one source as acting drillmaster of the Third Division of the State Guard, then as "acting captain" of Guibor's Battery, and voluntarily commanding the battery during most of the Battle of Wilson's Creek, where he was wounded at the end of the action. Barlow's account seems to disagree with this information. Peterson et. al., *Sterling Price's Lieutenants,* pp. 110, 191. Another sources explains that Corkery did serve as a drillmaster until the State Guard retreat to the Arkansas border, when he resigned and joined Guibor's Battery, serving then as an orderly sergeant at Carthage and Wilson's Creek. Moore, *Missouri,* pp. 264-65. Corkery's service record states that he was a second lieutenant of artillery in the Missouri State Guard from August 1, 1861 to March 25, 1862, when he was accepted as first lieutenant in Confederate service. *Compiled Service Records,* reel 81. Joseph Mudd of the State Guard wrote that Guibor was captured early in the action and escaped just before the battle ended. In his place, Corkery commanded the battery, as Barlow had not sufficiently recovered from his wound at Carthage. Joseph A. Mudd, "What I Saw At Wilson's Creek," *Missouri Historical Review,* vol. 7 (1913), p. 101. General Parsons' report of Wilson's Creek explains Guibor's capture, but credits Barlow with the leadership of the battery during his absence. *OR* 53, p. 434.

33. Parsons' report of August 14, 1861 lists Foley, Douglas (spelled Douglass by Parsons), Hicks, Corkery, Brown, Dayton, O'Neil, Studdart (spelled Studdard by Parsons), Shockley, and Zumalt. Report of Brig. Gen. Parsons, Springfield, MO, August 14, 1861 in *Confederate States Army Casualties: Lists and Narrative Reports, 1861-1865,* micro 836, reel 3, National Archives, Washington, D.C.; *Compiled Service Records,* reels 179-192. The Missouri State Guard Hospital Register provides the following additional information on each casualty: Private C. D. Zumalt, age 28, born in the United States, residence St. Louis, a farmer, wounded in the leg, on furlough August 29; Artillery sergeant Corkery, age 21, born in Virginia, a resident of St. Louis, a machinist, wounded in the thigh, on furlough October 4; Private H. H. Studdard, age 21, born in the United States, residence Missouri, a farmer, wounded on August 10, on furlough August 30; Private Michael O'Neal, age 24, born in Ireland, residence Missouri, a clerk, wounded in the arm and leg, returned to duty September 22; Private R .J. Brown, age 18, born in the

United States, residence Missouri, a farmer, wounded in the thigh, on furlough September 6 on sick leave of absence. *Missouri State Guard Records, Hospital Register, 5 July 1861-25 December 1861,* Missouri Historical Society, St. Louis.

34. The city of Joplin, Missouri, did not exist at this time, but the area was the site of extensive lead mines. A later newspaper account stated that the artilleryman went to the St. Joe lead mines to quarry lead for the army. St. Louis *Republic,* April 21, 1895.

35. Barlow included a list of casualty figures at this point in his narrative: "Gen. McCulloch reports the total loss of the combined forces as killed, 265; wounded, 800, total 1,065. This is based on reports made to him, of which Gen. Price reports a loss in the Missouri command of: Killed, 156; wounded, 517; total, 673. This leaves a total loss for McCulloch's troops proper of 392. This estimate is further substantiated by the following official figures: Maj. A. D. Cline, McCulloch's adjutantgeneral, reports the total loss of Arkansas state troops as: Killed, 33; wounded, 113; total 146. Col. Louis Hebert, commanding Third Louisiana, reports his loss at: Killed, 9; wounded, 48; total, 57. Col . E. Greer, commanding South-Kansas Texas regiment of cavalry, reports: Killed, 4; wounded, 22, total, 26. Of a total loss by Gen. McCulloch's troops of 229, against a loss by those under Gen. Price of 673. This tells where the brunt of the fighting fell." These figures were published in *OR* 3. Casualty figures for the Missouri State Guard, Arkansas State forces and some Confederate forces for this battle are still in dispute.

36. In the official report of General Parsons to Sterling Price on the Sixth Division's role at Wilson's Creek, the division commander noted that Barlow won for his company the "praises of all who witnessed his operations. I feel it my duty to present the name of the gallant young officer to your special notice." *OR* 53, p. 434.

37. Lyon's body was accidentally left behind on the Wilson's Creek battlefield by the retreating Federal army. After it was discovered by the Confederates, it was brought to Springfield under a flag of truce. Mary Phelps was the wife of Congressman John Smith Phelps of Springfield, Missouri. E. F. Perkins and T. M. Horne, *History of Greene County, Missouri* (St. Louis, 1883), pp. 822-23.

38. Lieutenant Crow, the only officer not previously identified, is probably assistant division quartermaster Captain James Crow of the Sixth Division. Peterson et. al., *Sterling Price's Lieutenants, p. 173.*

39. Thirty-six year old Dr. Edward C. Franklin served as surgeon of the 5th Missouri Volunteer Infantry. He entered the service in May, 1861 and remained at Springfield to care for the Federal wounded after the Battle of Wilson's Creek. *Compiled Service Records of Volunteer Union Soldiers Who Served in Organizations from the State of Missouri,* Record Group 94, micro 405, reel 422, National Archives, Washington, D.C. Presley Beal, a local undertaker, constructed Lyon's coffin. Perkins and Horne, *History of Greene County, Missouri,* 360. Then Major John M. Schofield served as acting adjutant general of Lyon's Army of the West during the Wilson's Creek Campaign. *OR* 3, pp. 55, 57.

40. Samuel H. Melcher became the assistant surgeon of the 5th Missouri Volunteer Infantry in May, 1861. He remained at Springfield after the Battle of Wilson's Creek to tend the Union wounded. He also examined General Lyon's body after it was found by the Confederates on the Wilson's Creek battlefield. *Compiled Service Records of Volunteer Union Soldiers Who Served in Organizations from the State of Missouri,* Record Group 94, micro 405, reel 423, National Archives, Washington, D.C.

41. Charles C. Rainwater served as a second lieutenant in Company E, 4th Infantry Regiment, Eighth Division, Missouri State Guard, then as an aide-de-camp and assistant division commissary of subsistence in the division. Peterson et. al., *Sterling Price's Lieutenants,* pp. 210, 212, 235.

42. Major Dorn is identified only as a member of the "Southern Army" who lived in Springfield sometime around the Battle of Wilson's Creek. Mrs. Kennedy was the daughter of Union Lieutenant Colonel Marcus Boyd, commander of the Greene and Christian County Home Guard Regiment. Perkins and Horne, *History of Greene County, Missouri,* pp. 302, 345, 360.

43. A reference to the field carriages designed by Frenchman Jean Baptiste Gribeauval in the late eighteenth century, which featured a double trail, an elevating screw for the tube and two sets of notches for the trunnions. The design was widespread in America by the War of 1812. For detailed drawings and further information, see Harold L. Peterson, *Round Shot and Rammers* (New York, 1969), pp. 36, 51-55. James A. Harding was appointed Quartermaster-General of the Missouri Militia in February, 1861. Biographies of this officer may be found in Goodspeed Publishing Company's *History of Cole, Moniteau, Morgan, Benton, Miller, Maries and Osage Counties, Missouri* (Chicago, 1889), pp. 854-56; and Howard L. Conard's *Encyclopedia of the History of Missouri,* 6 vols. (New York, 1901), vol. 3, pp. 175-76. Barlow's account of his stay at Ball's Mills during the winter of 1860-61 with the Southwest Expedition may be found in Brown and Company's *History of Vernon County, Missouri* (St. Louis, 1887), pp. 264-68.

44. John S. Cavender was then captain of Company G, 1st Missouri Infantry. *Compiled Service Records of Volunteer Union Soldiers Who Served in Organizations from the State of Missouri,* Record Group 94, micro 405, reel 372, National Archives, Washington, D.C.

45. Kansas Senator James H. Lane, organizing Federal forces in the area of Fort Scott, Kansas, believed that Price intended to attack the garrison, and ordered 1,200 of his men to reconnoiter the State Guard about 12 miles east of Fort Scott. On September 2, a brief skirmish ensued, both sides suffered light losses, and the Federals retreated back to the fort, then abandoned the post. Once Lane determined that Price was headed for Lexington, he entered Missouri and sacked the town of Osceola. *OR* 3, pp. 162-65; Wendell Holmes Stephenson, *The Political Career of General James H. Lane* (Topeka, KS, 1930), pp. 109-11. Price's report of the Drywood action is in *OR* 53, pp. 435-36.

46. James Mulligan, colonel of the 23rd Illinois Infantry, fortified College Hill (around the Masonic College) overlooking Lexington with about 3,500 men. On Septem-

ber 12, Price's men made the initial contact with the Federals, who retreated to their fortifications, and the Missourians went into camp at the local Fairgrounds. Skirmishing then continued until the 18th, when, after their ammunition and reinforcements had arrived, the State Guard laid siege to the fortifications. Parsons' Sixth Division occupied an area south and eventually southwest of the Federal positions. Colonel James A. Mulligan, "The Siege of Lexington, Mo.," in Robert U. Johnson and Clarence C. Buel, eds., *Battles and Leaders of the Civil War,* 4 vols. (New York, 1884-89), vol. 1, pp. 308-09; Albert Castel, *General Sterling Price and the Civil War in the West* (Baton Rouge, 1968), pp. 50-56; Harold F. Smith, "The 1861 Struggle for Lexington, Missouri," *Civil War History,* vol. 7 (1961), pp. 158-64.

47. General Parsons described how Guibor opened on the Federal entrenchments and college building, "doing them serious injury," but also prompting a vigorous response from the Federals. At twilight, Parsons withdrew his command to the Fairgrounds. *OR* 53, p. 448. Price explained that the attack was broken off due to the near exhaustion of his ammunition supply, and the fact that his men needed rest and food. *OR* 3, p. 186.

48. Excellent accounts of the siege of Lexington may be found in Robert S. Bevier, *History of the First and Second Missouri Confederate Brigades, 1861-1865* (St. Louis, 1879, reprinted by Inland Printer, Ltd., Florissant, MO, 1985); Smith, "The 1861 Struggle for Lexington, Missouri," pp. 155-66; *OR* 3, pp. 171-93; and Mulligan, "The Siege of Lexington, Mo.," pp. 307-13.

49. According to Parsons, Guibor fired three shots down the streets of the town as "a feeler" for the enemy. The battery advanced, occupied several "unimportant positions," then was established within 500 yards of the Federal works. Here Guibor's men kept up a "galling" fire during the day and at intervals at night. *OR* 53, p. 449. It is difficult to determine the precise movements and locations of Guibor's Battery at specific times during the siege. The map in *"Battles and Leaders"* locates the battery southwest of the Federal works, near the Court House. Mulligan, "The Siege of Lexington, Mo.," p. 309. A map reproduced by the Lexington Historical Society in 1903 likewise placed the battery in this location, but also southeast of the Union entrenchments. A description in the same work by Captain Joseph A. Wilson further confuses the issue by stating that two of Guibor's guns were placed where Wentworth Military Academy stands, while one under the command of Sergeant A. A. Lesueur was located behind the Traders' Bank, with Guibor's fourth gun loaned to Captain Churchill Clark, who posted it on South and Sixteenth Streets and fired into the front of the college. This work also adds that on the first day Clark had two of Guibor's guns on the "old Tutt place, on the east." In the *Battles and Leaders map,* "Judge Tutts' House" appears directly east of the Federal works. Lexington Historical Society, *The Battle of Lexington* (Lexington, MO, 1903), 11-12. A civilian eyewitness placed the battery near the intersection of Third and Tenth Streets on September 18, with Parsons' Division the following day, then "back again west afterwards." Susan A. Arnold McCausland, "The Battle of Lexington As Seen by a Woman," *Missouri Historical Review,* vol. 6 (1912), p. 131.

50. Lieutenant Colonel James T. Edwards was an aide-de-camp to General Parsons. Captain Thomas G. Buchanan was appointed an assistant chief of ordnance in the Sixth Division, Missouri State Guard in November, 1861. His regular assignment during the siege is unknown. Peterson et. al., *Sterling Price's Lieutenants,* pp. 173-74.

51. Edwin D. McBride, a native of New Jersey, served as a sergeant of artillery in Guibor's Battery in Missouri state service, then enlisted in Confederate service at Van Buren, Arkansas as a first lieutenant on March 25, 1862. *Compiled Service Records,* reel 81.

52. On the morning of the 19th, Parsons' Division was ordered by Price to cross the Missouri River and meet a large body of Federal reinforcements thought to be marching to Mulligan's relief. After he determined this was a false rumor, Parsons returned with his division to their former positions the same day. *OR* 53, p. 449. The "White Cloud" is named the "Clara Bell" in other sources. Lexington Historical Society, *The Battle of Lexington,* map insert.

53. In the maneuver that gives Lexington the name "Battle of the Hemp Bales," some of the State Guard began using hemp bales from a local warehouse on September 19 as movable cover. The idea caught on, and the next day the Missourians advanced with their bales dangerously close to the fort, and Mulligan offered to surrender. Castel, *Sterl ing Price,* pp. 54-55.

54. On the 20th, Guibor's Battery moved into a position only about 200 yards from the Federal fortifications, and commenced firing again "with decided effect." *OR* 53, p. 450.

55. In his official report of the siege, Parsons' praised Lieutenant Barlow, stating that although he was sick in the country at the beginning of the siege, he left his bed and resumed his post, rendering "the most efficient service." Ibid.

56. Fremont arrived in Jefferson City on September 27, 1861, in command of an army estimated at 20,000 men, intending to prevent Price from leaving Lexington and moving down the Missouri River. Fremont's force eventually pursued the rebels to the southwest and captured Springfield the following month, but failed to bring the main body of Price's army to battle. Allan Nevins, *Fremont: Pathmarker of the West* (New York, 1955), pp. 532-33.

57. Captain James C. Gorham's 2nd Light Artillery Battery, Sixth Division, Missouri State Guard, was organized after the siege of Lexington and fought at Pea Ridge. The battery was reorganized for Confederate service following the latter battle. Peterson et. al., *Sterling Price's Lieutenants, p.* 192; Stewart Sifakis, *Compendium of the Confederate Armies, Kentucky, Maryland, Missouri, the Confederate Units and the Indian Units* (New York, 1995), pp. 77, 146.

58. According to one source, the battery was reorganized in Memphis in December, 1861, recruited from the St. Louis men captured at Camp Jackson and exchanged, and mustered into Confederate service. Guibor then returned to Price's army with six guns in time to fight at Pea Ridge in March, 1862. Other sources dispute the fact that Guibor's Battery was formally in Confederate service by the time of Pea Ridge, and place the date

of their muster later in March. See Moore, *Missouri,* pp. 307-09; Sifakis, *Compendium,* pp. 80-81, 147; William L. Shea and Earl J. Hess, *Pea Ridge: Civil War Campaign in the West* (Chapel Hill, 1992), p. 338; Ozarks Genealogical Society, *Confederate Organizations, Officers and Posts, 1861-1865, Missouri Units* (Springfield, MO, 1988), p. 6. The Compiled Service Records for the men of Guibor's Battery note their organization from the State Guard at Van Buren, Arkansas, on March 25, 1862. *Compiled Service Records,* reel 81.

59. Some sources maintain that the battery was disbanded in early 1865. Sifakis, *Compendium,* pp. 80-81. Other sources state that Guibor, and presumably the members of the battery, were surrendered with Gen. Joseph E. Johnston's army in North Carolina in April, 1865. Moore, *Missouri,* p. 308. The most likely scenario is that the battery was disbanded and the survivors later surrendered with Johnston's Army of Tennessee. St. Louis *Republic,* April 21, 1895. Guibor himself was declared unfit for field service in September, 1864 and surrendered at Meridian, Mississippi in May, 1865. *Compiled Service Records,* reel 81. Details of Barlow's later service are sketchy, but he apparently left Guibor's Battery by the fall of 1862 and commanded a section of the Watson Louisiana Battery in the action at Corinth, Mississippi in October of that year. *OR* 17, pt. 1, pp. 375, 413. In late April or early May, 1864 he took command of a temporary Louisiana light battery at Montgomery, Alabama. Composed of furloughed and detached troops, the unit operated in east Louisiana and in the "District South of Homochitto," but apparently saw no action, and desertions forced the battery to be replaced with "details from the cavalry." In October, 1864, Barlow's Battery was ordered to be consolidated with Bradford's Mississippi Battery, so Barlow resigned, turned over his guns to the Mississippians, and his detached cavalrymen returned to their units. *OR* 39, pt. 2, pp. 610, 888; pt. 3, p. 872; Bergeron, *Guide to Louisiana Confederate Military Units,* p. 27.

60. Barlow returned to St. Louis sometime between 1868 and 1877. In 1880, his household consisted of his wife, three children, his mother-in-law and a servant. "Printer" was given as his occupation. *Tenth Census of the United States, 1880, Population Schedules for St. Louis, Missouri,* Ward 17, Micro T9, National Archives, Washington, D.C., reel 733. Barlow's newspaper obituary noted that he was "one of the best known men in St. Louis," and mentioned his work as secretary of the Ex-Confederate Home Association in Higginsville, Missouri. The *Post-Dispatch* also mentioned that Barlow had been made a U.S. "gauger" at the start of each of President Grover Cleveland's terms. According to the newspaper account, Barlow was survived by a nineteen year-old son. St. Louis *Post-Dispatch,* December 28, 1896.

61. From Price's official report of the siege of Lexington. *OR* 3, p. 188.

". . .a resort of Lincolnite pirates."

SHIP ISLAND
The Unwanted Key to The Confederacy

Gregory D. Bova

On Sunday, January 13, 1861, in the Gulf Coast town of Biloxi, Mississippi, the "Biloxi Rifle Guards," led by Captain John B. Howard, marched from the Lameuse Street Armory down to the wharf and boarded the schooner *Major Rainey*. Whatever chill was in the Gulf's damp winter air was warmed by "Secession Fever," begun four days earlier when Mississippi's legislature voted to leave the Union. Casting off the mooring lines, Captain Howard and his men sailed twelve miles out into the Gulf of Mexico, intent on capturing a Federal fort currently under construction on Ship Island.[1]

Arriving at their destination a short time later—they were the second group of Mississippians to visit the island that day—Howard claimed the island and the fort for the state of Mississippi. The Stars and Stripes were lowered and in its place was raised state flag of Mississippi. The officer of the U. S. Army's Corps of Engineers, the lone United States military representative on the island, was on leave. Only the civilian workmen bore witness to the Biloxi Rifle Guards as they became the first infantry unit in the state to initiate offensive action against the Federal government. Their bloodless mission accomplished, ten members of the Guards remained while the rest of the company sailed home.[2]

The fort's partial construction included its foundation and the first of two planned tiers for mounting guns. The lower tier was still open to the cold Gulf winds and fine blowing sand. Workers' quarters and workshops surrounded the unfinished structure.[3]

First Lieutenant Frederick Prime, engineer-in-charge, was in New York when word reached him on January 5 of secessionist activity in the Gulf. Stopping in Washington, D. C. for instructions, Prime returned to New Orleans prior to an inspection tour of the coastal forts of Alabama, Mississippi and Florida. He arrived in the Crescent City on January 10, the day after Mississippi seceded and three days before Ship Island's occupation.[4]

On January 11, the day Florida voted itself out of the Union, Prime traveled directly to Pensacola, steaming past Ship Island just two days before the Biloxi Rifle Guards' visit. Detained and arrested by state authorities in Pensacola, he was paroled after promising to return to New Orleans. He learned. however, that forts Barrancas and McRee were occupied by Florida state militia, but Fort Pickens remained in Federal hands. Back in New Orleans on January 17, Prime discovered that Ship Island was occupied by Mississippi troops. He recently had requested funds to close out the work at Ship Island, but it now was apparent the unfinished fort would remain in Southern hands.[5]

Despite his successful expedition, Howard learned on January 20th that the state could not furnish "an efficient armament for the fort." Fearing for the island's occupants, he dispatched a schooner to remove the garrison. Before departing they once more "claimed" the island, fort and the engineering matériel for the State of Mississippi.[6] Federal engineer Frederick Prime faced a similar circumstance. With the political situation along the Gulf Coast deteriorating, Prime considered himself "relieved from all connection with these works."[7] He told the governor's representative, however, that "the works on the Fort are suspended not because of the seizure of the island by Mississippi volunteers, but because of the inability of the Government to meet its engagements. . . ."[8]

Located midway between Mobile, Alabama to the east and the Mississippi Delta to the west, Ship Island was one of a chain of sandy barrier islands skirting the coast of Mississippi and Alabama. The island, seven miles long and but one-half mile wide, was twelve miles off shore and composed entirely of sand. Its evolution was shaped solely by the wind and tide. Hummocks—mounds of sand—rose nearly ten feet above sea level. Verdant sea grass grew abundantly, and on the island's eastern end, scrub oak dotted the surface.[9]

The chain of islands were of significant strategic importantce. Their cccupation by Southern forces would transform the Mississippi sound into a protected inland waterway, a haven from Union warships. Alternatively, in Union hands the scattered islands could prove an effective barrier to Confederate blockade runners. The island's water barrier and low profile gave it a distinct

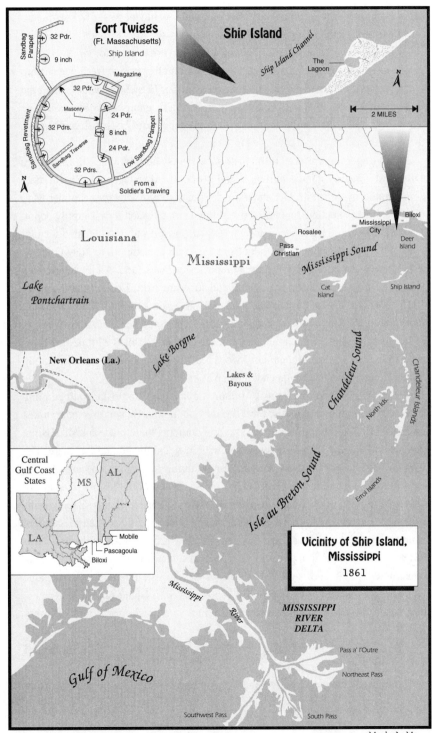

Fort Twiggs
(Ft. Massachusetts)
Ship Island

Sandbag Parapet

32 Pdr.

9 inch

Magazine

32 Pdr.

Masonry

24 Pdr.

Sandbag Revetment

32 Pdrs.

8 inch

Low Sandbag Parapet

24 Pdr.

Sandbag Traverse

32 Pdrs.

N

From a
Soldier's Drawing

Ship Island

Ship Island Channel

The Lagoon

N

2 MILES

Louisiana

Mississippi

Rosalee

Mississippi City

Biloxi

Pass Christian

Deer Island

Mississippi Sound

Lake Pontchartrain

Cat Island

Ship Island

Lake Borgne

Chandeleur Sound

New Orleans (La.)

Lakes & Bayous

North Ids.

Chandeleur Islands

Central
Gulf Coast
States

MS

AL

LA

Mobile

Pascagoula

Biloxi

Isle au Breton Sound

Errol Islands

Vicinity of Ship Island, Mississippi

1861

Mississippi

River

MISSISSIPPI
RIVER
DELTA

Pass a' l'Outre

Northeast Pass

Gulf of Mexico

Southwest Pass

South Pass

Mark A. Moore

advantage over any approaching attacker, who would necessarily steam into range exposed to the island's defending ordnance.

First discovered and described in 1699 by French explorers, the island provided vessels with a suitable harbor and two small ponds of fresh water. Ship Island became the first landfall and transfer point for Frenchmen establishing the Louisiana colony.[10] Over the next two and a half centuries, its strategic role would rise and fall with the fortunes of the French, Spanish, British and finally, the Americans.

One important episode in the history of the island took place in December 1814 and illustrates its geographic and strategic advantages. A British fleet commanded by Admiral Alexander Cockrane, together with troops under Maj. Gen. Edward Pakenham, anchored off Ship Island and used it as a supply depot. With their communications secure, the British moved out and defeated a small fleet of American gunboats in Lake Borgne before pressing on to New Orleans. The following month the British were repulsed by Maj. Gen. Andrew Jackson's American forces at Chalmette and forced to retire from Louisiana in January 1815.[11] Returning to Ship Island, the British again utilized it the following month in their attack on Fort Bowyer on Mobile Point, Alabama. After five days of bombardment the fort capitulated and the British occupied Mobile in February 1815. They remained there until word reached them in March of the signing of the Treaty of Ghent, which ended the War of 1812.[12]

Without a war to highlight its military advantages, Ship Island slipped into semi-obscurity over the next several decades. A lighthouse was erected to assist navigation in Mississippi sound and several attempts were made by Mississippi congressmen in the early 1800s to construct a naval shipyard and fort there. The Corps of Engineers opposed construction, claiming there was nothing of military value to protect along Mississippi's coast. In addition, the fort would have covered only one of the many channels between the barrier islands. Enemy ships using other avenues of ingress and egresss could easily sail between Mississippi sound and the Gulf of Mexico's deep waters. Pensacola, Mobile and New Orleans were the major ports in Ship Island's vicinity and forts were being constructed there. Not until Mississippi's senator, Jefferson Davis, became United States Secretary of War in the 1850s was Ship Island finally designated, despite grumbling from the Corps of Engineers, as a site for a new masonry fort.[13]

Tension increased between North and South through the early months of 1861 until it finally erupted in Charleston Harbor. Along the Gulf Coast men and supplies were deployed to meet the threat believed to be coming from

Tennessee and down the Mississippi. As local militia companies—such as the Biloxi Rifle Guards—departed, local inhabitants and newspaper editors questioned the wisdom of depleting the Gulf Coast of its troops. Conventional wisdom claimed that "Black Republican" hordes would sail down the Mississippi River and attack New Orleans, but coastal residents could not ignore the Union naval blockade ominously forming off their shores.

On May 18, Jefferson Davis, the provisional president of the fledgling Confederate States of America, received a short and enthusiastic telegram from Col. Robert J. Barrow, commander of the 4th Louisiana Infantry Regiment. Blustering with bravado, Barrow offered to attack Ship Island. "If you order me I am willing to storm the 'gates of hell' but I do not wish to sacrifice my men. Will I have the means of protection?"[14] Before the Louisiana troops could occupy the island, Confederate colonel William Hardee telegraphed on May 22: "Buildings at Ship Island burnt by my orders. Letter written." Hardee, in command at Pensacola, ordered the buildings torched to prevent them from becoming a "resort of Lincolnite pirates."[15] Hardee, unaware that the Confederate government intended to occupy the island, believed he had the authority to order the buildings destroyed. At that time of the war there was no clear division of command amongst the various coastal commands, a circumstance that would change very shortly.

The ensuing panic along the Gulf coast that followed Hardee's directive led many residents to believe the Federals had landed on Ship Island and were preparing to invade the mainland. The Biloxi Rifle Guards was ordered back from Jackson, Mississippi, and other regional militia companies had their orders changed. The 3rd Mississippi Infantry was another possible source for use on the southern coastline, but the still-forming regiment was not yet ready for operations.[16]

On May 27 the Confederate government appointed Maj. Gen. David E. Twiggs to command the newly-formed "Military Department Number 1," a geographical–administrative entity which comprised the entire state of Louisiana and the southern portions of Mississippi and Alabama.[17] As a Union officer the elder Twiggs—he was born in the last decade of the preceding century—had surrendered his former command in Texas to state troops, thereby earning the undying condemnation of the United States Congress. The septuagenarian would soon find himself in as much difficulty in New Orleans as he had experienced in Texas. Confederate commanders in the Crescent City had their own developing plans on how to defend the region and launch counter-offensives against a threatening enemy. Unfortunately for the Southerners, there was little cooperation or coordination between the state militia, privateers and Confederate officials.[18] As a result, the citizenry of New Orleans who had originally welcomed Twiggs soon turned a cold gaze in his direction when the weeks passed by and he refused to implement any plan of action.

On June 9, 1861, the 4th Louisiana Infantry reached Pass Christian, Mississippi. Two companies remained there, two each were at Biloxi and Pascagoula, and four companies camped at Mississippi City.[19] Ship Island remained ungarrisoned and residents of the gulf coast breathed a sigh of relief as they tried to rebuild their summer tourist trade from New Orleans. But that month the *USS Massachusetts* and several tenders began patrolling the Mississippi sound around Ship Island. The Union blockade announced by President Lincoln in April was becoming a reality, porous though it still was, in the waters of the gulf. Captain Melancton Smith, the *Massachusetts'* commanding officer, sent a reconnaissance party to the barrier island on June 17. One officer and three seamen spent the day inspecting the unfinished fort and strolling the lonely beaches on the narrow sandy island. Returning to their ship that evening, they reported the island deserted.[20] With his curiosity satisfied Smith sailed off. He did not have any instructions to hold the island, and lacked the manpower to do so in any event.

"I have not been able to garrison Ship Island for want of heavy guns," Twiggs wrote to Secretary of War Leroy Pope Walker the following day, completely unaware of Smith's reconnaissance. "I have troops for that purpose at Mississippi City, some ten or twelve miles distant."[21] The editor of the New Orleans *Picayune* asked sarcastically, "Where is our fleet of gunboats, and why are they allowed to lie idle when there is plenty of opportunity for them to exercise their skill and bravery by having a small tea party with the lighter craft of the enemy?"[22] The truth was a grim one for the South, for there were no Confederate gunboats to send anywhere. In order to deny Federal warships a routine and completely safe passage in and out of the sound, Twiggs ordered the navigation lights on Ship and Cat islands extinguished. He rescinded the order when he the inky darkness inconvenienced coastal and Confederate shipping more than it hindered the Federals.[23]

On June 23 five coastal vessels and barges were seized by the *Massachusetts*, thereby igniting another round of panic amongst area residents, who expected the Federal army to land occupation forces. Smith noted the captures in his log, adding, "I interrupted the mail communication between New Orleans and Mobile, by turning back the steamboat *Oregon*, one of the boats running regularly with mails."[24] In New Orleans, sixteen-year-old Clara Solomon wrote in her diary, "Pa says the mail will be suspended between New Orleans and the watering places; as yesterday a boat was fired into, and obliged to put back; fortunately the enemy was not close enough or they would have sunk the boat."[25]

The Union navy's seizure of local shipping venturing too far from shore had a demoralizing effect on coastal residents. Only the shallow Mississippi sound— which was just six to thirteen feet deep and extended for miles off shore—kept the larger warships from attacking the coastal towns and capturing more vessels. One citizen, a Mr. A. E. Lewis, reflected the coastal residents' collective mood in a letter written to Mississippi Governor J. J. Pettus:

> To be candid, I must say that portions of our Coast were and are *now* quite accessible to the enemy. When I saw the enemy's vessels in the Sound (visible from my house) I telegraphed to Gen. Twiggs in New Orleans. . .believing the Southern part of Mississippi as much of a *border* as Virginia, Mississippians should protect Mississippi. . . .[26]

Two weeks later on July 6, Twiggs informed Secretary Walker that he had "sent an armed steamer to the sound. Will have two or three more to arm to-day."[27] The converted mail steamer *Oregon* (now the *CSS Oregon),* together with the *CSS Swain*, steamed under Capt. Edward Higgins' command.[28] Formally of the United States Navy, Higgins was commissioned a captain in the 1st Louisiana Artillery and later was appointed Twiggs' aide-de-camp.[29] His naval service put him in good stead to command the *Oregon* and *Swain*. The former, which had plied the Mississippi sound prior to the war, had returned sporting an 8-inch columbiad and one 12-pounder howitzer. The *Swain* was also a shallow-draft steamer and armed with a 32-pound rifle and a howitzer. Higgins used the crew of the *CSS McRae,* plus a motley mixture of recruits and marines, to man the vessels. Ninety sailors served on the converted gunboats, along with a detachment of 55 marines, a sergeant and thirty privates from a Louisiana infantry company.[30]

The vessels steamed to Bay St. Louis, Mississippi, where the *Oregon* and *Swain* loaded cotton bales to protect their vulnerable deck boilers. Satisfied his ships were ready for action, Higgins sailed toward the *USS Massachusetts'* suspected cruising waters in the Gulf of Mexico. He reached Ship Island on Saturday, July 6, but could not find a trace of the *Massachusetts* or its tenders.[31] The *Massachusetts*, however, had reached Ship Island on the Fourth of July. Finding "everything quiet," Smith had proceeded to Pass a' l'Outre on July 6 and Southwest Pass on the 7th (both are part of the Mississippi River's Delta region). While Higgins had been preparing for combat, the *Massachusetts* had sailed southwest to investigate suspected Confederate activities at the Chandeleur Islands. To Higgins' surprise Ship Island was vacant of any Union forces. The Federals had not even left a token garrison on the island. It was Higgins' good fortune, however, that the *Massachusetts* was nowhere to be found. Had he battled the Federal warships his make-shift fleet would likely have been roughyl handled.[33]

With the Federal warship removed from the scene three choices faced the commander of the tiny Confederate fleet. He could always return to New Orleans, although that move might relay the impression that he was afraid to engage the enemy. Second, he could sail around the Mississippi sound in a reconnaissance, although such a move would burn up his fuel and put him at a disadvantage should he come upon the *Massachusetts* or other enemy warship. Or, he could occupy Ship Island. For Higgins the decision was relatively simple. His mission was to drive enemy forces from around the island and out of the sound, and he realized the strategic importance of occupying the barrier island. Higgins' initiative would become an embarrassment to the Federal navy and eventually cost one Union flag officer his command.

Once he reached his decision Captain Higgins moved quickly to implement his plan. After landing his small force and the four guns carried by the *Oregon* and *Swain,* he prepared to defend the island. It did not take long for him to realize that his small force would be no match against a determined enemy. Leaving behind most of him command, he departed for New Orleans with both vessels to get additional troops and guns for the island, leaving Lt. Alexander F. Warley of the Confederate navy to oversee the disposition of the force.[34]

Warley went to work with a vengeance. The Confederates re-enforced the lower tier of the unfinished Union fort, which gave them a commanding field of fire from northwest to southwest of Ship Island, as well as towards Cat Island further west. "I instantly commenced to get the 8-inch, the 32-pounder, and howitzers in battery, the men running up the heavy guns through the sand," Warley later reported."[35] Laying the platforms and building sandbag breastworks, the Southerners created a credible defensible position. Eventually thirteen pieces of artillery, including the 32 and 64-pounders and a 96-pounder Dahlgren used against Fort Sumter, were landed on the island. On Monday July 8, Captain Higgins returned with a company of 75 infantrymen to assist Warley.[36] That same evening a sail was discovered approaching the island.

The summer sun was already setting by the time the cannon, men and supplies were off-loaded and Higgins embarked on the voyage back to New Orleans. The *Massachusetts* had completed its rounds of the Chandeleur Islands and was steaming back toward Ship Island, unaware of the Confederate activity that had erupted in her wake. As she steamed closer her crew discovered the unwelcome occupants. Warley noted thatthe vessel fired a lone cannon about 9:00 p.m., made signals with white lights and then "beat to quarters."

At about 8:30 p.m. the *Massachusetts* reached Ship Island and Commander Smith noticed that the lantern was extinguished in the island's lighthouse. Spotting another light further inland (probably a campfire), Smith ordered a shot thrown in its direction. The discharge thundered across the shallow water, its reverberating echo the only response. The growing darkness made further firing futile. Anchoring well-off the island, Smith waited for dawn before closing in.[37]

As the dawn light of July 9 streaked the early morning sky, Warley saw the outline of a two-masted, steam-propeller vessel. He assumed it was the *Massachusetts* with a tender astern, both at anchor. Since neither ship was flying a flag, Warley waited until sunrise, 5:10 a.m., and then opened fire with an 8-inch gun, followed thereafter by a blast from a 32-pounder.[38] Compelled to show his colors under the rain of iron, Smith immediately got underway as Confederate shells fell short of their intended target. Instead of withdrawing, Smith guided his warship close inshore, discovering in the process "3 secession flags, 39 tents, and 4 batteries in process of erection." He also noted that the defenders were using cotton bales and sandbags for additional protection.

At 5:30 a.m. the contest began in earnest. Smith returned fire once he got within effective range of the Confederate guns, but even with maximum elevation the *Massachusetts'* shots fell short. Two rounds from the island's batteries whizzed over the *Massachusetts'* forecastle and engine house, striking the water near the vessel.[39] According to Confederate accounts, the Federal ship was "firing wildly mostly and doing no harm," although at least one shell found the correct range.[40] A young Confederate naval officer remembered that a "thirty-two pound shell. . . came whizzing from the steamer and knocking the sand in our faces. . . [exploded] amongst us."[41] After firing seventeen rounds, Warley ceased fire as the *Massachusetts* moved out of range. At the same time the *Oregon* and *Grey Cloud* arrived off shore with the garrison's relief supplies.[42]

Captain Higgins earlier had reported to General Twiggs on the tenuous hold the Confederates had on Ship Island. More guns and ammunition had been loaded aboard the *Oregon* and *Grey Cloud*, and the expedition was placed in charge of Maj. Martin Luther Smith. Knowing Warley's men needed gunpowder and shot which, unfortunately, had been loaded on the slower *Grey Cloud,* the materials were immediately transferred to the *Oregon* and Smith pushed on to Warley's relief.[43]

Having exhausted his shells with 15-second fuzes, Commander Smith broke off the engagement and sailed back to the Chandeleur Islands. Lieutenant Warley believed the *Massachusetts* pulled off after receiving three or four damaging shots, but Commander Smith reported that he withdrew because "the engine of this vessel is all above water" and thus dangerously exposed to enemy fire.[44] The approach of the *Oregon* and *Grey Cloud* may also have influenced Smith's decision to depart.

Later in the day as the Confederate ships unloaded their supplies, the *Massachusetts* briefly returned. The confident Warley immediately responded to the challenge, firing four rounds at the irksome ship. The *Massachusetts* returned one shot from her pivot gun before retiring.[45] The first battle for Ship Island was over and the Confederates were still in possession of the sandy real estate. Despite the expenditure of 26 rounds by the Southerners and 17 rounds by the Federal warship, no casualties were reported by either side. Commander Smith reported to his superiors that "the rebels have 1 rifled cannon, 2 guns of heavy caliber, one 12-pounder, and a force of 300 to 400 men." His officers concurred, some even estimating the number of Confederate troops to be as high as 800.[46]

While the Union naval officers' estimation of the fort's armament was accurate, they overestimated the size of the garrison. The Confederates, however, were doing their part to enlarge the island's land force. Several companies from the 4th Louisiana were shifted to the island to augment its strength, while Lieutenant Warley was relieved of command by Lt. Col. Henry Watkins Allen, who by virtue of his rank was now the commanding officer of the island's defenses. The island's new commander was a college graduate, former attorney and born adventurer. Bored with civilian life, Allen joined the Texas army during the 1836 Texas Revolution. When the Civil War broke out he again volunteered for military service and was commissioned a lieutenant colonel in the 4th Louisiana Infantry.[47] When Allen and his Louisianans arrived at Ship Island, Warley removed his own men and departed on the *Oregon*. He left with words of high praise for all the participants of the recent engagement, extolling the virtues of each of the officers by name.[48]

Although the first fight over Ship Island was small and bloodless, Lieutenant Warley's demonstration proved that the island could be held and maintained if the Confederates were willing to expend the necessary ships, men and supplies. Two boats seized by Louisiana's Governor Moore and turned over to General Twiggs had been armed, but they cruised the lakes near New Orleans instead of the Mississippi sound.[49] Had Twiggs dispatched the boats into the sound, he would have strengthened his water-based forces and the Federals would not have had an opportunity to get near the lakes in the first place. Still, Twiggs had good news to share with Secretary Walker: "Two heavy shell guns and four 32-pounders mounted on Ship Island. No attempt of the enemy to return." The general was relieved that the Yankees had sailed away, but he knew that they would come back. Elated by their easy success, the defenders returned to the mainland with tales of fierce battles, thundering cannon and a twice-retreating enemy.

On July 13, the Union navy and fledgling Confederate navy met in a brief clash near the island when the smaller Southern ships attempted to lure Smith closer inshore. As Commander Smith later reported, "On the morning of the 13th instant, while at anchor 3 miles from Ship Island light, two armed steamers, the *Oregon* and *Arrow*, were discovered under full steam, heading for this vessel." The Federal commander got underway at the sight of the Confederate gunboats. The *Massachusetts'* first shot caused both gunboats to return fire. Smith discharged his guns at long range, knowing that the smaller Confederate pieces could not return fire at those distances. According to Smith, "[t]he steamers turned back in unbecoming haste at the first fall of shot near them." The *Oregon* and *Arrow* wisely sought safety in the shallows, where the deeper-draft Union warship could not follow. Smith also reported that the Confederate crews had expended ammunition uselessly, and he encouraged them to continue by throwing an occasional shot in their direction. The object of the Confederate vessels "was not to engage," Smith wrote, "but to toll me up in range of the batteries on shore."[50]

As the light sparring took place, work on the Ship Island defenses continued apace. Twiggs reported on July 19 to the secretary of war that "Ship Island is now strong enough to resist any force that will probably be sent against it for the present. There are five companies of volunteers on the island." Tempering his enthusiasm, he continued to fear a Federal descent down the Mississippi against New Orleans. When that happened, "which will most probably be in the fall," he warned, ". . .the communication between Ship Island and the mainland will be interrupted, and the garrison of the island will be compelled to yield without striking a blow."[51]

While Twiggs worried about the island's possible strategic isolation, his opponents were distressed over the island's apparent strength. Commander Smith believed that "[t]he Ship Island Passage. . .is now guarded by a very formidable fortification and corresponding force," confirming Twiggs' earlier evaluation to Secretary Walker.[52] The perception that the island was strongly defended kept Union warships at a healthy distance from Fort Twiggs and the western end of the island. As long as the Federals kept away from Ship Island, they kept away from New Orleans.

The consequences of having lost Ship Island to the Confederates became painfully clear to Union authorities in early August 1861, when the Union Navy Department received a report from its "blockading committee." This committee recommended strategies for blockading and seizing portions of the Confederate coast for future military use. Union possession of Ship Island was seen by the committee as an important prerequisite to any attempt to take New Orleans. To add insult to injury, the report further stated that "[t]he military possession of Ship Island is no less important to our naval operations in Mississippi Sound than to the blockade of New Orleans."[53]

Without a base of operations close to New Orleans, the Union army did not have a viable location from which to build up its forces. As long as the Confederates held Ship Island—or at least kept the Union forces from occupying it— the ports of New Orleans and Mobile were safe. Key West was too far away tor use as a staging area for Union forces moving against New Orleans. While Mobile could possibly be threatened from a base on Key West, Federal authorities rightfully did not consider that port as important as New Orleans and the opening of the Mississippi River.

Ship Island was deemed so valuable that when the Union lost control of the island, the naval officer responsible for its safekeeping lost his career. On August 23, 1861, Secretary of the Navy Gideon Welles expressed surprise and regret to Flag-Officer William Mervine (Captain Smith's commanding officer and the commander of the Gulf Blockading Squadron) that such a key position as Ship Island was permitted to be fortified and retained by the Confederates. Early the following month Mervine received a tersely worded order relieving him of command after having held the post for a mere four months.[54]

While Washington was upset over the loss of the key island, the residents of New Orleans could not see any advantage to keeping the place. Fighting Federals so far from the city—or for that matter so far from any city—seemed to be a waste of men and matériel. Any Union invasion, they claimed, would come from the north, with enemy gunboats moving down the Mississippi River.[55] There were better defensive positions around New Orleans in need of the troops and guns exiled on the spit of sand along the lonely gulf coast. Placing too much emphasis on the British rebuff at Chalmette by Andrew Jackson in 1815, many believed no one could take New Orleans by coming through the lakes or upriver past the tandem of Fort Jackson and Fort St. Philip.[56] For his part Twiggs could not make up his mind as to which line of reasoning to follow. His vacillation irritated and angered both civilians and military men alike. To resolve his dilemma, he ordered Col. Johnson Kelly Duncan, the commander of the forces at forts Jackson and St. Philip, to travel to Ship Island to review the situation.[57]

"The occupation of the island is objectless," Duncan wrote after a brief inspection of the place. He said there was no control over any channel of the sounds worth the expense. Risking men and matériel could result in a shameful and humiliating defeat, he warned, without intimidating the enemy or gaining any substantive objective. Duncan urged that the island be abandoned immediately. He even directed officers of the Louisiana Artillery to return to their several posts on the coast. "They are of much less use at Ship Island than at Forts Jackson and Saint Philip," he wrote.[58] Twiggs admitted to Secretary Walker that he had never been to Ship Island but, he noted, "every intelligent person whom I meet, acquainted with the locality, concurs with the views of Colonel Duncan, that there are several other entrances to the sound besides Ship Island Channel, and that small steamers and gunboats can pass through them without difficulty." Nevertheless, Twiggs concluded, "I shall hold the island until ordered to relinquish it." The old soldier had done a passable job of transferring the onus of responsibility to another's shoulders.[59]

Others, however, believed that retaining the island was entirely feasible. Major Martin L. Smith, whose substantial engineering skills would soon assist major Confederate field armies, saw no reason for abandoning a position enclosed by the heavy brick walls of the fort. He also pointed out that the island's occupation was directed by President Davis. Its abandonment could not be carried out without Davis' express authority. Should it be vacated, how will the sound be defended? he wondered. Will gunboats be available to cruise the Gulf of Mexico's waters?[60] Major Smith obviously did not want to give up the island without a fight. The occupation of Ship Island extended Southern strategic control of the region another twelve miles into the Gulf of Mexico, forcing Union warships to give a wide berth to the island's western end. The Mississippi sound was safer with the Confederates at Ship Island than with no one occupying it. It would be even worse if the Federals controlled the island.

Twiggs' decision, which he had so much trouble making, was finally made for him. On September 13 he was ordered to "[t]ake immediate measures to evacuate Ship Island, and cause the guns to be removed at once."[61] Special Order No. 91 ordered Colonel Duncan "to repair at once to Ship Island and direct the evacuation of that post in accordance with verbal instructions from the major-general commanding."[62] From the ports along the Gulf of Mexico, from New Orleans to Ocean Springs to Mobile, ships were commandeered with nary a word to the public for fear of panic and alerting the Federal navy. As in July, the Union navy sailed slowly from the east while Duncan sailed from the west. The United States Navy would not know about the evacuation for some time, but coastal residents would learn about it soon enough.

In fact, the first to feel the heat from the evacuation were the citizens of the Mississippi gulf coast. While the troops were removed in an orderly fashion, rumors stampeded wildly along the coast. Citizens from Pascagoula to Bay St. Louis thought the troops were evacuating in the face of a Union invasion. In New Orleans, Sarah Solomon noted in her diary, "the Pass [Christian] was deserted after the evacuation of Ship Island, as the people were fearful for their safety."[63]

The confusion began immediately. Confederate Gen. John B. Dahlgren moved the newly formed 3rd Mississippi Infantry from Camp Dahlgren at Pass Christian across Bay St. Louis to Shieldsborough.[64] Although he had contemplated moving the regiment for some time, Dahlgren had no idea the troops were evacuating Ship Island because Twiggs failed to notify him. By coincidence, his men were moving at same time Duncan began evacuating the island. Dahlgren's re-deployment and Duncan's evacuation provided the impetus for the few summer residents to hastily depart. The belief that "Lincolnite pirates" were about to land and torch the coastal towns was reinforced when several Union vessels appeared off the eastern end of Cat Island.[65]

Twiggs had more than he could handle and he knew it. Knowing the prevailing opinion was against him and that his abilities were diminished because of age and infirmaries, he wrote the secretary of war and asked for assistance. "There will no doubt be an invasion of this place by the Black Republicans early in the fall," the general gloomily predicted. To assist him with preparations that could prevent that from happening, he requested "two brigadier-generals be ordered to report to me at as early a day as possible."[66]

Duncan, meanwhile, ordered anything of use at Ship Island removed. Another race was on, this time to gather up and leave Ship Island before the Union navy returned. The *Massachusetts,* traveling with a host of escorts and tenders, was once again sailing toward the place. The evacuation continued throughout the night of July 15 and ended near sundown the following evening. All of the guns, carriages, equipment, implements, ammunition, commissary and quartermaster stores, engineer tools and all other public and private property was evacuated. After ordering the large lumber supply burned, Duncan torched the stairs of the lighthouse after breaking the lantern and removing its lens.[67]

It was fortunate that the Confederates began to remove the property on the same day that the orders to evacuate were received. One day's delay would have witnessed the arrival of the *Massachusetts* and its escorts during the critical phase of the evacuation, when the men and guns were exposed on the open beach. It was a near-run thing, for the *Massachusetts* arrived just as the last of the men and matériel were loaded and the Southern vessels steamed away. According to Commander Smith, "The rebels on Ship Island set fire to the barracks and some of the shanties recently erected there for the accommodations of the troops," he wrote. "The rebels destroyed the light-house by burning the interior and breaking the plate glass of the lantern, and then took steam for the mainland."[68]

Colonel Higgin's letter, addressed to Smith, was found posted on the fort bulletin board. Dated "Fort Twiggs, Ship Island, September 17, 1861," it read:

> By order of my Government I have this day evacuated Ship Island. This my brave soldiers under my command do with much reluctance and regret. For three long months your good ship has been our constant companion. We have not exactly "lived and loved together," but we have been intimately acquainted, having exchanged cards on the 9th day of July last. In leaving you to-day we beg you accept our best wishes for your health and happiness while sojourning on this pleasant, hospitable shore. That we may have another ex-

Harpers Weekly illustration of "Fort Massachucetts" on Ship Island

Harper's Pictorial History of the Civil War

FORT MASSACHUSETTS
SHIP ISLAND

change of courtesies before the war closes, and that we may meet face to face in closer quarters, is the urgent prayer of very truly, your obedient servant, H. W. Allen, Lieutenant Colonel, Commanding Ship Island [69]

The fact that this letter is dated September 17 raises an interesting question concerning when Commander Smith actually landed on Ship Island. Twiggs' telegram and Smith's log entry indicates the *Massachusetts* and its escorts were off Ship Island as early as the evening of September 16, but Smith did not occupy Ship Island until two days later. His delay may have been caused by his belief the Confederates still held the island in force and were re-enforced by five Confederate vessels (*Oregon, Grey Cloud, Creole, A. G. Brown, California* and *Arrow*) he spotted on the sixteenth.[70] He may have felt the odds favored the Confederates and decided to wait and see what the they were doing.

The actual date that Smith occupied Ship Island may be inferred by another telegram that Twiggs sent to the secretary of war on September 18, in which he noted that "[t]he enemy's fleet did considerable shelling yesterday at, as they supposed, a masked battery on Ship Island."[71] Smith would not have shelled a "masked battery" on September 17 if he knew the Confederates had already departed. This may explain why Smith's report was dated September 20th and why the report was lacking any specific dates except when he mentions the fires he saw on the night of the 16th. In hindsight, he knew the fires were caused by Confederates burning their shanties. Smith's caution cost the Union navy an opportunity to capture the Confederates and their precious ordnance.

The Rebels escaped almost as easily as they occupied Ship Island. Whether Smith's carefully worded report eschewed the scrutiny of Flag-Officer Mervine's successor, William W. McKean, is not known. Nevertheless, Smith left the *USS Preble* and the *USS Marion* to guard Ship Island. "These vessels will occupy their present position unless I am otherwise instructed," he informed McKean. Once before he had left Ship Island unoccupied and the Confederates had taken it over. Now, the fortunes of war had handed him the island back and this time he would ensure that the Southerners would not get it without a fight. Ironically, the fort would become known as "Fort Massachusetts," in honor of the vessel which "captured" the island.

But what should the Federals do with their new prize? McKean asked his superiors in the Navy Department exactly that. Should he hold the fort or destroy it? If the Navy wanted it held, "in what way and from where [are] the necessary guns and men to be procured?"[73] The flag officer was obviously

unaware of the committee's report on Ship Island, but Secretary Welles quickly
sent word that the island's strategic importance required it to be held.[74]

The bloodless skirmishing over the occupation of Ship Island has dissuaded
study of its consequence on the evolution of the war in the Mississippi sound.
True, it was not of the size and scope of operations that would follow, such as the
passing of Forts Jackson and St. Phillip or the Battle of Mobile Bay. Yet the
impact of the Union's possession of Ship Island—and the Confederacy's voluntary evacuation of the place—was enormous. Within three months the first of
three Union brigades would arrive there to comprise the military arm of the
Department of the Gulf, under command of Maj. Gen. Benjamin F. Butler.[75] In
addition, the Union navy would use Ship Island as a naval depot for the soon-to-
be created West Blockading Squadron, Flag-Officer David Farragut's command.[76] In April 1862, four months after Butler's brigades arrived on the island,
Forts Jackson and St. Philip were bombarded and bypassed. New Orleans was
assaulted from the south, and the city's eventual surrender was a stunning blow to
the Confederate government. The loss of the Crescent City set the stage for
Union control of the entire length of the Mississippi River. The loss of New
Orleans swam in the wake of the fall of Ship Island.

Ship Island would remain in Union hands for the rest of the war. Besides
being used as a naval depot, it also housed political prisoners as well as captured
Confederate soldiers and sailors. Ship Island's final irony came many years after
the war when Jefferson Davis moved to Biloxi to write *The Rise and Fall of the
Confederate Government* and *History of the Confederacy*. On a clear day, Ship
Island's outline could be seen from the library of his home, Beauvoir. Decades
earlier, as the secretary of war during the Franklin Pierce administration, Davis
had requested and received appropriations to build a fort at Ship Island. He
believed it was an important military site and vital to his nation's security.

And so it was.

Notes

1. Grady Howell, Jr., *To Live and Die in Dixie, A History of the Third Mississippi
Infantry* (Jackson, MS, 1991), p. 20.

2. Ibid., p. 21 and Richard P. Weinert, "The Neglected Key to the Gulf Coast," *The
Journal of Mississippi History*, Vol. 31, No. 4 (1969), p. 282.

3. U.S. War Department, *The War of the Rebellion: The Official Records of the
Union and Confederate Armies*, 128 vols. (Washington D.C., 1890-1901), Series III, Vol.
1, p. 32. Hereinafter cited as *OR*.

4. Edwin C. Bearrs, "Gulf Islands National Seashore: Fort on Ship Island (Fort Massachusetts) 1857-1935," (1974)

5. *OR* 1, p. 329.

6. Ibid.

7. Ibid.

8. Howell, Jr., *To Live and Die in Dixie*, pp. 21-23.

9. Weinart, "The Neglected Key to the Gulf Coast," p. 269.

10. Ibid.

11. Ibid., pp. 279-281.

12. Ibid.

13. Annual Report of Secretary of War for Fiscal Year 1855, *Executive Documents of the Senate for the 1st and 2nd Sessions of the 34th Congress* (Washington 1856), Serial 811, p. 11.

14. *OR* 53, p. 686.

15. *OR* 53, p. 690.

16. Howell, *To Live and Die in Dixie*, p. 32-33.

17. *OR* 53, pp. 690-691.

18. Ibid., pp. 715-717.

19. Ibid., pp. 711-712.

20. U. S. Navy Dept., *Official Records of the Union and Confederate Navies in the War of the Rebellion*, (Washington, 1896), Series I, Vol. 27, p. 690. Hereinafter cited as *ORN*.

21. *ORN* 16, p. 826.

22. *Picayune*, June 25, 1861.

23. *ORN* 16, p. 827.

24. Ibid., 27, pp. 690-691.

25. Clara Solomon, *The Civil War Diary of Clara Solomon, Growing up in New Orleans 1861-1862*, edited by Elliott Ashkenazi (Baton Rouge, 1995), p. 35.

26. Howell, *To Live and Die in Dixie*, p. 35.

27. *ORN* 16, p. 830.

28. Weinart, "The Neglected Key to the Gulf Coast," p. 286.

29. Mark M Boatner, III, *The Civil War Dictionary* (New York 1987), p. 399.

30. Weinart, "The Neglected Key to the Gulf Coast," p. 286.

31. *ORN* 16, p. 830.

32. Ibid., 27, p. 691.

33. Ibid., 16, p. 581.

34. Ibid., pp. 581-582.

35. *OR* 53, pp. 708-710.

36. Ibid.

37. *ORN* 16, p. 581 and 27, p. 691.

38. *OR* 53, pp. 708-710.

39. *ORN* 16, p. 581 and 27, p. 691.

40. *OR* 53, pp. 708-710.

41. Read, C. W., "Reminiscences of the Confederate States Navy," *Southern Historical Society Papers*, vol. 1, no. 5, p. 333.

42. *OR* 53, pp. 708-710.

43. *ORN* 16, p. 583.

44. Ibid., 16, p. 581.

45. Ibid.

46. Ibid.

47. Boatner, *Civil War Dictionary,* p. 9.

48. *OR* 53, pp. 708-710.

49. *ORN* 16, pp. 581-582.

50. Ibid., pp. 602-603.

51. *OR* 53, p. 714.

52. *ORN* 16, pp. 616-617.

53. Ibid., 17, p. 629.

54. Ibid., 16, p. 660.

55. *OR* 6, pp. 728, 738; *ORN* 16, p. 826.

56. Ibid.

57. *OR* 53, p. 739.

58. Ibid., 6, pp. 730-734.

59. Ibid., p. 730.

60. Ibid., pp. 734-736.

61. Ibid., p. 738.

62. Ibid., 53, p. 739.

63. "The Civil War Diary of Clara Solomon," p. 158.

64. Howell, *To Live and Die in Dixie*, pp. 56-57.

65. Ibid.

66. *OR* 6, p. 738.

67. Ibid., 53, pp. 740-741.

68. Ibid.

69. *ORN* 16, pp. 678-679.

70. Ibid., pp. 677-678.

71. *ORN*, 16, p. 679.

72. Ibid., pp. 677-678.

73. Ibid., pp. 690-693.

74. Ibid., pp. 739-740.

75. *OR* 6, pp. 695-696.

76. *ORN*, 17, pp. 56-57.

"To see so many of our poor fellows—all of whom knew me, and most of whom
I knew—mangled and cut up, almost unmanned me."

WITH THE FIRE ZOUAVES AT FIRST BULL RUN

The Narrative of Private Arthur O. Alcock, 11th New York Volunteer Infantry

edited by Brian C. Pohanka

No Federal regiment marched to war with such high expectations for military glory as the 11th New York Volunteer Infantry, popularly known as The Fire Zouaves. The unit's rank and file was largely comprised of members of New York City's Volunteer Fire Department—men famed throughout Manhattan for their physical prowess, reckless courage and swaggering bravado. They were fiercely loyal to their respective engine, hose or hook and ladder companies, and those competitive organizations would some-times fight one another for the right to quench the conflagrations that posed a constant threat to the crowded cityscape. The exploits of these red-shirted dare-devils were widely recounted in the local press, and at a time when most Americans believed the sectional conflict would be settled in a matter of months, the firemen's strength and zeal promised to guarantee valorous deeds on the field of battle.[1]

While the "fire laddies" seemed ideally suited for the role of citizen sol-diers, the unit's charismatic colonel was martial enthusiasm personified. Though he had only just celebrated his twenty-fourth birthday,[2] Elmer Ephraim

Ellsworth was by any standard the most widely-known militia officer in America. Handsome, dashing and energetic, his very name was an inspiration to the zealous volunteers who rallied to the cause of the Union.

A native of Malta in Saratoga County, New York, Ellsworth grew up in the nearby Hudson River town of Mechanicville. At age seventeen he moved to Illinois, where he joined the state militia and studied law in the office of Abraham Lincoln, who became a lifelong friend. A chance encounter with a French army veteran—who regaled the young man with stories of the famed colonial troops called Zouaves—prompted Ellsworth to transform a lackluster Chicago militia company into the "United States Zouave Cadets." He outfitted his fellow enthusiasts in a Zouave uniform of his own design, and trained them in the complex, acrobatic maneuvers of a light infantry drill loosely based on French texts.[3]

In the summer of 1860 Ellsworth and his Zouave Cadets embarked on a six-week tour of some twenty cities, performing their superbly choreographed drills before admiring crowds that frequently numbered in the tens of thousands. Ellsworth became a national celebrity, and his company's success spawned a "zouave craze" that swept the country on the eve of Civil War. In those heady days of patriotic fervor that followed the bombardment and capitulation of Fort Sumter, the 11th New York was but one of dozens of volunteer units that adopted variations of the exotic French uniform; but no other regiment could boast the founder of the American zouaves himself as their commanding officer.

Anxious to be at the front before the fighting was over, Ellsworth managed to arm and equip his troops in a week's time, and on April 29, 1861—sporting jaunty gray uniforms with red fire shirts and kepis—the Fire Zouaves departed for Washington.[4] Arriving at the capital, the firemen's antics and occasional depredations soon made it clear that Ellsworth faced a considerable challenge in training and disciplining the "Pet Lambs," as he dubbed his troublesome soldiers[5] It was in large part to refurbish the unit's tarnished reputation that Ellsworth insisted his unit be assigned to the Federal force preparing to occupy the Virginia shore of the Potomac River.

In the predawn darkness of May 24, 1861, the Fire Zouaves boarded transports and embarked for Alexandria, the old colonial town that was a hotbed of secession sentiment. After landing on the city docks, Ellsworth personally led a small group of Zouaves several blocks inland, ostensibly to seize the local telegraph office. In a move that displayed more zeal than wisdom, Ellsworth abruptly altered his plans when he observed a huge Confederate banner flying above the Marshall House hotel. Ascending to the roof, Ellsworth cut the hal-

yards, and while making his way back down, was accosted in the stairwell by
the armed innkeeper James W. Jackson, who sent a fatal round into the Colonel's chest. Zouave Corporal Francis Brownell quickly avenged Ellsworth's
death—and in those deadly seconds both North and South were granted their
first popular martyrs of the war.[6]

Ellsworth's successor in command, Col. Noah Lane Farnham,[7] doubtless
hoped that the tragic incident at the Marshall House would have a sobering
effect on the unruly zouaves. A former executive in the Manhattan Fire Department and a veteran of the elite 7th Regiment State Militia, Farnham was determined to enforce military discipline. But his style of command made him far
from popular, and his best efforts went for naught. Three weeks after Ellsworth's
death, as they prepared to take the field with Brigadier General Irvin McDow-

Contemporary illustration of an officer and enlisted man of the 11th New York.
From *The Illustrated London News*, June 16, 1861

Courtesy of Brian Pohanka

ell's Federal army,[8] the 11th New York remained little more than an armed mob. The inevitable result of their unpreparedness and naivete occurred amidst the Union debacle at Bull Run on July 21, 1861, when the Fire Zouaves played a controversial part in the bloody fight for Henry House Hill.

One zouave who "saw the elephant" at Bull Run was Alfred O. Alcock, a former journalist serving as a private in the 11th New York. His detailed account was serialized in *The New York Atlas*, and a portion of that account is reproduced here.

Alfred O'Niel Alcock was a native of Wales, and though his exact date of birth has yet to be determined, census and military records indicate the year was likely 1820.[9] He resided in the village of Llangorse, Breconshire, where on November 13, 1845 he married 24 year old Anne Marsden, the daughter of Reverend Benjamin Marsden, who officiated at the local Church of England. They emigrated to New York City in 1848 with their year old son, and settled in Yorkville—a community to the east of Central Park, which was in the process of being absorbed by the expanding metropolis. Between 1852 and 1858 three more children were born to the Alcocks, and the outbreak of war found them residing on 83rd Street between 3rd and 4th Avenues.[10]

Alfred O. Alcock was employed as editor of the Fire and Military Department of *The New York Atlas*, a weekly journal that was one of several Manhattan papers providing extensive coverage of Fire Department matters. A volunteer fireman himself, Alcock's effusive if occasionally rambling columns reflected no small degree of wit and literary ability. John Leverich, the Fire Editor of the New York *Leader*—who joined the Fire Zouaves as captain of Company E—noted that his friend Alcock "always displayed much ability with the pen, as well as all the characteristics of a 'jolly good fellow.'"[11]

Initially considered for the captaincy of Company A, Alfred Alcock chose to go to war as Colonel Ellsworth's military secretary, a position for which he was well suited. Though officially recorded on the muster rolls as a private in Company A, most of Alcock's time was spent preparing regimental orders, morning reports and requisitions. Never one to shy away from publicity,[12] Ellsworth encouraged his acting secretary to continue his journalistic endeavors, and Alcock kept up a prolific correspondence with *The Atlas*, penning weekly articles that recounted the experiences of the 11th New York in the field. It was probably through the instigation of his friend Captain Leverich that Alfred Alcock found himself performing similar duty for the *Leader*—writing equally detailed columns under the pseudonym "Harry Lorequer."[13]

Following Ellsworth's death in Alexandria, Alcock's friends in the Fire Department petitioned to have him promoted a sergeant on the regimental staff. But some sort of personality clash seems to have arisen between Alcock and Ellsworth's successor, Col. Noah Farnham, and the former military secretary was returned to the ranks of Company A.[14] Perhaps in deference to Alcock's age—at 41 he was among the older men serving in the 11th New York—he was detailed to the regimental surgeon, Dr. Charles Gray,[15] as acting medical orderly and supervisor of the stretcher bearers. It was in that capacity that Alfred O. Alcock found himself en route to the great clash of arms that would transpire on the plains of Manassas. The journalist/soldier was captured in the aftermath of that military disaster, and following ten months of captivity in Southern prisons recorded his experiences in a series of articles published in *The Atlas*.[16] The first portion of his lengthy account appears below.

————————

Receiving orders at our camp at Campbell's Run, three miles from Alexandria, Va., on the Orange and Alexandria Railroad, to march for Manassas, our Regiment left tent and baggage, and joining the column of McDowell, made a detour to the left of the Railroad, and performing a semi-circle, including two whole days march—a distance of about twenty-three miles, and as rough a country as ever fell to the lot of man to traverse—we reached Fairfax station on the 17th July, 1861. It was on this march that our Regiment first knew the hardships of military life in the field, and the same power of endurance became manifest then that afterwards exhibited itself in so many ways, and which will require notice so often in the course of this narrative.

At Fairfax station the Rebels fled before our advanced skirmishers, and we occupied their deserted camps where we arrived just in time to extinguish the fires kindled by them with a view of destroying the station and the buildings adjoining. Here we found a small Catholic church [17] which Perrin and I saved from destruction. In it, on a cot in front of the altar, lay the putrid body of a Rebel soldier, left unburied by his comrades in their hasty flight; and near the fence of the enclosure surrounding the church, was found the body of another soldier partially covered with earth, the feet protruding temptingly under the nose of an old sow, who most unwillingly left her expected booty.

Immediately that a halt was called and pickets posted, as there was no necessity for lighting fires, all hands looked round for something to cook, and a drove of some twenty hogs being observed in a neighboring field some half dozen men of different Regiments, deployed themselves and gave chase. There was some fun in this, and the prospect of a good dinner of fresh pork made the affair quite pleasant. It was not long before two of our fellows had their share (as they always had) and as the return of two or three scouts came in laden with legs and shoulders—these secured with their bowie knives almost before the poor animals they originally belonged to were dead. Our hunger was satisfied by these means, however, and that was the main point just then.

There some scenes during our brief stay at Fairfax station worthy of notice, most of them showing that the rough life of a soldier in the field is in *reality* very different from the descriptions we read, and which are manufactured by the romancists [sic], to please people as ignorant as themselves on the subject; but as I shall have occasion to describe one or two—which may be taken as a fair sample of all the rest—in another place—I pass these by and go to sleep in the ambulance wagon, tired out. Dr. Gray and Perrin [18] also occupy the same roost—and "as thick as three in a bed," subluniary [sic] affairs become a blank to us until the sun is high on the morning of the 18th, and Ferguson,[19] the orderly, loudly summons us to a breakfast of coffee, and the inevitable pig, prepared by Dick Marshall [20] of "ours."

JULY 18TH.—Breakfast disposed of, and in expectation of a day's rest, we sauntered round the locality, searched the post office for papers without results, and found six rebel soldiers in an outbuilding at a farm house. They have had measles. The doctor prescribes for them. They belong to an Alabama regiment, and were left behind for want of means of transportation. Find the railroad obstructed in a very queer manner about a quarter of a mile on the Alexandria side of the station. The railroad passes through a deep cut there, and the earth had been dug from the steep embankment on each side and thrown on the track, and while this was doing, whole trees, and poles, varying in size from three inches in diameter to a foot, had been thrown in, the whole making a conglomerated mass of some twenty feet high, and perhaps sixty yards long, most difficult to remove.

At 2 o'clock, P.M., hear the first gun fired by the enemy on our left, and as we supposed at a distance of about seven or eight miles. All is excitement. Accoutrements are seized and the men equipped in a few minutes, and a courier arrives with rapid orders for an advance to Centreville. Our regiment with the 1st Michigan under Colonel—now acting Brigadier General Wilcox [sic],[21] start in good order, and after a march of seven miles, some of which were at double quick, in the anxiety to reach the point where the continued firing indicated that a battle was going on—we reached Centreville completely worn out, just in time to be too late to participate in the fight of the 18th.[22]

It was just getting dark and a heavy black thundercloud was looming up majestically in the distance, as, on our approach to the place appointed for the bivouac of our regiment, I met my friend Wilkes of the *Spirit*,[23] who in a few words told me that the enemy had "given us fits." And now the realities of campaigning began to take the romance out of those who thought it a very fine thing to go soldiering, in fine uniforms, long swords, "puss feathers," &c., &c.

The spot occupied by our men was on the side of a very small and sluggish muddy stream, about half a mile on the Washington side of the wretched and literally "one horse" village of Centreville; indeed it consisted of an old stone church, a blacksmith shop, a closed up and deserted tavern, and some twelve or fourteen houses. From the low swampy ground where we bivouacked, to Centreville, there was a continuous ascent until at the village a height of considerable altitude was obtained, the summit of which was crowned with a very poor attempt at an earthwork, pierced for four guns. No guns were there, however, and the whole thing had a deserted and forlorn look. One frame building was behind the breastwork, deserted also, and empty. But I must return to the affairs of the regiment, having finally and forever, I hope, done with the "deserted village" of Centreville.

By the side of a little brook there our poor weary fellows were soon to be seen trying to light fires from the wet wood and brush, carrying thick muddy water from the stream, or washing their swollen feet therein, while the jetty blackness of the firmament was occasionally relieved by the ruddy glare of a successfully kindled fire, enabling us to look around on the disheartening scene. Several shots in rapid succession attract my attention to a crowd of men, in the centre of which I find an ox just shot, and three or four active fellows with sleeves rolled up, and bowie knife in hand, are tearing the hide off the still bleeding beast, while the half famished crowd around are slyly cutting off gabbets of the still quivering flesh with their knives, and beating a hasty retreat amidst the jeers, shouts, cheers and curses of their comrades. The nasty morsels are hastily roasted—a ramrod the spit—and eaten without bread, or salt—with a gusto that would astonish a habitué of "Windust's," or the "Captain."[24]

This was the supper of nine-tenths of the men of our brigade on the night of the 18th July. Where now, thought I, as I afterwards wandered over the wet boggy field from fire to fire, is the romance of the soldier's life? Where the nice camp equipage, the charming scenery, the *piquant* little dinners, and the savory *soupers*, enjoyed by gallant fully bedizened and bespangled sons of Mars, beneath the umbrageous shade of impending trees—the air the while redolent of the wild flowers' perfume, and resonant with the titter of the birds, the purling of the brook, and the happy song or chorus of brother soldiers? Where are all those things that we have *read* about? Ask the weary, footsore, travel-soiled, half starved man yonder lying on his wet coat on the bare and muddy ground, who only sleeps because nature is exhausted; and he will tell you that the stern realities of a soldier's life are unknown to the crowd of scribblers who so flippantly write of them.

JULY 19TH.—Very warm. Expecting orders to advance every moment. Very little bread for the men and very bad water. Colonel Farnham very ill.[25] We visit the earthwork and view the country beyond Centreville towards Bull Run Mountain. The Colonel's illness increases. He occupies the ambulance wagon—he has very high fever. All expect orders to advance. The enemy are stated to be 50,000 strong, at Manassas. We take a wagon ride to Alexandria, with Doctor Gray. Distance twenty-one miles. Pass through Fairfax Court House by moonlight. Nothing had been injured there. It is a handsome little village with churches and pleasant country houses. Many of the ladies and children are standing on the stoops and piazzas, as we pass through. All in perfect quiet. We sleep in our old hospital near Campbell's Run.

JULY 20TH.—Go to Alexandria and visit Captain Tyler.[26] Obtain hospital stores and leave for the camp at 3 P.M. After a long and weary ride, we finally reach the camp at Centreville about 10 P.M., and find that all the troops are under orders to march at 2 A.M. All is preparation. No one sleeps. Very little to eat, except beef. Colonel Farnham is still very ill. Walk round the field visiting the officers of the different companies, all night. Got a cup of coffee and a roasted potatoe [sic] by good luck from Captain Tagen,[27] of Co. G. Lieutenant D. Divver[28] walks with me. During our conversation relative to the condition and good spirits of the men in view of the expected fight, poor Divver said to me, "Many a one of us will be cold to-morrow night." Who will say that "coming events *do not* cast their shadows before."

JULY 21. 2 A.M.—The orders to march, at this hour, have been counter-manded until 4 A.M. At length the regiment is formed, and has to wait until half past 5 before they get under way. We finally march—a weary and toilsome march, mostly at double quick, for some eight or nine miles, when we cross a shallow brook (Bull Run). We come suddenly on Sudley Church,[29] a plain and unpretending brick structure, about fifty by forty feet. This is at once taken possession of, and cleared of its seats and pews, for a hospital. Heavy, quick firing has been heard for the last two hours on our left. Dr. Gray remains in charge of the hospital. Mitchell [30] "no where." At the request of Dr. Gray, I take four men with the stretchers and follow the regiment to the field, at double quick. Firing is now very heavy.

We reach Dogan's House, at the Cross Roads,[31] at about half past eleven o'clock, and are immediately ordered to advance across the brook known as Cub's Run.[32] The enemy open with artillery, from masked batteries, as we march down the hill, on open ground. The shot and shell fly thickly around.

Crossing the brook, the regiment is now ordered to lie down in a stubble field, in which there are many small bushes, to shelter themselves from the heavy fire of musketry that now hails over us. Wait for some time for orders. (In crossing the brook I fall across a log and receive a severe injury, but it appears slight at the time.) About half past twelve o'clock P.M. orders are given to our regiment to charge up the hill at the enemy, who are firing on us.

Now the battle begins in earnest.

I have never dreamed of writing a history of the battle of Manassas, and so only mention here such portions of the scene as came under my own immediate observation. No one man can see the whole of a battle. Events of importance are occurring at the same times at points along the lines of the contending armies, which are very far apart. Under these circumstances, those of our regiment who find their names omitted, will recollect that it is because I did not see them, and, consequently, know nothing of their conduct or actions.

Of Col. Farnham I can say that he bore himself like a brave man, and did not shrink from the hottest of the fire, and was all along at the head of his regiment. Late in the action he was slightly wounded.[33] Col. Cregier [34] was everywhere, and no braver spirit was on that field, nor one in whom men had more confidence. Major Loeser [sic][35] was coolness itself; and this is a trait in a soldier's character than which none is more valuable. Capt. Leverich, of Co. E, was in his place with his company—as was also Capt. Wildey [36] of Co. I—the tall single feather in his cap making him a conspicuous mark. Capt. Downey, Lieut. Barnard, Lieut. Mathews, Lieut. Berry, Lieut. McFarland, Lieut. Divver, and Lieut. Bowerman.[37] Sergeant-Major Goodwin [38] I saw also, as he was making his way wounded from the field.

I had spoken to Eugene Ebling,[39] of Co. A, our regiment, but a few minutes previous to word being brought me that he was shot through the head. When I saw him last he was loading his musket. We were then engaged with the Fourth Alabama rebel regiment.[40] Ebling, poor fellow! I knew him well. He enlisted with me at the Arsenal in Thir[t]y-fifth street. Whole-souled, generous,

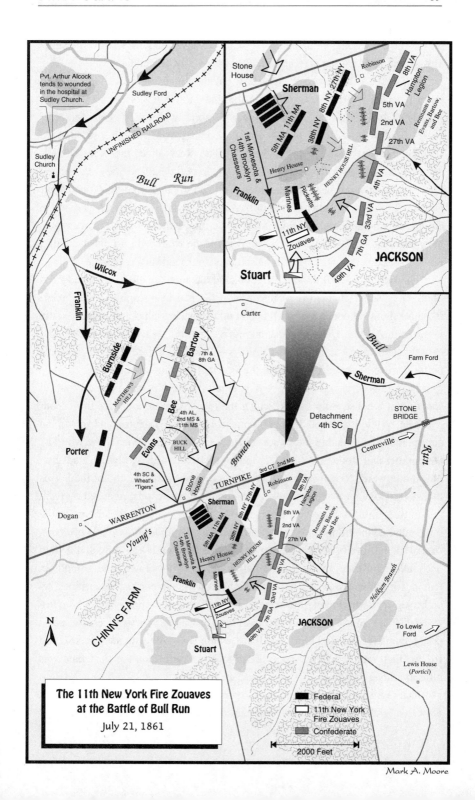

Pvt. Arthur Alcock tends to wounded in the hospital at Sudley Church.

Sudley Ford

UNFINISHED RAILROAD

Sudley Church

Bull   Run

Wilcox

Franklin

Stone House

Sherman

8th NY 27th NY

Robinson

8th VA

Hampton Legion

5th VA

2nd VA

27th VA

Remnants of Evans, Bartow, and Bee

1st Minnesota & 14th Brooklyn Chasseurs

5th MA 11th MA

38th NY

Henry House

Pickets

HENRY HOUSE HILL

4th VA

Franklin

Marines

11th NY Zouaves

33rd VA

7th GA

49th VA   7th VA

JACKSON

Stuart

Carter

Bull

Farm Ford

Sherman

STONE BRIDGE

Bartow

7th & 8th GA

Burnside

MATTHEWS HILL

Bee

4th AL, 2nd MS & 11th MS

Evans

BUCK HILL

Branch

Detachment 4th SC

Porter

Stone House

4th SC & Wheat's "Tigers"

TURNPIKE

Centreville

Run

3rd CT 2nd ME

Robinson

8th VA

Hampton Legion

Dogan

WARRENTON

Sherman

5th MA 11th MA

38th NY   8th NY 27th NY

5th VA

2nd VA

27th VA

Remnants of Evans, Bartow, and Bee

Young's

1st Minnesota & 14th Brooklyn Chasseurs

Henry House

Franklin

Marines

HENRY HOUSE HILL

4th VA

Holkum Branch

N

CHINN'S FARM

11th NY Zouaves

33rd VA

7th GA

49th VA   7th VA

JACKSON

To Lewis' Ford

Stuart

Lewis House
(*Portici*)

The 11th New York Fire Zouaves at the Battle of Bull Run

July 21, 1861

■ Federal

□ 11th New York Fire Zouaves

▨ Confederate

2000 Feet

Mark A. Moore

brave—he only too soon fulfilled what seems to have been his destiny—to show how soon a good soldier can be made, and how nobly he can die.

The rebel artillery served very fast, but the range not good. I threaten to shoot the men with the stretchers, for their cowardice in not coming forward. The threat has the desired effect. Divver is mortally wounded. Poor fellow! I knew it, but to satisfy him I put a tourniquet on his arm. He died that night at the hospital. Stewart's [sic] cavalry charge.[41] The story about the New Orleans Tigers raising their knives is all false.[42] Our regiment and they exchanged volleys, and men fell fast on both sides. No hand to hand fighting. None of our men are wounded by either knives or bayonets. Stewart's [sic] cavalry are much cut up in their encounter with our men, while they inflict but little injury on us. Keep the stretcher parties at work, carrying off the wounded into the shade of a few trees, and put on innumerable tourniquets, on friends and foes alike.

The fight is now at the hottest point, and our men are almost parched from thirst. Give some of them my canteen, which I had from time to time replenished for the wounded. See Dr. Mitchell on horseback, well out of range, quietly viewing the battle. Cannot resist taking a hand in, so taking a musket and cartridge box from one of our poor fellows—Dukes, of Co. K [43]—who can have no further use for them. I fired some thirteen shots "on my own hook."

Two guns of Ricketts' battery in position on our left made some beautiful shooting at a house from behind which the rebels kept up a deadly fire on our regiment. While I watched their good practice for a few minutes, and was in the act of stooping to enable me to see under the smoke, the poor fellow who had the rammer and stood about ten feet to my left, was cut in two by a round shot, which afterwards took a spoke out of the gun wheel, mangled one of the horses that stood in the rear, and then went whistling into the woods, ricochetting from tree to tree, until its force was expended. Another poor fellow belonging to the same gun had the front of his throat shot away by a round shot while I was there, so that his head fell backwards, hanging by the flesh and skin only; and he had only fallen prostrate on the ground before another shot plowed the ground six feet in front of where he lay, and striking him on the hip completely stripped his entire leg of flesh, leaving the bone exposed. The gallant lieutenant who commanded these guns,[44] whom I had often met at Capt. Tyler's office at Alexandria, recognized me, and requested that I would shoot the wounded horse. I did so, and then returned to our men. Shortly after, I heard that the lieutenant was himself among the slain.

The regiment engaged the 4th Alabama, the 'Tigers,' the 8th Virginia, and Stewart's [sic] Cavalry, successively and then retired across the brook in good order, when they made a stand in line, and fired some first rate volleys. It was after this, and when other regiments had *commenced* it, that ours retreated. Then came the disorder and confusion. While the regiment was in the act of firing the volley, I went to the hospital with two wounded men on the stretchers,[45] and then remained with Dr. Gray, assisting him in operations and dressing wounds, until he left, while I was bringing some instruments from the church. There were then but three surgeons in the hospital. I could easily have escaped at that time, as I had captured an excellent horse, but I could not leave our wounded men, who were continually calling me by name. Almost immediately after, a party of cavalry, headed by a lieutenant, surrounded us, and we had to surrender.

The scene in the hospital at Sudley's Church defy all my powers of description. On my arrival, Dr. Gray, who was only assisted by Harry L. Perrin, our hospital steward, was operating with his usual rapidity and skill, and I was at once pressed into his service. In the church—from which everything in the way of seats, pews, &c. had been previously removed—the scene of human suffering was terrible. Every part of the floor was covered with the wounded—dying and dead. Poor Stephen Griswold, surgeon of the 38th N.Y. Vol.,[46] here earned a fame only second to that I shall hereafter describe. So close together did the wounded lay upon the floor, that it was with the greatest difficulty I could pick my way through them; and here the surgeons had to perform some of the most difficult, and to the scientific observer, some of the most beautiful operations.

Under a small table immediately in front of the pulpit was a heap of legs and arms, that had been amputated, quite sufficient to load an ordinary sized wheelbarrow. At the end of the table, to the right, lay the almost nude body of a man who had been shockingly mutilated by a round shot, and who had died in horrible agony before anything could be done to relieve him. The anguish depicted on this poor fellow's countenance, and the contorted attitude in which the death struggle left him, can never be effaced from my memory. To the left of the table, and partially reclining against the wall of the building, lay another corpse, naked from the waist up. He had been shot by a minie ball through the lungs, and had died from internal hemmorhage [sic]. His placid, pale features affording a marked contrast to the to that of the unfortunate already described. He had evidently passed away without a pang, just as a child would fall asleep.

But the cries of the wounded and dying were the most heartrending that can be imagined: indeed they cannot be realized by those who have not seen such sights, and heard the wail of mortal agony. "Water, water for God's sake!" was the one universal cry, and "Oh! for Heaven's sake don't step on me," was continually moaned into my ears from the poor sufferers, as I carefully picked my way amongst them, assuring them that they would all be attended to in due time, and giving each a small cup full of the desired but difficult-to-be-obtained fluid.

Around the door outside the church most of the wounded of our regiment were sitting or lying on the ground, and it was here, to the left of the door, that Dr. Gray had his operating table; and it was here too, that my feelings almost overcame me. To see so many of our poor fellows—all of whom knew me, and most of whom I knew—mangled and cut up, almost unmanned me. And they knowing of my intimacy with Dr. Gray, kept continually begging of me most piteously to get him to attend to each one first. Altogether the scene was one of unmitigated horror, and one which, ever so well described, can only be realized by those who have witnessed it. Hospital scenes, and scenes on the battle field since the battle of Manassas, have been so run into the ground, that I have skipped lightly over both in order to carry out my purpose of describing our life in prison, and so to continue my journal.

After begging the Rebel Cavalry Lieutenant who captured those at the hospital to permit me, Ferguson and Carmody [47] of our regiment to remain by our wounded men, stating to him that there were many who would die from loss of blood before morning, whom we might save, and using every entreaty that I could to obtain this end, the vindictive traitor brutally refused to listen to me, and said that we should all go to Manassas Junction and that the wounded must look out for themselves until their surgeons could arrive. I could not help at the moment, regardless of the revolver he presented at us, telling him bitterly that "the rebels now intended to add cold-blooded murder to the catalogue of their crimes." But all was no use; so I had to bid a hasty farewell to our poor fellows—receiving from Ira Wilson (who was badly, and he feared at the time mortally wounded) a little pocket diary to be given to his uncle, (Commissioner Wilson of the New York Fire Department) in case he never reached home. Wilson, however, recovered—rejoined me at Richmond, when his book was returned, and finally he came home with me.[48]

On thus being forced to leave those I had been associated with—and leaving them, too, in such a sad condition, my feelings were such that I actually did not care what became of me. There was no alternative, however, and as there was no commissioned officer of our regiment to be seen, and as by years and experience I was the oldest by far of the men present, I took upon myself to collect the members of our regiment together, to console them in their misfortune, exhort them to cheer up, not to allow the rebels to think they were downhearted,—to keep together,—to share the same fate,—to assure them that I would be with them wherever we were sent, and finally wound up by telling them that it was my belief that our government would have us all exchanged in three weeks or a month. How we were disappointed in this expectation will appear hereafter.

On the march to Manassas—a distance of about eight miles, we had to cross a portion of the battle-field, and passed by scores of dead men and bodies, many of them horribly mutilated. We also met many wounded, and among them two of our regiment to whom I gave a drink out of my canteen despite the threatening order of the officer in command of our guards to "fall in there and go on, you d___d Yankee." One of these men I saw afterwards at Richmond, and though I did not recognize him, he did me, and was most profuse in his thanks. I believe he was sent home with the first lot of those who were wounded, and I think his name was Clark.[49]

The dust on the roads was full six inches in depth, and as we had had nothing to eat since the night before, our powers of endurance were sadly tried. We kept good hearts, however, and notwithstanding the rebels made us carry one of their wounded men in a blanket for over two miles, we reached Manassas Junction—the camp of Beauregard—at about ten o'clock at night, in good spirits, but weary, weak, hungry, and covered so with dust that we could scarcely recognize one another. Once arrived here we were put into an enclosure formed by a cordon of guards, in the open air—as villainous a looking set of rascals as were ever brigands in the Abruzzi. Here upon the bare ground, which, however, the now fast falling rain—mixing the dust into mortar—rendered comparatively soft, we lay down like pigs in a sty, and slept the sleep of physical exhaustion until morning.

Our misery now began. The suffering here endured baffles description. All of us were weak and hungry, and the demand for water was incessant, while the supply was so scant, that the men were fain to suck such portions of each others' clothing as became saturated by the rain. For myself I really believed that I should have died that morning of sheer debility, but could not bring myself to utter a word of complaint. And the kindness of our men to me I shall never forget. Stewart [50] of the 1st Michigan regiment, bugler to Colonel Wilcox [sic], and McArthur [51] of "ours," after procuring the vile fluid mud, called water, *sold to them by the guards at fifty cents the canteen-full*, would not touch a drop until they first saw that I had what I wanted. It is in such circumstances that the true characters of men are developed. At about 11 o'clock, a few biscuits, and some pieces of horrid fat, rancid bacon, were thrown to the crowd of prisoners, who had now been thirty-six hours without eating a morsel of any kind.

12M.—Leave on train for Richmond at 1 P.M. People—men—some women and children, jeer and taunt us at the different depots. Call us "d—d Yankees," and say we ought to be all hanged, at the same time want to buy buttons from our uniforms and wish to buy our red caps. A little bread was given us on the cars, and on.

TUESDAY, JULY 23 —At about 9 o'clock in the evening, we reached Richmond, having traveled about 100 miles in 33 hours. To be sure, we remained on the road at a dead stand still all Monday night, and this was very pleasant in one of the baggage cars, crowded to its utmost capacity. Along the road at the various stopping places, crowds of people including many ladies (?) were assembled to see the "Yankee prisoners," as they passed, and the salutes that greeted us were not of the most pleasant character, many of them unfit for publication.

One lady much amused me, she was escorted to the cars by the Major of the party who had us in charge. The Major was a Louisianan by birth, and the lady was evidently an old maid and not even tolerably well-looking. Upon seeing our party of Zouaves, as we stood in the open door of the baggage car, she asked us if we did not think we had been "well whipped at Manassas." In reply, I told her, that "we had certainly lost the battle, but that good reasons could be given for it." She tauntingly replied that "the women in Virginia could beat us." To this I replied that I would be willing to admit the superiority of the women in every point of view. (what else could I say?) The Major smiled and said something to the lady, which I could not hear, nevertheless the lady continued.

"Why we are getting up a regiment of women in Virginia, who will whip you all out of it, in no time." Maddened by her manner I replied that "if they were all as good looking as she was, we would all run away without being whipped." The Southern lady (?) who could find in her heart to torment and abuse the poor prisoners, felt the reproof and colored up; and the Major, now evidently anxious to get his companion out of the unpleasant predicament in which she had placed herself, again whispered in her ear, and led her reluctantly away, the men in the meantime vastly enjoyed the discomfiture of the "slab-sided old cat," an appellation more expressive than elegant, I must admit, though richly deserved.

At last we got through the hissing, yelling crowd that beset our weary march through the city, and reached the Tobacco Factory of Harwood, where we were huddled together on to the different floors, officers and men, until there was scarcely room for us to lie down on the floor. This we did, however, at once, and but a very few minutes elapsed ere many of us were asleep. Guards were placed everywhere, in the rooms, on the stairs, in the street, and all round the building, while a crowd of the rabble of Richmond made night hideous by their shouts and malediction on the "d—d Yankees." After we had remained in this condition for about two hours, a number of men came up laden with loaves of bread, and tins of fried bacon, all of which was speedily devoured. We were ravenously hungry and made short work of the eatables. Fortunately some pails of water were also brought, so that for once were enabled to slake our burning thirst. Those who fell asleep on our arrival were woke up to join in the feast, as we had only had a few dry hard biscuits given us during our entire journey from Manassas. During the night several shots were fired by the guards outside the building, at what or whom we never discovered.

JULY 24th. —To-day we are removed from Harwood's to Ligon's Tobacco Factory, and here it may be said that our prison life commenced. . . .

Alfred Alcock's family and friends in New York were initially informed that the private had been killed during the Federal retreat from Bull Run. It was mid August before they learned otherwise, by means of a letter Alcock managed to smuggle out of his place of confinement.[52] But while he had escaped enemy bullets, prison life nearly did him in. Covered in filth, plagued with lice and tormented by thirst, for weeks he suffered the debilitating effects of dysentery and exhaustion. He had recovered sufficiently by September 9 to accompany his comrades when several hundred Federal prisoners were transferred from Richmond to Charleston, South Carolina. After five miserable days in the city jail, on September 18 the captives were transported to Castle Pinckney, a masonry fortification just offshore in Charleston harbor.

Over the next three and a half months the disheveled Union prisoners—some two dozen of whom were 11th New York Men—were able to regain a modicum of comfort. They got on well with their Confederate guards, the Charleston Zouave Cadets, and set up comfortable—if crowded —quarters in the casemates of Castle Pinckney. Alcock was appointed acting sergeant of the 17 soldiers housed in Casemate Number One, and the entrance to their improvised barrack was bedecked with a sign denoting the casemate as the "Hotel de Zouave."[53] But after months of imprisonment the Federal captives were justifiably embittered that the government had yet to effect their release, and in the few letters that Alcock managed to get north he expressed his outrage at this seeming abandonment. Several of these censorious missives were published in *The Atlas*, causing some to cast doubts on Alcock's loyalty.

On January 1, 1862, most of the Union prisoners were moved from Charleston to Columbia, South Carolina, and in late February they were transported back to Richmond. On May 8, Arthur Alcock was among a large group of captives that were exchanged and transported to Baltimore, Maryland, where he excitedly telegraphed his good fortune to his family. But before returning to New York, Alcock and the other Zouaves were ordered to Washington, D.C. for muster out.

In the months following the battle of Bull Run the 11th New York had returned to the front but continued to suffer from disciplinary lapses that at times brought the regiment to a condition bordering on anarchy. By late May the entire unit was back in New York and in the process of disbandment.[54]

Soon after arriving in the capital Pvt. Alcock was stunned to learn that he was facing a potential court martial for his published complaints against the government. Luckily the evidence of his fellow captives quickly exonerated Alcock of any charge of treason, and he was officially mustered out of the 11th New York on May 24, 1862.[55]

Overjoyed to be reunited with his wife and children—who had suffered no small degree of economic hardship in his absence—Arthur Alcock resumed his position as Fire Editor of *The Atlas*. In mid August of 1862 the paper began to serialize a book-length account of his experiences titled "The Prisoners of War: Ten Months in the Rebel Prisons. . .A Journal of Facts." Five installments of Alcock's account were serialized in *The Atlas*, but following the September 13 issue, no further articles appeared. The precise reasons for this have yet to come to light, but as Alcock seems to have given up editorship of the fire column at that time, he may well have severed his relationship with the paper.

The circumstances of Alfred Alcock's career over the next year remain elusive, but we do know that early in 1864 he decided to re-enlist in the Union army. On February 27, 1864, Alcock walked into a recruiting station at Manhattan's Tammany Hall and signed up for a three-year term with the 10th New York Infantry. The depot's examining surgeon was none other than Dr. Charles Gray—former surgeon of the Fire Zouaves—who was awaiting a new assignment with the 11th New York Cavalry. Alcock gave his age as 41—he was actually nearly 45—and his physical description characterized him as 5 feet 7 1/2 inches tall, with blue eyes, light hair and a light complexion. Before starting for the front Alcock received a sixty dollar bounty plus one month's pay of thirteen dollars.[56]

Arthur Alcock joined the ranks of Company A, 10th New York at the unit's winter quarters near Morton's Ford, Virginia. Like his former regiment the 10th New York was clad in Zouave attire, and "The National Zouaves," as they were known, had seen extensive action in the war's eastern theater.[57] Re-enlisting as a four-company veteran battalion, by April, 1864 the 10th New York was increased to six companies, and served in the approaching campaign as one of nine units in Col. Samuel S. Carroll's brigade of Brig. Gen. John Gibbon's division of Maj. Gen. Winfield Scott Hancock's II Corps.

Alcock's regiment was heavily engaged at the battle of the Wilderness, losing 95 men in the fight of May 6, 1864.[58] Four days later, Col. Carroll's brigade took part in an assault on the Confederate defenses near Laurel Hill, one of the engagements comprising the battle of Spotsylvania. At 4 p.m. the 10th New York advanced in the first of three successive lines of battle. They traversed a burning patch of woods, pushed their way through a tangled barrier of *abatis*, and stormed on toward the enemy earthworks. There, as Carroll reported, the charge recoiled in the face of "a concentrated and murderous fire."[59]

Thirty-six soldiers of the 10th New York were cut down in the failed assault, and the dead included the battalion's commander and color sergeant.[60] Arthur Alcock was among the severely wounded, struck by a minie ball that slammed into his left leg above the knee, breaking the bone. Evacuated to the rear Alcock endured the amputation of his mangled limb, and as soon as he was able to travel was sent north. On May 28 he was admitted to the Armory Square General Hospital in Washington, D.C. But Arthur Alcock was unable to rally from his injury, and on June 16, 1864 he succumbed to his wound.[61]

It is the editor's sincere hope that this article, and the forthcoming publication of Arthur Alcock's letters and memoirs, will serve to honor the memory of a sensitive and literate volunteer who soldiered in the ranks of the Federal zouaves.

Notes

1. For a fascinating account of the 19th century New York Volunteer Fire Department and life in old Manhattan, see Kenneth Holcomb Dunshee, *As You Pass By* (New York, 1952).

2. Ellsworth was born April 11, 1837.

3. Published sources on Ellsworth and the American "Zouave Craze" include Charles A. Ingraham, *Elmer E. Ellsworth and the Zouaves of '61* (Chicago, 1925); Ruth Painter Randall, *Colonel Elmer Ellsworth* (Boston, 1960) and Michael J. McAfee, *Zouaves: The First and The Bravest* (Gettysburg, 1991).

4. The first uniform worn by the 11th New York more closely resembled the French *chasseur* pattern than traditional zouave garb. One surviving example is the uniform of Fire Zouave Corporal Francis Brownell, in the collection of Manassas National Battlefield Park, Virginia. The quality of this first clothing issue proved less than adequate for active service, and was the subject of frequent complaints by 11th New York men. By mid July the uniform was largely replaced with a blue version of the zouave pattern. See McAfee, *Zouaves*, p. 61, and Newspaper Clippings File, 11th N.Y.V., New York State Division of Military and Naval Affairs, Military History Collection, Latham, NY.

5. Randall, *Colonel Ellsworth*, p. 246. Initially quartered in the unfinished U.S. Capitol building, the athletic firemen delighted in scaling the scaffolding and swinging on ropes across the open dome. *The New-York Times*, May 8, 1861. In a less amusing vein, others were accused of burglary, theft and assault. *New York Herald*, May 5 and May 10, 1861.

6. Southerners viewed slain innkeeper James W. Jackson as the victim of Northern aggression, and his death is commemorated by a bronze plaque located at the site of the Marshall House at Pitt and King Streets in Alexandria. Anon., *Life of James W. Jackson: The Alexandria Hero, The Slayer of Ellsworth, The First Martyr in the Cause of Southern Independence* (Richmond, 1862; reprinted by Walton H. Owen, Falls Church, VA, 1985). Brownell, who eventually received the Medal of Honor for avenging Ellsworth, became a hero in his own right, and was granted a commission in the 11th U.S. Infantry. Frank E. Brownell, "The Death of Colonel Ellsworth," *The Story of American Heroism....As Told by The Medal of Honor Winners and Roll of Honor Men* (Chicago, 1896).

7. Farnham was born June 6, 1829, in New Haven, Connecticut, and joined the New York Fire Department in 1851. Commander of Mutual Hook & Ladder Company Number 1, he became one of the youngest Assistant Engineers to serve on the Department's Board of Directors. Like Ellsworth Farnham was an accomplished fencer and gymnast, and had befriended Ellsworth during the latter's zouave tour in 1860. Farnham was nicknamed "Pony" because of his short stature. Newspaper File, New York Division of Military and Naval Affairs.

8. The 11th New York was one of four infantry units assigned to Colonel Orlando B. Willcox's brigade of Colonel Samuel P. Heintzelman's division.

9. In June of 1860 the U.S. Census recorded Alcock's age as 39. His age was not noted at the time of his enlistment in the 11th New York on April 20, 1861. When Alcock re-enlisted in the 10th New York on February 27, 1864, he incorrectly stated his age as 41. In her pension application, Alcock's widow stated he was "about 45" at the time of his death, in June, 1864. National Archives and Records Administration, Washington, D.C., 1860 U.S. Census, New York City, 19th Ward, District 3, M 653, Roll 815. *Annual Report of the Adjutant-General of the State of New York For the Year 1899*, Volume 6 (Albany, 1900), p. 68, Hereinafter referred to as *NYAGR*. Record Group 94, Records of the Adjutant General's Office, Compiled Service Records, Pvt. Arthur O.

Alcock, 10th New York Infantry, National Archives, Washington, D.C.; Pension File, Arthur O. Alcock and Anne M. Alcock, National Archives.

10. Arthur and Anne Alcock's eldest son, thirteen year old Alexander, appears in the 1860 Census, but seems to have died sometime prior to 1867. The other children were Richard Thomas Ferne Alcock, born May 20, 1852; Mary Anne Alcock, born February 5, 1857 and Benjamin Marsden Alcock, born October 21, 1858. 1860 Census and Pension File, National Archives, Washington, DC.

11. *The New York Atlas*, May 10, 1862. Thirty-two year old John B. Leverich, a member of Gotham Hose Company Number 7, was commissioned Captain of Company E, the Zouaves' Color Company, on May 7, 1862. He resigned his commission in the 11th New York on October 4, 1861, but re-enlisted in the unit as Captain of Company G on May 3, 1862. Mustered out with his company June 2, 1862, he was commissioned Lieutenant Colonel of the 163rd New York Infantry on September 12, 1862. When the 163rd was consolidated with the 73rd New York, Leverich was mustered out, January 20, 1863. Frederick Phisterer, *New York in the War of the Rebellion*, vol. 3 (Albany, 1912), p. 1869 and vol. 4, p. 3907.

12. Ellsworth's senior military secretary, acting Lieutenant Henry J. Winser, was a pre-war reporter for *The New-York Times*. Both Winser and *New York Herald* correspondent Edward H. House accompanied Ellsworth on the colonel's ill-fated foray to the Marshall House.

13. Harry Lorrequer is the protagonist in a humorous novel by Irish author Charles Lever, *The Confessions of Harry Lorrequer* (Dublin, 1839). Lever described his book as "a notebook of absurd and laughable incidents."

14. Despite, or perhaps because of Col. Farnham's attempts to maintain discipline in the wayward 11th New York, and certainly in large part due to Farnham's refusal to promote him, Alcock had little good to say about his new commanding officer. On August 27 he wrote, "I have suffered grievous wrongs at that man's hands which I could not redress while I was in his power...." *New York Atlas*, October 13, 1861.

15. At age 28, British-born Charles Gray had already experienced an adventurous career, having served in the Crimean War, the Sepoy Rebellion and a military campaign in China. Gray was mustered in as surgeon of the 11th New York on May 7, 1861, and was mustered out of the Fire Zouaves on June 2, 1862. He saw subsequent service as regimental surgeon for the 7th New York Infantry and 11th New York Cavalry. Phisterer, *New York in the War*, vol. 3, p. 1868. Newspaper File, New York Division of Military and Naval Affairs.

16. Alcock's account was serialized in *The Atlas* on August 16, 23 and 30, and September 6 and 13, 1862.

17. Constructed in 1858, St. Mary's Catholic Church still stands in modern-day Fairfax Station. The building saw duty as a field hospital during the Civil War, and Red Cross founder Clara Barton tended the wounded there during the campaign of Second Manassas.

18. Twenty-seven year old Henry L. Perrin enlisted in the 11th New York on April 20, 1861, and was appointed hospital steward on May 7. He was captured with Alcock at First Bull Run, and mustered out May 24, 1862. *NYAGR*, p. 1186.

19. John Ferguson, age 24, enlisted April 20, and was mustered in as private, Company I, May 7, 1861. Detailed as a medical orderly, he was captured at Bull Run and mustered out May 24, 1862. Prior to the war he was a member of Hook and Ladder Company Number 2. *NYAGR*, p. 1121, and *New York Atlas*, June 7, 1862.

20. Richard D. Marshall, age 40, mustered into the 11th New York as private in Company I, and was discharged for disability December 27, 1861. *NYAGR*, p. 1162.

21. Colonel Orlando Bolivar Willcox (1823-1907) graduated from West Point in 1847, and left the army ten years later to practice law in Detroit. He commenced his Civil War service as commander of the 1st Michigan Infantry, and commanded a brigade at Bull Run, where he was wounded and captured. Following his exchange he rose to the rank of brevet major general, and led a division in IX Corps. Ezra J. Warner, *Generals in Blue: Lives of the Union Commanders*,
(Baton Rouge, 1864), pp. 558-559.

22. This was the engagement at Blackburn's Ford on Bull Run, between Col. Israel B. Richardson's brigade and the brigade of Confederate Brig. Gen. James Longstreet. A Massachusetts soldier recalled seeing several Fire Zouaves in the fight, presumably men who had headed to the sound of the guns on their own hook. Warren H. Cudworth, *History of the First Regiment Massachusetts Infantry*, (Boston, 1866), p. 43.

23. George Wilkes was serving as war correspondent for the New York *Spirit*, a paper that generally featured sporting events. Presumably Alcock knew him from journalistic circles in Manhattan.

24. Edward Windust's Tavern at 11 Chatham Street was a popular New York restaurant, with connections to the Fire Department; Nassau Hose Company Number 46 was founded there. Dunshee, *As You Pass By*, p. 132. "The Captain" obviously refers to another Manhattan hostelry.

25. According to Pvt. Lewis H. Metcalf of Co. E, Farnham was suffering from some type of fever. Lewis Herbert Metcalf, "So Eager Were We All," *American Heritage*, vol. 16 (June, 1965), p. 34.

26. Capt. Robert O. Tyler (1831-1874) was an 1853 graduate of West Point, serving as depot quartermaster in Alexandria. He subsequently served as Colonel of the 1st Connecticut Heavy Artillery and was promoted Brig. Gen. in 1862, commanding a brigade in II Corps. Warner, *Generals in Blue*, pp. 515-516.

27. Twenty-seven year old Michael A. "Mick" Tagen, a member of Eagle Engine Company 13, New York Fire Department, was commissioned Captain of Co. G, 11th New York, on May 7, 1861. He resigned August 1, 1861. Phisterer, *New York in the War*, vol. 3, p. 1871, and Newspaper File, New York Division of Military and Naval Affairs.

28. Daniel "Danny" Divver, a 23 year old tanner, was mustered in as Second Lt. of Co. G, 11th New York, and like Capt. Tagen was a member of Eagle Engine Company

13. Described as "a tall, handsome figure of a man," Divver was fatally wounded in the fight at Bull Run, as Alcock later describes. Phisterer, *New York in the War*, vol. 3, p. 1867 and Dunshee, *As You Pass By*, p. 175

29. The original Sudley Church was constructed in 1814. Severely damaged during the two battles of Manassas, the building was razed after the war and rebuilt as a frame structure.

30. Henry H. Mitchell, 22, was appointed assistant surgeon of the 11th New York on July 1, 1861, and not officially mustered in until August 9. He resigned his commission the following day. Phisterer, *New York in the War*, vol. 3, p. 1870.

31. This is most likely a reference to the Stone House at the intersection of the Sudley road and Warrenton turnpike. It remains a notable landmark of Manassas National Battlefield Park.

32. The stream crossed by the 11th New York in their advance on Henry House Hill was Young's Branch, a tributary of Bull Run. Cub Run, another tributary, is over a mile east of where the Fire Zouaves deployed.

33. While attempting to rally his regiment, Col. Farnham was knocked from his horse by a bullet that glanced off a button on his kepi, and inflicted a cut on his scalp. Though stunned, Farnham was able to remount, and continued in command of the Fire Zouaves during the retreat to Washington. Ten days after his injury Farnham's condition worsened, and on August 14 he died at the Washington Infirmary. An autopsy revealed the presence of a blood clot and abscess on his brain. *The Medical and Surgical History of the War of the Rebellion*, Volume II, pt. 1 , pp. 109-110 (Washington, 1870).

34. Lt. Col. John A. Cregier, age 45, was mustered in as major of the 11th New York May 7, 1861, and promoted lieutenant colonel on June 7. He resigned September 21, 1861. Prior to the war Cregier was Assistant Engineer with Hose Company Number 40, and was an executive with the Mercantile Insurance Company. Phisterer, *New York in the War*, vol. 3, p. 1866, and Newspaper File, New York Division of Military and Naval Affairs. Soon after the fight at Bull Run, Capt. Michael C. Murphy of Company C wrote, "Old Cregier rode along the lines as coolly and collected as when walking up Broadway smoking a Havana....one of my men was cut in two by a rifled cannon ball, throwing the upper part of his body against Cregier's horse, covering saddle and all with the blood and intestines of my poor lad." Letter of M.C. Murphy, July 30, 1861, *New York Atlas*, August 4, 1861.

35. Charles McKnight Leoser (1839-1896), a graduate of the West Point Class of May, 1861, was appointed adjutant of the 11th New York in May, 1861, and promoted major in June. After Farnham's death and Lt. Col. Cregier's resignation, Leoser became colonel of the Fire Zouaves. He resigned on April 17, 1862, and resumed his regular army rank of First Lt., 2nd U.S. Cavalry. Phisterer, *New York in the War*, vol. 3, p. 1869. Mary Elizabeth Sergent, *They Lie Forgotten: The United States Military Academy, 1856-1861, Together with a Class Album for the Class of May, 1861* (Middletown, NY, 1986), pp. 161-163.

36. John Wildey, age 36, was mustered in as captain of Company I on May 7, 1861. He was discharged January 1, 1862. A member of Engine Company 11, Wildey was a saloon owner and had served as private in the 7th New York State Militia. Phisterer, *New York in the War*, vol. 3, p. 1872, and Newspaper File, New York Division of Military and Naval Affairs.

37. Captain John Downey of Company D was captured at Bull Run. The other officers are First Lt. Edward Bernard, Company I; Second Lt. John Matthews, Company K; Second Lt. Lloyd W. Berry, Company E; First Lt. Joseph E. MacFarland, Company H and First Lt. Richard N. Bowerman, Company E. MacFarland and Bowerman had both been members of the 7th New York Militia; MacFarland later served as lieutenant colonel of the Fire Zouaves, and Bowerman —who later led a brigade in V Corps — attained the rank of brevet brigadier general. Phisterer, *New York in the War*, vol. 3, pp. 1865, 1867, 1869, 1870. Roger D. Hunt and Jack R. Brown, *Brevet Brigadier Generals in Blue* (Gaithersburg, MD, 1990), p. 68.

38. Thirty-one year old Thomas F. Goodwin was mustered in as regimental sergeant major of the 11th New York on May 7, 1861. He was a marble-cutter and foreman of Hook and Ladder Company Number 15. At Bull Run he was wounded in the right ankle, but managed to reach Centreville, where he boarded a Washington-bound ambulance. Discharged for disability on December 27, he subsequently re-enlisted as First Lt. of Company I, March 1, 1862. He was mustered out June 2, 1862, and subsequently served as Captain in the 132nd New York Infantry. Phisterer, *New York in the War*, vol. 3, p. 1868. Military Service and Pension files, National Archives.

39. Twenty-eight year old Eugene W. Ebling enlisted as a private in Company A, 11th New York, and was promoted corporal on May 7, 1861.

40. The 4th Alabama Infantry of Brig. Gen. Barnard E. Bee's brigade, had been severely handled during the first stages of the fight at Manassas, but later returned to action on Henry House Hill. However it is more likely that the Confederate unit engaging the Fire Zouaves at the time Ebling fell was either the 33rd Virginia or Col. William "Extra Billy" Smith's mixed force of troops from the 49th Virginia, 4th South Carolina and 11th Mississippi. William C. Davis, *Battle at Bull Run* (New York, 1977), pp. 200-101. See also, John Hennessy, *The First Battle of Manassas: An End to Innocence* (Lynchburg, 1991), and Ibid., "The First Hour's Fight on Henry Hill," (mss., 1985).

41. In one of the most celebrated incidents of the battle of First Manassas, Col. J. E. B. Stuart charged the right flank of the deploying 11th New York with two companies of his 1st Virginia Cavalry. While casualties were relatively light in the brief melee, and most of the New Yorkers continued the fight, the Confederate charge threw the Fire Zouaves into a disorder from which they never recovered. Hennessy, *The First Battle of Manassas*, pp. 80-81. William W. Blackford, *War Years With Jeb Stuart* (New York, 1945), p. 30. Metcalf, "So Eager Were We All," pp. 37-38.

42. Major Roberdeau Wheat's Louisiana Battalion — the "Tigers" — did launch a counter-attack on the advancing Federals, but engaged elements of Col. Ambrose Burn-

side's and Col. Andrew Porter's brigades, not Willcox's brigade. Hennessy, *The First Battle of Manassas*, pp. 54-55, 60.

43. No soldier named Dukes appears on the roster of the 11th New York. Two Company K men were killed in the fight: Cpl. William Waters and Pvt. Ernest Hesler. In addition Pvt. George Weidmuller was missing and never accounted for, so it is likely he was also a fatality.

44. The officer was First Lt. Douglas Ramsey of Capt. James B. Ricketts' Battery I, 1st U.S. Artillery.

45. In another account, Alcock noted that he returned to Sudley Church on horseback soon after the wounded Lt. Divver was carried off on a stretcher. Letter of August 11, 1861, in *New York Atlas*, August 18, 1861.

46. Stephen Griswold, age 34, was mustered in as assistant surgeon of the 38th New York Infantry on June 8, 1861. Captured while tending the wounded at Bull Run, he died while a prisoner of war at Charleston, S.C., November 30, 1861. Phisterer, *New York in the War*, vol. 3, p. 2182.

47. Twenty-nine year old Arthur F. Carmody was mustered in as a drummer in Company B, 11th New York, May 7, 1861, and detailed as Col. Farnham's clerk on June 1. Taken prisoner at Bull Run, he was mustered out May 24, 1862. Service record, National Archives.

48. Ira Wilson, age 21, was mustered in as a private in Company C, May 7, 1861. He was severely wounded in the shoulder and captured at Bull Run. Wilson was mustered out following his parole on May 24, 1862. *NYAGR*, p. 1221. Service record, National Archives.

49. Twenty-six year old Pvt. William H. Clark of Company H, 11th New York, was wounded in the right thigh and captured. Military and pension files, National Archives.

50. On May 1, 1861, George C. Stewart, age 26, was mustered in as a musician in Company A, 1st Michigan Infantry. Captured at Bull Run, he was exchanged and mustered out on May 20, 1862. *Record of the 1st Michigan Infantry in the Civil War* (Detroit, n.d.), p. 128.

51. Alexander McArthur, age 23, was mustered in as private in Company I, 11th New York, May 7, 1861. He was mustered out following his exchange on May 24, 1862. *NYAGR*, p. 1163.

52. Alcock's letter of August 11 appeared in *The New York Atlas*, August 18, 1861. A subsequent letter of August 27 did not reach New York until October 7, and was published in the *Atlas* on October 13, 1861.

53. Charleston photographer George S. Cook made a series of views showing the Federal prisoners at Castle Pinckney, and their guards of the Charleston Zouave Cadets. Though specifically unidentified, Alfred Alcock almost certainly is among the group of Fire Zouaves gathered in front of Casemate Number One.

54. The 11th New York arrived at Governor's Island, New York harbor, on May 19, 1862. On June 2 the Fire Zouaves were ordered to be mustered out "on account of

general demoralization, the desertion of more than half its members, and at the request
of the officers & men remaining with it." New York *Leader*, May 24 and June 7, 1862.

55. *New York Atlas*, June 7, 1862.

56. Arthur A. Alcock, military service record, National Archives.

57. The 10th New York had seen action with the V Corps before being transferred
to II Corps, Army of the Potomac. See Charles W. Cowtan, *Service of the Tenth New
York Volunteers (National Zouaves) in the War of the Rebellion* (New York, 1882).

58. U.S. War Department, *The War of the Rebellion: Official Records of the Union
and Confederate Armies*, 128 vols. (Washington, D.C., 1890-1901), series I, vol. 36, pt.
1, p. 121. Hereinafter cited as *OR*. All references are to series I unless otherwise noted.
Phisterer, *New York in the War*, vol. 3, p. 1844.

59. *OR* 36, pt. 1, p. 447.

60. Cowtan, *Tenth New York*, pp. 261-265.

61. Arthur O. Alcock, service and pension files, National Archives. *Medical and
Surgical History*, vol. III, pt. 2, p. 489.

A Conversation with Historian John Hennessey

Interviewed by Mark Snell

Although he is best known for his book *Return to Bull Run: The Campaign and Battle of Second Manassas* (New York, Simon and Schuster, 1993), an exhaustive study of that campaign and battle in late August, 1862, John Hennessey's first book was *The First Battle of Manassas: An End to Innocence*, (Lynchburg, VA, H. E. Howard, 1989). John is considered the foremost expert on both battles, and he agreed to be interviewed about First Manassas when I caught up with him one hot July afternoon in his office at Fredericksburg and Spotsylvania National Military Park, where he is the assistant superintendent.

A native of Rutland, Massachusetts, John is a graduate of the State University of New York at Albany. He is a long-time employee of the National Park Service. In addition to his current assignment at Fredericksburg, John also served as a historian at Manassas National Battlefield and as an exhibit planner at the Park Service's Harpers Ferry Center. A fervent battlefield preservationist, he resides in Fredericksburg with his daughter, Caroline, who is just shy of her sixth birthday.

MS: What was your primary reason for undertaking a study of First Manassas?

JH: Back in the days when I actually worked at Manassas National Battlefield, I admit I wasn't very interested in the battle. We did all the tours—that's what people wanted to see—but the real mystery and intrigue for me was out beyond Sudley Road and out beyond Dogan Ridge on the battlefield of Second Manassas. After I left Manassas—actually, in my last months there—I started to get very interested in [First] Manassas as a human story more than a military event. And that's really what it is—it's a human story. It's one of the great human stories in American history.

MS: So the human side of the fighting caught your attention.

JH: That's what stimulated me to start looking at this battle for the first time. It's always been portrayed so stereotypically: civilians come out from Washington, sit around the field and munch on fried chicken while all these people die in front of them. Supposedly these men [the Union and Confederate soldiers] had no concept of what they were doing or how to do it, and they just ran up there and panicked and turned around and went home. In fact, the reality of the battle was a good deal different, and that became apparent to me as I started to dig deeper into the story. So I was very interested in filling the historical as opposed to the mythological void on First Manassas.

MS: I recall once you were leading a tour on the battlefield of First Manassas and you mentioned that there were no civilians anywhere near the battlefield except those few who lived there, and that senators and representatives and other spectators never even got close to the battlefield. Would you elaborate on that?

JH: Most of the civilians never got more than five miles from the battlefield, maybe twenty to fifty got within a mile and a half. The only civilian that I know who was on the battlefield was the Governor of Rhode Island, Gov. William Sprague, who led [Colonel Ambrose] Burnside's men. In fact, Sprague was scouting for Burnside, as Burnside crossed at Sudley Ford and Sudley Spring's Ford. Today it seems kind of comical to think that someone like [Virginia] Governor George Allen or [New York] Governor George Pataki would lead the Virginia National Guard or the New York National Guard into battle. But at that time, William Sprague, who was a very ambitious politician, very visible, very mindful of his public place, wanted to associate himself with what everybody thought was going be the greatest, defining event of a generation, and so he was right out there in front. Almost everything about this battle speaks to the fact that it was part of the infancy of this war, and there are no subtle shades to this fight. It's just completely different than anything else you're going to run into at anytime during the Civil War.

MS: Just for my clarification, Sprague was Burnside's honorary aide-de-camp in this battle?

JH: Right. He attached himself to Burnside, who was a colonel, as kind of an aide, and rode all over the battlefield and led the troops onto the field. In fact, he was among the first Union men to see the Confederates moving to confront the Yankees on Matthews Hill. So he actually played a role in the battle. It wasn't purely symbolic or ornamental, but it sure is a vivid testament on the nature of this event, that the Governor of Rhode Island would be among the first troops on the battlefield.

MS: What problems did you encounter as you researched and wrote this book?

JH: Well, actually the problems researching for the First Battle of Manassas derive from the fact that it was the first event of its kind for this generation. With the emotion wrapped up in it and the intensity of the moment, none of those men were experienced in the events of which they wrote. Recollections of the event are copious—thousands and thousands of words were written about First Manassas in the battle's aftermath. So in that sense, in terms of letters [sent] home describing the fighting, there are few battles of this war that have a larger body of material with which to work.

MS: That is a nice problem to have!

JH. It is. Yet at the same time, there are few battles of this war that are harder to understand than what happened on the battlefield that Sunday afternoon. That's largely because of the emotion of the men involved and the intensity of the experience for them. Also of course, in most instances they could not see beyond a few feet and thus could not understand just how what they were doing fit into the larger picture. They had no concept of the larger picture at all. The confusion is also a reflection of how the battle was fought. Once again, it goes back to this being the first of its kind. It was a battle that was fought by commanders as well schooled as anybody in the country at that time, and yet [these were] men who, by later standards, would demonstrate a very painful lack of awareness of how to fight a battle on a major scale. Every battle is a collection of little battles and this was especially so for First Manassas. These mini-engagements were especially disjointed and disconnected, and relating one to the other and fitting them all together is very difficult.

MS: Like a giant jigsaw puzzle.

JH: Exactly. In case of First Manassas you've got tens of thousands of pieces to deal with. Yet, of those pieces, you have descriptions for maybe 400 to 500 at most. Though you only have a tiny percentage of the picture before you, as the writer you have to paint that entire portrait. Filling in those gaps and theorizing as to what probably happened in those areas that you really don't know anything about is a real challenge in writing about any battle. There are things about this battle that, despite my best efforts and the best efforts of a lot of people, we are just not going to understand.

MS: What events in particular?

JH: The actions on Henry Hill are a good example. There were probably 15,000 or 16,000 human beings involved in the fighting there, which lasted maybe two to two and a half hours. The fighting was going in every which direction at different times. This was not a battle where the concept that we have today of little rectangles on a page works very well. That doesn't work on any battlefield, really. The information contained on tactical maps is an over simplification of what took place. The reality was much more complex than I could ever portray on paper, and that was especially so with First Manassas and within that battle, Henry Hill. I think I have a pretty good idea of what happened on Henry Hill. There are some vagaries and uncertainties that will never be resolved.

MS: So how do you handle this sort of problem?

JH: You can take two basic approaches. One approach is to throw everything out at the reader and say, "here, you decide what happened." Or, spread everything out on the table yourself and try to figure out, to the best of your abilities, what took place, keeping in mind that the person whose material you are reading knows more about it than any other person in the world. You reach your conclusions and take the responsibility of giving your best opinion of what happened.

MS: You employed the latter approach in both your books.

JH: Yes. I subscribed to Alan Nevins' theory that you present the fruits of your labor and not the labor itself. I spared the reader all that agonizing over source materials conflicting and all that. I just laid everything out, and came up with the solution or the rendition of events that made the best sense to me given the source materials I had. I wrote a couple of supporting papers for the First Manassas project that kind of hash out all the "innards" of the battle, primarily for my own benefit. I wanted to figure it all out, and provide documentation for readers who wanted to dig deeper. I think battle books ought to present the historian's most well-reasoned conclusions. He is the person who knows more about it than anybody else and that person should take the responsibility of laying it out for his readers.

MS: Along that line of thought, how does your study of First Manassas fit into the overall historiography of this campaign?

JH: Well, I did what I did on First Manassas for a very specific reason. My purpose was not to retell an oft told story. Jack [William C.] Davis, in his book, *Battle at Bull Run*, does a magnificent job of giving the context of the battle. I worked at the battlefield for many years and I had a hard time relating what the paper [primary and secondary sources] said happened on the ground on which we were standing, and I stood on it every day! So my purpose in writing the book on First Manassas was to take the heart of the battle itself—those parts of the battle that aren't really reflected solely in documentary evidence, but require a real hard look at the terrain in relating how the account fits with that terrain—and to decide how all that fits together. Jack did a magnificent job for everything that leads up to the battle and everything that follows the battle. My job was to take his work on the battlefield to another level, based on having spent, literally, years walking the battlefield and trying to mesh these accounts together. When I wrote my book on Second Manassas, one of my hopes was that the story would stimulate others to look more closely at that battle and to answer questions that maybe I didn't even think to ask. I suspect Jack probably had the same idea when he wrote his First Manassas book. So I took his work and started to ask a different set of questions, and to relate the events on the ground and try to be a little bit more definitive on how all of these things fit together. Occasionally when you write military history you have to retreat into a vagueness because you just don't know [the answers]. Essentially, what I tried to do is reduce the amount of vagueness that exists about what happened on the battlefield.

MS: Who do you find to be the most fascinating figures in this battle, both on the Union and the Confederate sides, and why do you feel they're fascinating?

JH: I think one of the most interesting or appealing things about this battle are the personalities involved. Especially on the Confederate side, there was so much hope wrapped up in personalities, especially General [P. G. T.] Beauregard, who commanded better than half of the Confederate army at First Manassas. If you had to cast a character to lead the Confederacy's largest army into its first major battle, you'd have a hard time picking a better personality than Beauregard. He embodied the Southern ideal of what a soldier ought to look like, what he ought to sound like, what he ought to ride like. He also embodied success—he was in command when Fort Sumter fell in April 1861. Beauregard was very much a popular figure, a perfect match of aspiration, image, and of the person trying to carry that image forth. General Joseph Johnston is a little bit less flamboyant in that sense but, nonetheless, he embodies much of the Southern gentleman, maybe a little bit stiffer, [and] less flamboyant than Beauregard, but certainly a Virginian through and through.

MS: And on the Union side. . .

JH: On the Union side—in fact, for the campaign at large—there's nobody more fascinating than Irvin McDowell. Here was a man who was a staff officer before the war and who had commanded maybe a handful of men at any time in his past. Within a short time he was thrust into the position of commanding the largest army that ever trod on North American soil until that time. More importantly, McDowell was charged with bringing about, by virtue of one campaign, a swift conclusion to a rebellion that had been festering in this nation for sixty years. You can't put someone in a more difficult position than that, and to do it with the press clamoring and putting constraints on his ability to train his army and get it ready for combat. He didn't have that luxury. So he was in a very, very difficult position. McDowell, to me, is really the decisive personality of the battle. No single personality affected the outcome more than his. Despite the forces working against him, which were considerable, he had an opportunity to do something that day that would have fulfilled any Northerner's vision of what should have happened on that field. When the Union army stopped on Matthew's Hill at noontime and did not continue bowling forward across to Henry Hill and breaking whatever Confederate resistance might have been there, General McDowell redefined the day and redefined how it would come out. . .

MS: Why did he stop?

JH: He never explained. You can only conjecture today, but it was unquestionably the decisive moment of the battle. The other interesting fact about McDowell is that the rest of the day he had the uncommon luxury on a Civil War battlefield of being a commander of an army who could ride from one end of his battle line to the other in about five minutes and do the "duck-duck-goose" routine. By that I mean he could literally tap commanders on the head and say, "you do this, and you do this, and you do that."

MS: But he did not exercise that level of command, did he?

JH: No, he did not take advantage of that opportunity. Once the battle for Henry Hill began it sputtered along. Sixteen or seventeen Union regiments went into the fight that day and no more than two of them went in together—there's really one man who deserves the responsibility for that sort of piecemeal tactics, and that's Irvin McDowell.

MS: Haven't others excused his actions?

JH: Many times. Some said his army was untrained, and that is true; others point to his plan and call it "brilliant," and that is perhaps true. But the fact is that he had the ability to accomplish a decisive victory that day and he did not accomplish it. You can ascribe it to a lot of reasons, but somewhere in Irvin McDowell there's a personal failing that prevented him from pushing and exploiting success that his men had fought so hard to win earlier in the day. Irvin McDowell had a great deal to do with the outcome of this battle.

MS: You are not a McDowell fan.

JH: No, I am not. At Second Manassas he committed probably the greatest tactical blunter on any eastern Civil War battlefield, a mistake that led very nearly to the destruction of the Union army. So Irvin McDowell has, in my mind, a very checkered record. He's a very interesting man, [with] lots of forces working against him.

MS: Despite the important role he played in both the Manassas battles, we don't know much about him.

JH: He's an enigma in many ways. We don't have his letters, we don't have any writings by him Yet, we might think a little bit more sympathetically of him if we had such documents. I'd love for someone to go out and launch on that, try to undertake some sort of study of McDowell—even if they don't come up with his personal papers—to take a hard look at him. I've not [undertaken a study of him] except within the context of these couple of battles, and my look at him is not particularly favorable.

MS: If not Irvin McDowell in command, who should have commanded Federal army at First Manassas? And, I'd like you to answer this question in the context of not knowing what we know now, but judging instead these officers based upon their qualifications at the time the campaign was launched.

JH: There was nobody qualified to do what Irvin McDowell was asked to do, there just wasn't. Some of the older officers with Mexican War experience were pondered as possible leaders, [such as Winfield] Scott. Some expected him to take the field, which wasn't physically possibile for him. Maybe one of the few Union officers with a track record of experience who would have done well was Edwin Vose Sumner. He had seen a lot of service out west, he had the rank to qualify himself, [and] he was not a political "being" in any sense of the word. Sumner was a very "no nonsense" sort of fellow, and not a particularly inspirational character, but certainly one who warranted consideration for the whole thing [command of the Union army].

If you search through those men under McDowell's command—running down through the list of officers he had in his stable—the aren't many there to have chosen from. You've got some fairly well known names, like [William B.] Franklin, [Erasmus D.] Keyes, David Hunter, Daniel Tyler, and [William T.] Sherman. Either these people had significant personality flaws, as was the case with Daniel Tyler and David Hunter, or they didn't have the rank, like Sherman or Franklin, or they didn't have the reputation or personality, as is the case with someone like Keyes.

Here is another way to look at it. If Beauregard captured the Southern view of what an officer ought be like, Samuel Peter Heintzelman, a very prominent officer of the Union side, was the opposite of that. He was exactly what you would not want in command of the nation's greatest army. Heintzelman had the rank and some of the experience, at least in the pre-war variety. Physically and otherwise he was also not the person to head the army. Contemporaries called him a "mass of wrinkles" and went on about how awkward he was. He would not have been a commander who would have inspired the men in the ranks. There really wasn't anyone [to command the Union army at First Manassas] who leaps readily to mind. There were a few officers in the Confederate army, though, who probably would have done a pretty good job commanding the Union Army at First Manassas.

MS: In addition to the personalities, there were regiments that fought on both sides at First Manassas that could claim some fame, not just because of how they performed during the battle, but by how they performed throughout their terms of service. Which stand out?

JH: Well, pre-battle, the greatest "reputation" possessed by any regiment on either side was that of the 11th New York Infantry—the Fire Zouaves. They proved, not so much at First Manassas but in the aftermath of First Manassas, that reputations before actual service in the field mean absolutely nothing, because they essentially melted away and disappeared in the months after First Manassas. They had been commanded by Elmer Ellsworth at the beginning of the war, and had a number of officers of some experience, at least of militia experience. They were much ballyhooed and unit was composed of strong physical timber recruited from the fire houses of New York City. If you measure the quality of a regiment by its losses, which we like to do sometimes, it was one of the best on the battlefield because it lost more men killed than any other Union regiment in the battle, and they lost them in about five minutes. In fact, the regiment did not perform very well and [it] fell apart on the battlefield.

MS: Which others come to mind?

JH: Right next to the Zouaves on the battlefield was a regiment which, by contrast, would go on to become one of the most famous of all Union regiments in the Army of the Potomac—and that was the 1st Minnesota. It suffered a very similar fate as the 11th New York. In fact, they even wore red shirts, unlike the 11th New York which didn't have red fireman's shirts on. The Minnesotans suffered heavily that day and did not perform particularly well. They did not perform much better than the 11th New York. But, by virtue of really notable leadership under Willis Gorman and some of his subordinates, the 1st Minnesota went on to become, as almost everybody knows, one of the best, or at least [one of the] most bloody Union regiments in the war. We have a tendency to equate losses with [the] quality [of a regiment]. I'm not sure the two go hand-in-hand. There were some regiments that lost a lot of men because they didn't perform particularly well. I don't think the 1st Minnesota was one of them. Nevertheless, there is an interesting contrast there between the Fire Zouaves and the 1st Minnesota.

MS: Which Southern regiment or regiments stand out as having performed exceptionally well at First Manassas?

JH: The dominant regiments on the battlefield were [Thomas J.] Jackson's Virginia regiments [of] the Stonewall Brigade, as it would become known as a result of this battle. They certainly played a key role in the fight, as did Jackson. Individually, each of the regiments did very well that day, [but] none of them were spectacular. The 30th Virginia did something out of desperation that helped turn the tide of battle by capturing Griffin's guns. The 4th and the 27th Virginia regiments launched the first Confederate charge across the battlefield and captured Ricketts' guns. The 5th Virginia fought around the Henry house for a long time that afternoon. All of those regiments marked themselves as units to watch.

Other regiments did reasonably well, [but] probably the most notable single regiment on the battlefield that day—in terms of its performance—was Hampton's Legion from South Carolina. It was engaged during a critical time during the Confederate collapse on Matthews Hill, acted as a Confederate rear guard and beat back a couple of Union advances north of the Warrenton Turnpike. Later in the day the South Carolinians were heavily involved with Sherman's brigade around the Henry house and that's when Wade Hampton was seriously wounded. If you had to pick one regiment out of that pantheon of the most spectacular performers that day, you'd have to probably pick the Hampton Legion.

MS: And on the Union side. . .

JH: On the Northern side it's hard to pick an individual star. Much was expected in battle of the regular battalion commanded by George Sykes. The Regulars were involved heavily on Matthews Hill and did very well during the retreat also, forming a hollow square for one of the few times in the war. Beyond that, you are hard pressed to find an individual regiment on the Northern side that did exceptionally well.

MS: What about the artillery?

JH: Most of the Federal artillerymen viewed First Manassas as a disaster, and for good reason. They lost exactly half their guns during the First Manassas Campaign. Some of the guns were lost on the battlefield, but others were lost at the stream crossings. Artillery at First Manassas was characterized by a complete misunderstanding on how to use it on the part of superior officers. At First Manassas you literally see artillery batteries on the skirmish line, on Matthews Hill for example. On Henry Hill you see two lines of artillery, Union and Confederate, less than 350 yards apart. On no other battlefield do you see that. They learned serious and harmful lessons that led to the loss and destruction of a lot of human beings and organizations at First Manassas. Whatever brilliance there may have been, and there were some very good [artillery] commanders there—men like Romeyn Ayres and Henry Hunt, for example. James Ricketts and Charles Griffin rose to prominence at First Manassas. But they were all misused to some extent.

MS: Speaking of famous units, there's a new book by David Sullivan that just came out about the United States Marine Corps during the Civil War. He contends that the Marine battalion of the Army of Northeastern Virginia has been unjustly criticized by historians for their conduct in the battle. What's your opinion of this?

JH: I'm not sure that I have ever seen any real criticism of the Marine Corps battalion at First Manassas. Its fate was very much similar to everyone elses. In fact, its make-up and command was very similar to all the other regiments on the field. These guys were not the gruesome veterans who were the 19th-century equivalent of Iwo Jima [veterans]. Most were fresh recruits and had not been in the service very long. They carried the Marine Corps insignia and imprimatur to the battlefield, but not a lot else would distinguish them. I have not read David's book. I will say, though, that in the accounts of the battle written by hundreds [of participants], you almost never see the Marines mentioned. Maybe it's because people didn't recognize them for who they were, but you just don't see any mention of them at all.

One of the things that pains me a little bit about modern historiography is that we do have a lot of people—I'm not saying David Sullivan is doing this—but we do have a lot of people who have an ancestor in a regiment or have a particular reason to be interested in a unit, and they go out to rehabilitate that unit's name, sometimes with good cause. Stuart Osborne has done a magnificent job of rehabilitating or establishing the name of the 20th New York State Militia, for example. The fact is, there were bad regiments, and there were bad regiments who put in bad performances. There were also good regiments who delivered bad performances. We have a tendency sometimes to write history with a nostalgic vein that everybody did well. The fact is that everybody didn't [do well], especially at this battle. Everybody did their best, probably, but that doesn't mean they did very well. Whether the Marines did better than anybody else at First Manassas, I don't know—I've never seen any documentation to that effect. The official reports tend to indicate that they went up, stayed for a little while, turned around and left, like a lot of people did. That's OK. There's no great horror in all of that. In David Sullivan's work, maybe they did perform better than they have been credited. He's undoubtedly seen more source material than I have, and I would yield to his account of this. On the other hand, I don't think it's all that important. These guys shared a human experience—all of them—and they reacted just like everybody else to that battle.

MS: Has your research shed any new light on the First Battle of Manassas?

JH: I think so. I think the most important thing that I wanted to do goes back to the site. My passion in life is having people go to these places and understanding what happened there, right there where they are standing. Whether or not you're interested in the war as a whole is irrelevant to that experience. If you're interested in human beings even remotely, you can relate to that. You don't always need to know how it fits into the bigger picture, or what political implications there were of that experience. There is great emotional power in these stories.

So, my major goal in undertaking a study of both First and Second Manassas was to accord meaning to the ground, not just because of the vague meaning that this is where this battle took place, but this is what happened right here. There's an immediacy in that kind of understanding that carries a power way beyond a video or a book. The appreciation that fills you at a place like that is meaningless without the place itself. That was my major goal in a broad view: do a better job of relating to things on the ground, and being very specific, so that when you go to Manassas you'll be able to stand there and say, "this is what happened here, this is what it looked like, etc."

MS: What about the battle itself?

JH: I made a few contributions, none of them terribly earth shattering. I offered a deeper look at McDowell and his opportunities and failures of that day. Certainly I really tried hard to unravel what happened on Henry Hill [and] to put that in some sort of logical sequence. It's not ironclad, and I hope some day that the source material turns up that tells us definitively what happened. Some of what I've woven together may not stand the test of time. I actually hope that's the case. On the other hand, perhaps documentation will turn up that confirms what I have written.

MS: What about the Stonewall Jackson episode on Henry Hill?

JH: My work has incensed some Virginians concerning Jackson at First Manassas. The circumstances were not nearly as dramatic as people would have you believe, and the Virginians, of course, would like to put themselves at the center of every story. They put themselves at the center of Henry Hill, and unjustly so. I did some work on that, [as well as] clarifying the role of the spectators, which was a very important part of the battle in that it reflects the media, the hysteria—not quite hysteria, but excitement—that surrounded the battle. This was an event that had the press attention of a Super Bowl and the emotional impact of Pearl Harbor, in part reflected by the fact that people came out to watch it. We like to scoff at that today: these people wanted to come up and watch a battle! As I've suggested to you before, if you could guarantee to people today that they could get within two miles of the battlefield without getting hurt, they would be selling t-shirts out there and [it would] bring tens of thousands of people. In fact, the highest rated [television] show of 1991 was the beginning of the Gulf War, as we all sat in front of our televisions watching it unfold that evening of January 17. It's not a morbid curiosity that people have—it's a curiosity to see something that has the potential of altering the course of history. We have that curiosity today, and we'll have it 2,000 years from now. We've had it since time immemorial—there's nothing wrong with that. The fact that [there were] spectators at First Manassas is a reflection of the attitudes that this nation took to war.

MS: Perhaps that's our fascination with battlefields today—we can't see a battle unfold—but in our mind's eye, if we stand on that field, we can imagine, we can wonder why these men did this.

JH: It's more morbid than any video game or any film you'll ever see. Places are what make the difference when you do that. I could give the most vivid talk, I could possibly conjure up the First Battle of Manassas in a class-room in upstate New York, and it would be interesting, people would nod and they would listen. Six months later they wouldn't remember a word that I said. If I took that same talk and gave it sitting or standing out on the battlefield in the middle of Henry Hill, chances are they would remember some or much of it for their whole lives. Not because of anything I said, but because of the place I said it—it's the place that makes the difference. It's those places that drive me, really, to do what I do on a daily basis.

MS: John, how does this battle compare with other early-war battles in terms of strategic significance?

JH: There was a painful lesson going on in 1861 and 1862 and this was the first step in that lesson. When this war began, there was a firm belief that it was going to require, from the Northern point of view, one campaign to end it. Initially, everyone thought this campaign would end the war. That idea of a one-campaign war did not go away with the loss of this battle. We like to think it did, but it didn't. We see it later with McClellan and his grand planning for 1862—he was very much in the belief that one campaign would end the war. Of course, it would come to pass that one campaign was not going to end anything. This was the first step in that very painful learning process.

MS: And how did the battle affect the Confederacy?

JH: It was very important to the South strategically, in that it allowed the Confederacy to continue to defend itself at its northernmost border in Virginia. There was a strong instinct in 1861 not to yield a damn inch of Virginia to the damn Yankees if they could avoid it. The First Battle of Manassas fulfilled that image for the Confederates, and that was very important. In terms of pure strategy—if the Confederates had lost the Battle of First Manassas—they could have fallen back to central Virginia and done something else. Had First Manassas been a decisive victory for the North, it would not necessarily have transformed this war into a one-campaign war—that lesson still was going to come. It came faster because of the outcome of the Battle of First Manassas. When the armies retake the field nine months later, they come back far larger than before—in the case of the Union army [McClellan's force was] four times the size of the army that took the field at First Manassas. It's all part of a realization. But in terms of the moving of blocks on a map, First Manassas didn't amount to a hill of beans strategically.

MS: Were the early campaigns in Missouri and elsewhere out west, for example, more important than this battle?

JH: Absolutely! Forts Henry and Donelson have significant strategic implications, as did some of the early Missouri campaigns. First Manassas isn't about strategy—it's about tactics, in the sense that it's a vivid demonstration of how far these people had to go. First Manassas was really about humanity. If you want to look into the psyche of a nation on the edge of war, taking that first tentative step into an abyss of blood and horror, you can not truly appreciate the magnitude of how horrific this war was until you imagine—or until you can appreciate—the thoughts and feelings that run through those camps in Centerville on the eve of this battle. That contrast is just jarring: the belief that this was just going to be some sort of an adventurous, one-campaign undertaking that transformed into this grinding, horrific event that would physically, psychologically, socially, politically and economically transform our country. The contrast, the magnitude of that, is only truly understood if we can understand what their attitude was—what their psyche was—on the eve of this battle. That's really the impact of First Manassas.

MS: John, thanks for your time and candidness.

JH: My pleasure.

Book Reviews

The Civil War In Books: An Analytical Bibliography, by David J. Eicher. Foreword by Gary Gallagher. (University of Illinois Press: Urbana and Chicago), 1997. Appendix, index. HC. $29.95

"Over the course of 135 years since the Civil War began, more than 50,000 books and pamphlets have been published on the subject (through mid-1995). How can someone interested in the Civil War—whether for light reading or through the passion of building a Civil War library—sift through this mass of printed material and discover the most important, creditable, relevant, and interesting works?" (p. xxi), asks compiler Eicher in his Introduction. How, indeed? For one thing, "someone" can use this book. Previously, everyone could use *Civil War Books: A Critical Bibliography* (1967), compiled by Allan Nevins, James I. Robertson, and Bell I. Wiley, but a great many works on the Civil War have appeared since this product of the Civil War Centennial appeared nearly thirty years ago.

Eicher's work is divided into the following categories: Battles and Campaigns—with subsections for Naval Warfare, Civil War in the West, and All Others; Confederate Biographies, Memoirs, and Letters; Union Biographies, Memoirs, and Letters; and General Works. These sections include evaluations of "the most important 1,100 books on the Civil War" (p. xii). Out of shameless conceit, I shall use the entry on *Make Me A Map Of The Valley: The Civil War Journal of Stonewall Jackson's Cartographer*, which is item 242, as an example. The entry begins with a standard bibliographic identification of the publication, reviews Jedediah Hotchkiss' role in the war, evaluates his journal, notes there are a few errors in the introduction without identifying them, and cites more recent biographical works on the principal subject.

The Civil War In Books is a useful tool for research libraries, collectors, and scholars. It is subjective in selection and evaluation, obviously and inevitably, but useful nonetheless.

Archie P. McDonald   Stephen F. Austin State University

Maryland: The South's First Casualty, by Bart Rhett Talbert (Rockbridge Publishing Co., P. O. Box 351, Berryville, VA 22611), 1995. Foreword, photos, notes, biblio., index. 150pp. HC. $25.00.

Whatever *Maryland: The South's First Casualty* purports to be, it probably cannot be described as history. Polemic would be a better word. Although Bart Rhett Talbert asserts that the "primary source material from Maryland's Civil War era is meager compared to that of other states," he believes there is a "wealth of secondary source material on Maryland and the Civil War written by eyewitnesses and respected historians unencumbered by the prejudices of the late twentieth century" (p. xv). That previous writers may have also been encumbered by their attitudes when they wrote about Civil War Maryland is never mentioned. He accepts their interpretations because they espoused a pro-Southern, anti-Republican, and state's rights philosophy.

Talbert laments the fact that "uncontrollable factors withheld from Maryland the time to make decisions at her leisure." Opposed to "revolutionary change," the pro-Southern element respected the law and honored its agreements, unlike many in the North who ignored the national compact and "hurried to subjugate other states, breaking every agreement under the Constitution as fast as their troops could roll into the South."

During the secession crisis Governor Thomas Hicks and others of his ilk, whose "traitorous actions" kept Maryland in the Union, were "coldly calculating politicians or suffering from a serious lack of common sense." President Abraham Lincoln and his cohorts "manipulated" the Constitution to "legitimize their actions" (pp. 85-86). Worst of all, however, it was the "abolitionist core in the North, which precipitated the war by operating outside of the law, then carried on a war of conquest, subjugated an entire region of a free country, and has dictated to the people of that region how they should run their society ever since" (p. 86).

These are "inescapable" facts to Talbert. He sees conspirators everywhere. Even President James Buchanan, who generally is viewed as an ineffectual executive, is blamed for using the army to maneuver South Carolina into a situation where it would be accused of starting the war. In fact, Talbert seems to be suggesting that all would have been well between the two sections if only the North had allowed the South to secede quietly.

Besides his diatribes against the abolitionists, Lincoln, and the Republican Party, Talbert concentrates his ire upon the Union Army. From the beginning of the war when a conflict ensued between the citizens of Baltimore and the Federal soldiers who were on their way to Washington, the army violated every civil right known to man. According to Talbert, the Union Army so oppressed Marylanders during the Civil War that it banned the initials CSA from obituaries of slain Maryland Confederate soldiers. He concludes, with little analysis, that "military rule was harsh in Maryland." The "despot's heel" which suspended constitutional rights had a "real and lasting meaning that subsequent events and writings have obscured" (p. 65).

The major thrust of Talbert's book seems to be that previous historians have misinterpreted the history of Maryland in the years before, during, and after the war. He hammers the point that Maryland was, and is, a Southern state and that only the intervention of the Union Army prevented it from joining its sisters in the Confederacy. Not surprisingly, this is largely a non-issue. A plethora of historians, contrary to what the author argues, have held that Maryland was indeed a slave area, that the state had long associated and supported the philosophy of the other states in the South, and that it was Lincoln's astute maneuvering which kept the Old Line State from leaving the Union. The president could not allow the nation's capital to be militarily isolated.

The emphasis throughout this brief work is clearly pro-Southern, support for the philosophy of state's rights, and admiration for the valiant efforts of the Confederate States of America to fight a losing struggle for an outmoded idea. That slavery also entered the equation is slighted or not considered important enough to discuss by Talbert. He views it as a fully acceptable institution which the Republican Party desired to abolish to punish the South. The Republicans are depicted as being controlled by a group of abolitionist-driven fanatics. Their eventual leader, Abraham Lincoln, is portrayed as a deceitful and conniving individual who would violate civil and constitutional rights during the war.

If any scholar has been waiting for a first-class monograph on Civil War Maryland, they will have to continue to be patient. *Maryland: The South's First Casualty*, is neither first-rate nor even a good synthesis. A general indictment of this monograph includes the limited use of source material, and a quick perusal of the endnotes proves this assertion. Allegedly based upon extensive archival work, most of the citations are to secondary works published late in the nineteenth or early twentieth century. That fact alone suggests that this book will be a virtual assault upon the ideas of more recent writers. In addition, several outstanding works on Maryland and the period in question are ignored. For example, the controversial study of Maryland slavery in the transition period by Barbara J. Fields is conveniently missing. There are many similar omissions. Moreover, the extensive essay literature which has appeared in the *Maryland Historical Magazine* in the past two decades, among other historical journals, is not even cited. In fact, the bibliography is composed of works whose interpretations have long been discredited. This dictum holds true for whatever period of Maryland history Talbert discusses. He suffers from the same malaise of writers three or four generations ago. His book nicely fits the older Dunning school interpretation.

This work has little, if anything, to recommend it to either the scholar or the lay person. There is no new information, the interpretation is radically pro-Southern and distorted, and it glosses over so many national and state events that it is virtually useless. Of interest to some may be the short biographical vignettes of the more prominent Marylanders who served as Union and Confederate general and flag officers during the war. In addition, a very brief history of the Maryland units that served in the Federal and Confederate armies is provided. But even in this section, one has to be careful with accepting the material presented.

In short, this is a bad book and should never have been published.

Barry A. Crouch   Gallaudet University

Voices of the 55th: Letters From the 55th Massachusetts Volunteers, 1861-1865, edited and annotated by Noah Andre Trudeau (Morningside House, Inc., 260 Oak Street, Dayton, Ohio 45410), 1996. Maps, photos, footnotes, index, d.j. 258pp. HC. Contact publisher for price.

The plight of black soldiers during the American Civil War is an area that has been understudied despite the tremendous amount of Civil War literature that has been produced. Noah Andre Trudeau, the author of the well-received trilogy on the last year and one-half of the Civil War, *Bloody Roads South*, *The Last Citadel*, and *Out of the Storm*, has brought together one of the best collections of letters and reminiscences of black soldiers. In *Voices of the 55th*,

Trudeau skillfully uses the writings of the men of the 55th Massachusetts regiment to tell the story of this remarkable yet largely unknown infantry unit.

Formed as part of Massachusetts Governor Andrew's plan to raise two regiments of black troops, the 55th attracted men from all over the North, Midwest, and even the South. The 54th Massachusetts, since it was the first state-raised volunteer infantry regiment of black soldiers, received a majority of the press at the time and because of the popular film "Glory," has received most of the attention since. Yet, the men of the 55th faced many of the same trials and turmoil that were common to all black soldiers in service for the Union cause. As Trudeau writes, the "Black solders in the Civil War were truly fighting on two fronts: the Confederate enemy before them, and Northern racism behind them" (p. 101). It's clear from many of the letters that while the Confederate enemy was the more deadly of the two, the reality of racism weighed more heavily on the minds of the individuals of the 55th than the fear of facing Confederate bullets.

Trudeau highlights this racism through the use of a number of letters dealing with the inequality between white and black soldiers. Although enlisted as full-fledged soldiers in the Union cause, the members of the 55th were paid $10 a month as opposed to the $13 a month received by white soldiers. Like the men of the 54th Massachusetts, the men of the 55th refused any pay until they were paid equally by the Federal government. One soldier wrote that the pay issue was not the main reason why the members of the 55th were discouraged, but rather "because we have not been treated like men and soldiers of the United States, and this is why we are not satisfied. We did not leave our homes and friends for the sake of money, but in order that our suffering might work out a great good for ourselves and friends." Yet even with the racism they faced at the hands of their own government, these black soldiers remained dedicated to the cause, writing that even if they did not receive "equal treatment on earth, they were sure to receive their just in heaven when the bonds of slavery were finally broken for all" (pp. 102-103).

On November 30, 1864, the 55th faced its toughest challenge on the battlefield at Honey Hill on the banks of the Broad River in South Carolina. One soldier in the 55th claimed the battle of Honey Hill "was like rushing into the very mouth of death" (p. 165). Trudeau has collected a number of letters and descriptions of this battle, including a significant account written by Capt. Charles Soule, an officer of the 55th. The regiment lost 137 men at this engagement and performed very well. Soule wrote that at Honey Hill the 55th proved, like the 54th did at Battery Wagner, that "a black regiment, well disciplined and well officered could behave as gallantly under fire as the best troops in the service" (p. 193).

Trudeau's remarkable compilation provides a real insight into the hearts and souls of these men. They faced heavy challenges and struggled hard to overcome the obstacles presented to them by racism; however the men of the 55th, as Trudeau points out, did not lose faith in the endeavor they were undertaking. One soldier of the 55th, in a letter to a black newspaper wrote, "Our debasement is most complete. No chances for promotion, no money for our families, and little better than an armed band of laborers with lusty muskets and bright spades, what is our incentive to duty? Yet God has put it into our hearts to believe that we will survive or perish with the liberty of our country. If she lives, we live, if she dies we will sleep with her" (p. 88).

The editor's use of footnotes is a tremendous help in identifying the sources and the authors of many of the letters and is a welcomed change from the notation format in some of his earlier works. His footnotes are also useful for gaining insight into the history of the regiment and many of the individuals. Trudeau placed the letters in chronological order, allowing the reader to sense the changes in the men as their terms of enlistment dragged on. The 55th served almost exclusively along the coast of South Carolina and Georgia, with a couple of forays into northern Florida. Detailed maps highlight the regiment's military operations.

This is a significant contribution to the history of black troops in the American Civil War. This book will be of great value to anyone who wishes to get a better understanding of the struggles faced by black soldiers and a better understanding of what these soldiers fought for. Their words are the best way to understand their struggles. Thanks to Noah Trudeau, the men of the 55th Massachusetts have been given a voice that until now had been silent.

Andrew MacIsaac   Worcester, MA

Editor's Note: An in-depth article on the 55th Massachusetts Infantry, "History and Archaeology: Edward Wild's African Brigade in the Siege of Charleston," by Steven D. Smith, appeared in *Charleston: Battles and Seacoast Operations in South Carolina* (*Civil War Regiments*, vol. 5, no. 2).

The Secret War for the Union: The Untold Story of Military Intelligence in the Civil War, by Edwin C. Fishel (Houghton Mifflin, 222 Berkeley St., Boston, MA 02116), 1996. Maps, photos, notes, biblio., index. 734pp. HC. $35.00.

Late on the evening of July 2, 1863, Col. George Sharpe, chief of the Army of the Potomac's Bureau of Military Information, entered the headquarters of Maj. Gen. George G. Meade at Gettysburg. A weighty decision about the deployment of the Union army had to be made: should it retreat to Meade's favored defensive position at Pipe Creek or stand fast at Cemetery Ridge, Cemetery Hill and Culp's Hill? Sharpe, who was tired and weak from hunger, reported that every unit of Gen. Robert E. Lee's Army of Northern Virginia had fought at Gettysburg but for Pickett's Division. The report was based on exhaustive interviews of close to 1,400 Rebel prisoners taken during the colossal struggle for the strategic crossroads near the Pennsylvania border on the second day of the battle.

Major General Winfield Scott Hancock, who had been sitting quietly on a cot in Meade's tiny headquarters, raised his hand and said, "General, we have got them nicked!" (p. 528). Sharpe's intelligence, reported to the council of Meade's corps commanders, played a major role in the decision by the Federal high command to stay and fight at Gettysburg on July 3, 1863. It was the high point in the secret war of spies, prisoners interrogations, reconnaissance, and other intelligence activity which the Union had waged against the South since First Bull Run.

Author Edwin Fishel, a former intelligence officer with the National Security Agency, breaks new ground in this book. The widely-held belief that in intelligence and related matters the Rebels ran rings around the Yankees is pure fancy, due largely to the romanticization of cavalier mounted scouts and Southern lady spies. Federal intelligence activity was far more productive. In only one sector of intelligence, cavalry reconnaissance, did the Confederates outperform them.

Fishel's sources have never been used by Civil War historians. In October 1959, he discovered the operational files of the Army of the Potomac's Bureau of Military Information at the National Archives, arranged with bureaucratic neatness and neatly tied with red tape. He also found the intelligence files of Gen. Joseph Hooker, who decided not to return these documents to the War Department. Fishel also delved through The Secret Service Accounts at the National Archives, the payroll record for Allan Pinkerton's spies.

The author taps these resources to create a compelling picture of the evolution of Union army intelligence from First Bull Run through Gettysburg. He focuses exclusively on the Army of the Potomac, leaving out discussion of intelligence activities in the Western Theater. An intelligence organization did not exist in the U.S. Army when the war began. Civilian spies were the first asset used by the Federals. Major George B. McClellan hired Allan Pinkerton to make estimates of the Southern forces which opposed him. Pinkerton's operatives visited Richmond and Confederate army camps. Their calculations of Rebel army strength, usually far too high, profoundly influenced McClellan during the Peninsula Campaign. But Fishel dispels the traditional myth that McClellan retreated from Lee's much smaller army because of Pinkerton's intelligence: McClellan always believed he was outnumbered, and doubled or even tripled Pinkerton's estimates on the size of Lee's army.

"Fighting Joe" Hooker emerges as the father of modern military intelligence in Fishel's book. Hooker created the Bureau of Military Information under Col. George Sharpe, a New York lawyer. The organization was an "all source" operation, collating data from spies, prisoner interrogations, cavalry scouts, balloon observers, and flag signalmen. It ranks alongside the war's most significant innovations, such as the transportation of troops by railroad, and the development of ironclad warships. No comparable military intelligence unit existed again in the U.S. Army until World War II.

Sharpe's unit provided Hooker with an estimate of Lee's military strength on the eve of Chancellorsville that was only off by 2%. Using deception and Sharpe's intelligence, Hooker placed an army of 70,000 men in Lee's rear at Chancellorsville and seemed destined to win a decisive victory. But intelligence alone cannot win battles, and Hooker was ultimately beaten by the superior generalship of Lee and Thomas Jackson. Sharpe's bureau continued to function after Hooker was fired. Soldier-spies and Pennsylvania civilians kept the Army of the Potomac informed of Lee's movements during his invasion of the Keystone State and of the enemy's concentration near Gettysburg. Sharpe's intelligence unit continued to function when General Ulysses S. Grant took over the Union high command. Grant regarded Sharpe so highly that he promoted him to brigadier general.

The book is thoroughly researched and well-written. Bob Benjamin's maps supplement and illustrate the text. The only criticism about this important effort regards its exhaustive detail. Fishel chronicles the exploits of every Union spy hired between 1861-1863 and gives us his pay records. At times, this micro examination boggs down the flow of the story.

This attention to fine points is a minor flaw in a superb treatment of Civil War intelligence. The book is a fully crafted intelligence history of First Bull Run through Gettysburg, with intelligence's hits and misses, successes and failures.

Kevin E. O'Brien   Scottsdale, Arizona

Guide to the Battle of Shiloh (University Press of Kansas, 2501 West 15th Street, Lawrence, KS 66049-3904), 1996. Maps, illus., appendices, biblio., index. 253pp. Paper. $12.95

A trademark of the battlefield guidebook series known as "The U.S. Army War College Guides to Civil War Battles" has been a combination of comparison eyewitness Union and Confederate reports and detailed maps to interpret tactics, maneuvers, obstacles, achievements, and failures associated with several pivotal battles of the American Civil War. The editors of the Army War College battlefield guides have labored to provide generous directions to key points of interest on the battlefields and consistently used high quality maps to illustrate historic troop positions, roads, rivers, fields, wood lines, structures, and contour topography.

The previous battlefield guidebooks, particularly those compiled on Gettysburg, Antietam, Chancellorsville, and Fredericksburg, established a high standard in subject editing. Although the narratives have relied heavily on the *Official Records of the Union and Confederate Armies*, almost to the exclusion of other primary sources, the editors have been thorough in selecting the most detailed and thought-provoking reports to provide on-the-spot, event specific, historical context. Used in the field, these well mapped guidebooks have assisted both the novice and professional military history student to recreate both the setting and proportions of each battle. They help promote understanding of the physical and psychological obstacles which confronted the combat soldier. Unlike other guides on Civil War battles, the editors of this series have provided a unique blend of documentary sources and terrain descriptions, coupled with numerous "on the ground" tour stops arranged in chronological order to depict the battles as they actually unfolded.

With the publication of *Guide to the Battle of Shiloh*, the editors tackle the difficult and often confusing battle fought at Pittsburg Landing, Tennessee, on April 6-7, 1862. In targeting their standard guide format on the first grand battle in the West, the editor's traditionally high level of subject matter expertise has diminished. Several of the selected tour stops, where some of the most significant close quarter and savage fighting occurred at Shiloh, do not contain comparison observations of the two combatants—Union versus Confederate (i.e. stops 7, 8, 9, and 10 use only Union accounts, while stop 11 incorporates just Confederate). The entire second day of battle, Monday April 7, is covered in only four brief tour stops, with ten Federal eyewitness accounts, versus only one Confederate report (that of Gen. P. G. T. Beauregard), to detail the action and context of battle fought on Shiloh's second day.

In a battlefield guidebook series whose major goal is to provide sources of first-hand experience to better highlight and understand a soldier's view of battle, a secondary source was selected to represent primary battle knowledge and experience at Shiloh. Two excerpts from *The Life of Albert Sidney Johnston* (1878), Col. William Preston Johnston's biography of his famous father, the Confederate army commander at Shiloh, is used at stops 13 and 18a to help provide the Confederate perspective of the fighting in Shiloh's famous Hornet's Nest thicket. However, Colonel Johnston, who served as an aide to Confederate President Jefferson Davis in Richmond, was not present at Shiloh. The fact that Colonel Johnston did not participate in the battle is not cited for the guidebook reader, who might improperly assume that his Hornets' Nest narrative is a first-hand account of the battle. Excellent primary sources exist that recount the Confederate "face of battle" experienced in Shiloh's Hornet's Nest, but the editors opted to use Colonel Johnston's often cited secondary account.

Eighteen battle maps are provided, but unfortunately most of them contain noticeable errors. With this type of guidebook format, accurate and detailed maps are extremely important. Accurate maps greatly assist the user in taking the historical information provided in written eywitness observations and placing those human battle experiences on the ground where the actual combat was fought. However, the base map provided in this Battle of Shiloh guide is extremely difficult to read and contains few defining historic geographic feature names. Virtually none of the battlefield roads, fields, or creeks are cited properly. An accurate historic base map for Shiloh exists and was available to the editors. Prepared by National Park Service Historian, Edwin C. Bearss in 1973, the Shiloh base map illustrates the location of historic fields, wood lines, major roads, farm lanes, and over seventy homes and farm structures located on the Shiloh plateau in 1862. The detailed battlefield landscape information provided on Bearss' base map would have improved the War College guidebook maps significantly and allowed the reader to reference and understand the many physical changes which have occurred in the battlefield landscape since 1862.

The War College editors make some gross misinterpretations regarding physical changes to the Shiloh landscape. First, they fail to cite that almost ninety percent of the historic roads which traversed the Shiloh plateau are intact and are the same transportation corridors as at the time of the battle. The editors inaccurately state that the current roads, "even when built to take the (park) visitor around the battlefield, rarely follow the lines of advance or connect the positions of large formations at a given stage in the battle" (p. 7). This is simply not true and misrepresents the vital fact that upon the preserved landscape found today on the field of Shiloh, one can still follow the lines of maneuver on a surviving 1862 road system. Since the establishment of Shiloh National Military Park in 1894, the only significant changes to this system of historic roads is that the routes have been widened and paved to accommodate modern vehicles.

Another important terrain factor misrepresented in the Shiloh battlefield guide is the assertion that a main problem for the park visitor today is the "restricted field of observation compared with that in 1862" (p. 5). "Trees then were not so tall. . . ," claim the editors. In fact, the trees found in the forest covering the Shiloh plateau in 1862 were much taller and were, in general, much older than those growing today. In April 1862, a mature open forest existed, whereas today a shorter, younger, and much more dense growth of forest exists. Therefore, numerous tall trees dominated in 1862, and virtually little or no underbrush existed at ground level (a natural feature of old growth forests), except along watersheds and ravines, where heavy pockets of dense cover was encountered. The older mature (taller) forest accounts for the greater, or increased, field of observation and line of sight experienced by the Union and Confederate combatants at Shiloh, and not the War College editor's interpretation that the Shiloh area had been "logged" heavily to provide fuel for steamboats. This misinterpretation of terrain and landscape builds a fragile foundation for the "on the ground" historical accuracy sought by the editors.

In addition to cultural landscape misinterpretations, the maps included do not provide the contour topography which was included in earlier volumes of this battlefield guide series. Thus important ground elevations and terrain features that influenced the course of battle are not represented or identified. The resulting flat landscape depicted in the Shiloh maps promotes difficult, confusing, and inaccurate interpretations.

A large number of the army troop maneuvers and unit battle positions illustrated are grossly inaccurate. In some instances, artillery batteries are cited as infantry brigades (p. 87, "Burrows'" and "McAllister" [misspelled "McCal-lister" on the map] were actually Union artillery batteries, but are shown on the map as Federal infantry brigades, which in turn should have be labeled "Marsh" and "Hare"). On p. 106, "Stephens" is misidentified as a Rebel field battery when the unit was actually a Confederate infantry brigade. On several maps, individual combat units are misidentified. On p. 22 the camp of the "l6th Iowa" should be labeled the 16th Wisconsin, while the camp shown as the "16th Illinois," is actually that of the 61st Illinois (repeated on map for p. 91).

Finally, many of the unit positions and maneuvers drawn on the maps are inaccurate in both the context of time and space. For example, the location of Col. Madison Miller's brigade on p. 22 is 2,000 feet too far south, while on the same map, Col. Everett Peabody's first line of battle is also shown 1,000 feet too far south. On p. 91, the center and left flank of Gen. William T. Sherman's division, and the location of Gen. John A. McClernand's 3rd Brigade under Julius Raith, are about 1,500-2,000 feet too far south and placed on the wrong side of Shiloh Branch ravine. The maps on pages 58 and 91 place the initial morning advance of Gen. William H. L. Wallace's Union division one mile too far west; and on p. 120, the Union forces under Sherman and McClernand are both shown as west of Tilghman Branch (which is unlabeled) at 4:00 p.m., when they should be one half mile further east on the east side of the creek, having retired across Tilghman Creek an hour earlier. Also, no attempt was made to distinguish cavalry from infantry forces, as is illustrated on maps on pp. 87, 157, and 167, for Brewer's, Wharton's, and Clanton's Confederate cavalry organi-zations, which the reader could easily misinterpret as infantry brigades.

Traditionally, the interpretive concept and format used in the earlier vol-umes of "The U.S. War College Guides to Civil War Battles" guidebook series has been good, but with *The Guide to the Battle of Shiloh*, tradition, concept and format fall short in actual execution. Inaccurate maps and poor editorial inter-pretations weaken and reduce the effectiveness of this guide as an "on the ground" learning tool. A second edition is needed to correct the many unfortu-nate map errors and provide a far more accurate, comprehensive, and descriptive narrative.

Stacy D. Allen   Shiloh National Military Park

Nowhere to Run: The Battle of the Wilderness, by John Michael Priest (White Mane, 63 W. Burd St., P. O. Box 152, Shippensburg, PA, 17257), 1995. Photos, biblio., notes, index. 326pp. HC. $34.95

In recent years the effort to present a balanced historical perspective of our nation's past has led to a proliferation of publications that view events from the "bottom up." In the case of America's Civil War, this trend has led to the publication of numerous works similar in style to John Priest's current offering, *Nowhere to Run*, the first in a two-volume account of the Wilderness Campaign of May 4-7, 1864.

Priest's book, which is largely based upon the accounts of soldiers, offers readers their account of the courage, cowardice, pain, suffering, and sheer terror encountered by seasoned veterans in the Wilderness. "There are but one or two square miles upon this continent that have been more saturated with blood," wrote one soldier, words which seems to support Priest's contention that Robert E. Lee and Ulysses S. Grant had no grand military strategy except, perhaps, attrition. Grant, Lee, and many other officers are scarcely mentioned in *Nowhere to Run* since the author did not make any effort to coordinate the fighting related by the soldiers.

While analyzing the battle from the more traditional "battles and leaders" approach provides readers with a broad perspective and more insight into the course and conduct of fighting, it often overlooks the human dimension that determine whether grand strategies succeed. Priest's style supplies that missing dimension and provides a much deeper understanding of the realities of war, giving readers greater insight into what the fighting was like for the soldiers who had to wage it. The inherent disadvantage in this approach is that readers are often not provided with enough context to understand the interlaced mini-accounts, and thus lack perspective.

Priest has relied on a broad range of primary and secondary sources including regimental histories, reminiscences, diaries, newspaper accounts and an impressive array of archival material. These sources offer a gripping, indelible impression of the bloody Wilderness fighting. The sources are arranged in endnotes grouped by chapter, although they include a page heading indicating the section of the chapter in which the notes are found.

The narrative is arranged chronologically. The initial skirmishes are related in sequence in an attempt to transport the reader from one scene to another as the battle unfolds. This method, which leaves the reader with the impression that there was no tactical strategy, would be difficult to follow without the forty-five three-color tactical maps. The maps vary in scale from one-eighth of a mile to ten miles and, although on five of the maps the scale is unclear, they generally allow the reader to maintain an accurate depiction of the engagement's progression.

Nowhere to Run is replete with fascinating anecdotes and descriptive sequences. Of the fighting at Saunder's Field, one soldier wrote: "Wounded men, unable to crawl into the ditch between the lines or to reach the turnpike, screamed horribly as the flames ignited their clothing or touched off their cartridge boxes. . . .the sickening, tangible smell of frying human flesh hung over the woods" (p. 104). The horror of war is amplified in the account of Maj. Thomas Hyde of 7th Maine Infantry, who was hit by the decapitated head of a fellow bluecoat "full in the face, splattering his uniform with brains and blood. Hyde. . .spent the next fifteen minutes spewing the brains from his mouth and cleaning himself up" (p. 101). The author describes the seasoned veteran who searched amongst the graying corpses of his fellow soldiers and commented that "all these men had stood together with us in so many hard-contested battles but they would no more unsheath their swords or raise their voices in battle-cry in defense of rights, home and liberty" (p. 210). The soldier then proceeded to eat his lunch in the midst of the deteriorating bodies.

This handsomely-bound volume includes an Order of Battle taken from *Battles and Leaders of the Civil War*, as well as twenty-nine photographs accompanying the text. This work is not intended to replace Edward Steere's *The Wilderness Campaign*, or Gordon Rhea's recent book on the same subject. It is, however, a worthy addition to its genre and should enlighten those who seek to understand the history of a war that resulted in our several states becoming a union.

Tammie McDaniel   Oak Ridge, Louisiana

Pickett: Leader of the Charge, by Edward G. Longacre (White Mane Publishing Co., Inc., 63 West Burd St., Shippensburg, PA 17257), 1995. Maps, photos, end notes, biblio, index. 242pp. HC. $29.95.

Confederate General George E. Pickett enjoys a rare distinction among Civil War personalities by having a widely-known image and a virtually unknown personality. His association with one of the most famous charges of the war explains the former distinction, and a lack of sufficient personal papers accounts for the latter. While Civil War-era "Pickett letters" exist, most historians agree that Pickett's widow, La Salle Corbell Pickett, heavily embellished the original letters; some claim she fabricated them. Nonetheless, Michael Shaara's novel *The Killer Angels* and the film "Gettysburg" have helped to keep the image of George Pickett alive in the minds of Civil War enthusiasts.

Edward G. Longacre's *Pickett: Leader of the Charge* attempts to reconcile the differences between the general's image and his personality. Longacre argues that Pickett was a complex individual who was not as shallow or simplistic as historians have suggested. While Longacre successfully repudiates the image of Pickett as a one-dimensional simpleton, he does not effectively penetrate Pickett's enigmatic personality.

The lack of reliable primary sources significantly hampers any attempt to reach an understanding of Pickett's inner identity, as Longacre's account demonstrates. He presents many intriguing aspects of Pickett's experiences but is unable to provide an effective analysis when source material is lacking. When primary materials are available, Longacre presents an adequate analysis. For example, his discussion of Pickett's feelings after the death of his first wife is effective because it relies on an actual letter from Pickett to Elizabeth Heth Vaden. Analysis of other important issues suffers from the dearth of source material. The biography offers few insights into Pickett's early life or his relationship with his parents. His relationship with an unnamed "Indian maiden" while on Pacific Coast frontier duty and his subsequent abandoning of the child from that relationship receives little analysis because no record of Pickett's thoughts or feelings on the matter exists. On such key issues like secession, the reader gains little insight into Pickett's feelings but must instead accept a vague tentative view: "[b]orn and reared a Virginian, Pickett could not have escaped being affected by the controversy over slavery" (p. 150). The only specific evidence Longacre uses for Pickett's views on secession come from the embellished letters. Other qualifiers, including various forms of "doubtless," and "may well have," plague most analytic passages of the biography.

Longacre attempts to salvage some credibility from the embellished Pickett letters by claiming only to use the letters "when they tally with known facts, when they present a reasonably accurate account of events, and when they offer a plausible interpretation of Pickett's frame of mind" (p. 182n). Despite this commendable statement of restraint, Longacre relies heavily on the dubious letters as a historical source. When discussing the personal relationship between La Salle Corbell and George Pickett, Longacre uncritically accepts La Salle's version of the relationship, as described in her memoirs and the embellished correspondence. In many other cases throughout the biography Longacre bases his discussion on information from published and unpublished versions of the questionable Pickett letters.

The biography is more effective when considering the Civil War experiences of Pickett, but again the soldier's personality remains elusive. Longacre provides fairly detailed accounts of the role of Pickett's Brigade, the "Game Cocks," at the battles of Williamsburg and Seven Pines in 1862. Using after-action reports from the *Official Records,* the biography offers insight into Pickett's strategy and his management of the brigade, but little else. The chapter on the Battle of Gettysburg focuses on how Pickett might have felt before his famous charge, and whether he was justified in not accompanying his troops for the length of the assault. Longacre vindicates Pickett's absence by explaining that the responsibilities of a division leader did not include personally leading assaults. He further suggests that the actions of General Johnston Pettigrew and General Isaac Trimble, who had gone beyond the boundaries of their position by accompanying their troops on the charge, made Pickett appear irresponsible.

Longacre's discussion of Pickett's operations in the Department of North Carolina early in 1864 show that the general did have some abilities in military planning and was adequate but not spectacular in independent command. His actions in the Bermuda Hundred Campaign likely saved Petersburg from capture. However, Longacre notes that Pickett's behavior before the Battle of Five Forks, when he left the front to attend a shad bake with other generals, is indefensible. He suggests that Pickett may have been sulking after General Lee ordered him to defend a position that he thought could not be held.

Longacre's treatment of Pickett's war career is admirable in that it gives the reader a sense of Pickett's experience as a commander before and after his famous exploits at Gettysburg, but other important issues receive scant attention. Longacre makes suggestions about Pickett's relationship with other notable personalities, including Joseph E. Johnston, U. S. Grant, and George B. McClellan, but these relationships are not considered in any detail. This limited analysis is especially frustrating when considering Pickett's relationship with two crucial figures: James Longstreet and Robert E. Lee. Longacre suggests that Pickett's early rise in rank might be related to his friendship with Longstreet, which is alluded to throughout the biography but never fully explored. Pickett's relationship with Lee is treated similarly. The author suggests at various points that Pickett may have been developing an antipathy toward Lee, but the nature of their relationship remains sketchy.

Has Longacre made a contribution to Civil War historiography by presenting a more complex George Pickett? It is up to the reader to come to terms with this issue, as the biography ends abruptly with Pickett's death. No concluding assessment of Pickett's wartime performance or of his importance in the struggle is included. Longacre's discussion of Pickett's war experience suggests that the general was not a brilliant leader, but rather an average officer. The treatment of Pickett's pre-Gettysburg career shows that he led a fearless brigade that fought well and sustained a high casualty rate, but does not provide evidence that Pickett played a crucial role in its combat record. Pickett was recovering from a wound during the Antietam Campaign, and his division was held in reserve at Fredericksburg. At New Bern, North Carolina, Pickett met with frustration, and Five Forks resulted in his utter defeat. Longacre suggests that many of Pickett's combat failures were the result of poor planning by his superiors. While this assessment has some validity, the truly great leaders of the Army of Northern Virginia adapted and exercised their own initiative within Lee's broader plans.

Despite his suggestions to the contrary, Longacre's evidence seems only to reinforce the traditional view of Pickett's leadership skills. Longacre's best efforts notwithstanding, his study adds little to what is known already of Pickett's personality. The biography utilizes accounts of Pickett's peers and the scant material written by the general to bring together in one synthesis what is known about George E. Pickett. It is an admirable effort and the biography is an adequate starting place for readers with little knowledge of Pickett. However, those who seek new insights into the personality of the general will need to continue their search. The lack of family papers and reliable letters ensures that even after the publication of Leader of the Charge, the personality and thoughts of George E. Pickett remain elusive.

Jonathan M. Berkey   The Pennsylvania State University

Halleck: Lincoln's Chief of Staff, Stephen E. Ambrose (Louisiana State University Press, Baton Rouge, LA 70893), 1996. Maps, photos, biblio., index. 226pp. Paper. $11.95.

Since it was first published in 1962, Stephen Ambrose's biography of Henry Wager Halleck has stood as the "standard" work on that general's life and legacy. The reissuance of the book in paperback by Louisiana State University

Press should be welcomed by everyone who has wanted a copy for his library. Criticized during his lifetime and afterwards, Halleck nevertheless played an important part not only in shaping the North's ultimate victory but in developing a modern command system for the United States Army. The bulk of Ambrose's book deals with these two aspects of Halleck's life, and he succeeds well in describing them. Ambrose argues persuasively that the Union probably could not have won the war without Halleck.

In 1839, Halleck graduated third in his class from the United States Military Academy at West Point. There, he was influenced by Professor Dennis Hart Mahan, who was captivated by the military theories of Henri Jomini. Halleck later studied in Europe and wrote *Elements of Military Art and Science*, which became an extremely influential book. He stressed the Jominian concepts of concentration of forces and the use of interior lines of operations. Halleck served in a non-combat role in California during the Mexican War, and became secretary of state under the military governor. In that latter role his talents as an administrator began to evidence themselves. Winfield Scott secured Halleck's appointment as a major general in the regular army when the Civil War began.

Halleck expected the war to be short and to be fought in accordance with the teachings of Jomini. His first assignment was command of the Department of Missouri, where he found a situation bordering on chaos. Halleck quickly recognized the weakness of the Confederate defenses at Fort Henry and Fort Donelson and the strategic advantages of striking at the enemy's center. He was initially reluctant to move against the forts because he had his doubts about his commander in that area—Ulysses S. Grant. He planned to use the armies of Samuel R. Curtis, John Pope, and Grant to drive the Confederates away from the Mississippi River. His strategy worked well in the early months of 1862. Grant took Henry and Donelson and Pope captured New Madrid and threatened Island No. 10. Curtis, meanwhile, cleared Missouri and northern Arkansas of Confederate forces. Halleck attempted unsuccessfully during this period to be named commander of all forces in the West. When he could not get a request approved by General-in-Chief George B. McClellan, he tried to go over Mac's head to Winfield Scott or to the Department of War.

A hallmark of Halleck's command theories was established while in the West: he did not interfere with his commanders after he assigned them a task. Only the general in the field knew the true situation on his front, Halleck believed, so he was reluctant to insist too strongly on movements or tactics he thought the general should follow. "The departmental commander's duties, as Halleck visualized them, involved outlining the operation before it began and supporting the field commander with reinforcements and supplies while he executed it" (p. 38).

On March 8, 1862, President Abraham Lincoln named Halleck commander of the Department of the Mississippi and made McClellan commander of the Army of the Potomac. Halleck left St. Louis for Pittsburg Landing to take charge of the campaign against Corinth but reached Grant's army after the Battle of Shiloh had been fought. Halleck wanted only to capture the Mississippi town and to cut its railroad connections, not to destroy the Confederate army of Gustave Toutant Beauregard. In May, he lay siege to the town with the armies of Grant, Pope, and Don Carlos Buell. Beauregard evacuated his entrenchments late in the month, giving Halleck the almost bloodless victory he desired. Halleck began reorganizing his army, rebuilding railroads, and preparing to send Buell's army into eastern Tennessee.

On July 11, Lincoln named Halleck general-in-chief to coordinate the movements of Union armies. Halleck had succeeded in the West despite criticism, bringing efficiency to operations there. Though less than spectacular as a field commander, he had shown improvement. His primary accomplishments, however, were "as an organizer, a supplier, a planner, in short as a manager of war" (p. 63). Those talents continued to grow in Halleck's new situation: "He gave the President technical advice, translated Lincoln's civilian terms into military parlance for field generals, and assumed almost all the administrative details of running the army" (p. 65). While he got the blame for Lincoln's unpopular decisions concerning appointments and dismissals of generals. Halleck tried to make the army more professional. Many of the reforms he introduced struck at the politics in the army. Halleck did not achieve everything he desired, but he kept pushing. By the end of the war, the United States Army was the finest the young country had ever fielded. He deserves most of the credit for making that army what it was.

Halleck did not remain a strict Jominian. In the West he continued to stress the capture and holding of geographic points of importance. He recognized the significance of Vicksburg in 1862 and concentrated the Union army's efforts on its capture. After Grant captured the river fortress, Halleck continued to direct the Western armies against such places as Chattanooga and Atlanta. He realized that Confederate armies there would disintegrate if they could not be supplied, and he convinced Lincoln that this was the proper course of action. However, by the time of the Gettysburg campaign, Halleck had begun to modify his Jominian ideas in the Virginia theatre. He realized that the destruction of Robert E. Lee's army should be the real target of the Union army's effort, although the capture of Richmond would provide a moral victory for the North.

Grant became general-in-chief in March 1864, and Halleck was made chief-of-staff. He continued doing most of the same things he had in the past. He served as a liaison between the president and the generals in the field and between Grant and the various departmental commanders. This relationship worked exceptionally well and allowed Grant to remain with George G. Meade's army in the field. Additionally, Halleck and Grant worked together to remove from field commands such political generals as Nathaniel P. Banks and Benjamin F. Butler. Halleck was very successful in managing the Union war machine, and he played a significant role in the shift toward the concept of modern, total warfare.

Ambrose's book is well researched and well written. He succeeds in his goal of delineating the contributions Henry Halleck made toward the North's victory in the Civil War and toward the creation of a modern staff system in the United States Army. Ambrose does not gloss over Halleck's weaknesses but shows readers how he became a successful general despite his flaws.

Arthur W. Bergeron, Jr   Pamplin Park Civil War Site

Ken Burns' The Civil War: Historians Respond, by Robert Brent Toplin (Oxford University Press, 198 Madison Avenue, New York, NY 10016), 1996. Preface, introduction, notes. 197pp. HC. $24.00.

My claim as part of my expertise in reviewing Toplin's collection of essays by historians is the offering of a long-distance learning, educational television course based on Burns' series. I have offered it approximately twelve times and have established a dialogue with students in all stages of maturity and majors as well as different degrees of expertise, from the novice to the well-read Civil War enthusiast. Almost without exception the viewing audience, seeking academic credit and including black and white students, has responded positively to the eleven hours of "The Civil War." Moreover, Burns' series has served as a springboard for perhaps ten percent of the students to enroll in a more intensive, lecture-based course on the Civil War and Reconstruction which requires formal book reviews, essay tests, and for graduate students, scholarly research papers based on primary and secondary documentation.

From the perspectives of a professional historian, however, negatives may certainly be laid at the feet of both the film maker and the historian who co-wrote the accompanying book. Indeed, James M. McPherson's *Battle Cry of Freedom: The Civil War Era* seems more appropriate to provide an in-depth analysis on the War's events. For primary material flavor, the reviewer has utilized at times, Sam Watkins, *"Co. Aytch": A Side Show of the Big Show*, or B. P. Gallaway, *The Ragged Rebel: A Common Soldier in W. H. Parsons' Texas Cavalry, 1861-1865*, for the experiences of David Carey Nance in the Trans-Mississippi West.

My specific interest in the riverine warfare on the Western and the Trans-Mississippi waters could lend itself to a criticism of Burns' failure to document adequately this phase of the conflict. I could also lament "The Civil War's" over emphasis of the black troops' contribution to the Union cause by arguing that these troops did not see their first battle action until Port Hudson in May 1863, or later at Millikin's Bend the following month. Few would dispute, however, that the surrender of Vicksburg and the Confederate defeat at Gettysburg, both in July 1863, represented the key turning points of the War. Consequently, the contributions of blacks Americans to the Union cause from July 1863 until April 1865, may well have been to serve as cannon fodder, which some historians have argued rather convincingly, or for service on garrison duty, thus releasing previously trained white troops for battlefield service.

Finally, the film maker can be condemned for failing to recognize—as do many professional historians—that the War was lost in the Western Theater, which was underemphasized throughout the nine programs. Indeed, many of the errors, both profound and profane, other than factual ones described by the essayists, are still subject to ones' own interpretation of the four years of rebellion.

Several of the essayists, however, unjustly censure Burns for not making the film that they would have produced themselves. Catherine Clinton's contention that females made a significant contribution to the war effort cannot be denied. Except for those females in the hospitals, the Sanitary Commission and on the homefront, however, few females served in combat, a major topical theme which Burns freely admits held more attraction for viewers. Clinton's statement by a student, unidentified by race, that "he didn't expect to learn anything from a guy who looked like Opie" (p. 64), reveals more about the mind set, apathy, and ignorance of today's university students than about the fascinating panorama of American history and female contributions to the American landscape. Eric Foner may well be correct in his critique that Burns fell victim to the romance of reunion among veterans of the blue and grey as well as the two sections, but the era of Reconstruction is a film project unto itself. Indeed, it is possible to claim that Reconstruction had more of an impact on present-day Southern attitudes, black and white, in reference to racial, civil, political, economic, or other issues, than the Civil War.

C. Vann Woodward, a transplanted Arkansan, must be commended for his calming, gentile influence by asking critics in the professional academy to let Ken and Ric Burns be artists and not take sides in the continuing generational and ideological disputes among the academy of historians. There are enough scholarly publications and professional meetings for these interpretations and disputes to create as bloody a battleground of words as did the battlegrounds of the Civil War. The most abrasive essay, in this reviewer's opinion, penned by Leon F. Litwack, takes Burns to task for not incorporating the new history and showing the Civil War as a social revolution of far-reaching consequences. His particular concern is the meaning of freedom for blacks. The comparison of this television series with D. W. Griffith's film "The Birth of a Nation," however, seems a bit calloused. While a historian who reads Shelby Foote's *The Civil War: A Narrative History* may become frustrated with Foote's lack of footnotes and documentation, these volumes remain some of the mostly widely read on the War. Perhaps Foote, the novelist-turned-historian, is speaking of the white South and not the black South, but because of his literary training, he has written what the common-man-historian-in-the-streets of America will read, and not some pedantic tomb filled with ponderous documentation written by a scholar for other scholars. Because of the generational ebb and flow of political currents, Barbara Fields draws a critical analysis by stating that the Civil War has not ended; it is still being fought, and it may still be lost. The film maker, however, has little control over public attitudes other than to create an awareness among them of the rich historical heritage from which they stem.

Ken Burns has created a renewed interest in Civil War cinematography as may be witnessed by the numerous other films on the War being produced. His series also has stimulated new interest in Civil War historiography. Burns' recently-completed television series on the American West will probably do the same for the vast panorama of Western History that this series did for those non-professionals extolled by Carl Becker as "everyman his own historian."

Marshall Scott Legan   Northeast Louisiana University

Defender of the Valley: Brigadier General John D. Imboden, CSA, by Harold R. Woodward, Jr. (Rockbridge Publishing Company, P.O. Box 351, Berryville, VA 221-0351), 1996. Photos, notes, biblio., index. 149pp. HC. $25.00.

John Imboden, the author of this work correctly points out, has been to a great extent ignored by historians of the Civil War. Historians are not the only ones guilty of this. Relegated to the sidelines of the Shenandoah Valley and supplanted in overall command during times of crisis, Imboden seems to have been ignored by his contemporaries as well. He was promoted to the rank of brigadier general early in 1863 but advanced no further. Harold Woodward, Jr. makes a sold case in this welcome biography for our viewing Imboden as a talented and courageous soldier, as well as an intelligent, successful business-man and politician. Regrettably, there is no explanation provided for Imboden's failure to assume a more significant role in the drama that unfolded on the American stage between 1861-1865. Whether we are to accept Imboden's own self-effacing claim that he denied advancement remains unclear.

Woodward's biography of Imboden, which provides a brief but complete synopsis of the life and career of the general, is thoroughly researched and relies greatly on Imboden's own papers and writings. Imboden was educated at Wash-ington College in Lexington, Virginia, from which he was graduated in 1843. He also received some military training at the Virginia Military Institute while attending engineering classes. Thereafter Imboden began a successful career as an attorney in the thriving Shenandoah Valley town of Staunton. Imboden was active in politics and maintained a longstanding connection with the local mili-tia, forming the Staunton Artillery on the eve of the Civil War. Imboden was part of a conspiracy hatched by former Virginia Governor Henry Wise that involved seizure of the arsenal at Harpers Ferry prior to the state's secession. The group involved "agreed `to act without official authority'" (p. 21). Such resolve proved unnecessary as Virginia seceded before the men could act fully on their plans. Imboden later directed his battery admirably at Bull Run, and in the spring of 1863 received authorization to raise a regiment of partisan rangers for service in the Shenandoah Valley. He achieved some success in efforts to disrupt Federal operations, though there were a number of disappointments as well.

Early in 1863, Imboden's promotion to brigadier general was made contin-gent upon his raising a brigade for regular service and disbanding the partisan command. Many of the men chose to transfer to regular service with Imboden, and by the summer of that year he was given increased responsibility and command of the Valley District. Woodward details Imboden's efforts to stymie Federal advances through the innovative use of his vastly inferior numbers. When supported, as he was during Franz Sigel's and David Hunter's advances up the Valley in 1864, he received not only additional forces but accompanying infantry commanders who outranked him and assumed control. He was never provided an opportunity to prove himself in directing larger numbers of troops, a misfortune that was most evident at the Battle of Piedmont in June of 1864, where he undoubtedly could have handled the army more adeptly than did Brig. Gen. William E. "Grumble" Jones.

Imboden continued his service in the Valley under Jubal Early's command until December 1864, when he requested reassignment for medical reasons. He finished the war in command of Confederate prisons in an area that included the dreaded Andersonville Prison in Georgia. In that capacity he ordered reforms that improved the lot of the Union prisoners to some degree. Imboden never returned to law or politics after the war, and until his death in 1895, he had a successful business career in the railroad and mining industries. Toward the end of his life, Imboden authored a number of articles on Civil War events.

Woodward provides a sympathetic look at Imboden's career, stating that the cavalyman's "valuable contribution to the Confederacy's war effort [was] unquestionably immeasurable" (p. ix.). He has not heretofore received such lavish praise from historians, however, and is more often criticized for his incapacity to train and discipline his sometimes unruly troopers properly. Imboden's abilities probably can be characterized more accurately as occupying the middle ground between those two views. Nevertheless, Woodward's book is a solid work that will surely accomplish his desire to bring Imboden greater exposure among Civil War enthusiasts.

Edward J. Hagerty   American Military University

Echos of Battle: The Struggle for Chattanooga, by Richard A. Baumgartner and Larry M. Strayer (Blue Acorn Press, Box 2684, Huntington, WV 25726), 1996. Photos, maps, biblio., index, d.j., 480pp. HC. $40.00

Anyone familiar with the first-class books put out by Richard Baumgartner and Larry Strayer will not be disappointed with their latest endeavor, *The Struggle for Chattanooga*.

Similar in look and feel to their earlier *Echos of Battle: The Atlanta Campaign*, this volume blends an impressive combination of photographs and illustrations, many previously unpublished, with carefully selected soldier's accounts. The end product is a lavish and attractive oversize volume that offers a rather unique perspective on the intriguing battles for control of the rivers, hills, and valleys surrounding the critical gateway city of Chattanooga, Tennessee. While Chattanooga is the primary emphasis of the book, the authors wisely included coverage of the Tullahoma campaign and the fighting at Chickamauga, both of which set up the final and largely decisive battles of Lookout Mountain and Missionary Ridge. The latter two actions effectively wrested control of the heartland crossroads from the Confederacy, permanently denying the South any meaningful opportunity of again occupying the important city.

The uniqueness of *The struggle for Chattanooga* resides in its focus. In an effort to preserve "an authentic flavor of the times," the authors sifted through nearly 1,000 accounts, selecting "only those written in first-person style." Thus we learn from ordinary soldiers what they experienced in the tangled and smoky thickets of Chickamauga, climbing the towering heights of Lookout Mountain, or attacking the impressive and entrenched Missionary Ridge. Other anecdotes peppered throughout include fascinating (and previously unknown to this reviewer) examples of Maj. Gen. Patrick Cleburne's humor. When one of Cleburne's regiments was standing in line for inspection, the general stopped and examined one soldier's rifle. "Ben was not known for keeping a clean gun," wrote an eyewitness. After examining the filthy weapon, Cleburne handed it back to the private and stared into the man's eyes. "I hope I do you no injustice, my man, but I don't think you have washed your face for several days." Thereafter, "Ben's gun and face were always ready for inspection" (p. 295).

These and scores of similarly interesting (and informative) stories tell the tale of these important actions, inextricably bonding the reader with the subjects. The authors are quick to point out in their helpful introduction, however, that "this volume does not attempt to detail or analyze strategy, military operations or command decisions in the region between June and December 1863." In other words, if readers desire a more traditional battle study they must seek it elsewhere.

The Struggle for Chattanooga compliments rather than competes with Wiley Sword's *Fire on the Mountain*. This handsomely produced book is a satisfying and enriching experience. I highly recommend it.

Theodore P. Savas   San Jose, CA

Bloody Valverde: A Civil War Battle on the Rio Grande, February 21, 1862, by John M. Taylor (University of New Mexico Press, Marketing Dept., 1720 Lomas Blvd., NE, Albuquerque, NM 87131-1591), 1995. Photos, maps, notes, biblio, index, d.j., 185pp. HC. $29.95

The 1861-82 Confederate invasion of the Union territory of New Mexico, the westernmost campaign of the Civil War, remains one of the least known campaigns of that conflict. This situation has begun to change, however, due to several factors: nationwide publicity (even if only by mention) of the battles of Valverde and Glorietta in the popular Ken Burns PBS Civil War series; recent discovery and attendant publicity of the mass grave of Confederate soldiers killed and buried on the Glorieta battlefield; widespread and successful historical preservation efforts to save that battlefield; and a new generation of scholarly books that tend to analyze the campaign and its component actions utilizing a surprisingly large body of newly discovered diaries, reminiscences, letters, and other personal materials and artifact evidence.

These recent publications have included biographies of key participants and heavily annotated and edited diaries of other important figures, North and South, as well as overall histories of the campaign and the Confederate Sibley Brigade. This welcome swelling of the literature of the Civil War and the Southwest has not, however, included detailed studies of the two major battles of the New Mexico campaign. John M. Taylor's *Bloody Valverde: A Civil War Battle on the Rio Grande* corrects half that deficit, and does it very well indeed.

The Battle of Valverde, fought in south-central New Mexico Territory near Fort Craig, was the first of two formal battles and three lesser fights. It was also the largest battle of the campaign as well as the westernmost battle of the Civil War. On its outcome depended the continuation of the northward advance by Texan invaders to take the key military posts in northern New Mexico, including Fort Union, the supply center for the Federal military in the Southwest, and subsequent occupation of Colorado and Utah territories and southern California.

The author does an excellent job of setting the stage for the Battle of Valverde with a description of the organization of Confederate and Union personnel and units in their respective regions. He describes their arms and equipment as well, and details the advance of the Texans into southern New Mexico and Federal preparations for defence. Key leaders on both sides are evaluated in some depth. Confederate commander Brig. Gen. Henry Hopkins Sibley, for instance, already regarded by some as "a walking whiskey keg," was soon identified by his own troops as a coward and incompetent, beginning with his performance (or lack of it) at Valverde. Taylor rightly emphasizes, however, the expertise of Texan hero Col. Tom Green, who was in actual field command during the battle. The author also analyzes the effectiveness of Union commanders Col. Edward Canby and Benjamin Roberts in conducting the two major phases of the Federal operations on the battlefield.

As previously mentioned, this is the first complete and scholarly history of Valverde, and it gives every indication of being the definitive work as well. Taylor's major contribution to understanding the tactical movements lies in his formulation of a rational chronology. The battlefield itself was an extensive cottonwood bottom along the Rio Grande, thick with trees and power smoke on a cloudy, snowy, still winter day. The result was a series of separated actions often out of sight of the overall field commanders, which led to confused orders and misunderstandings, and later to similarly confusing official reports by the officers of both sides. The author has, through careful study and interpretation of all available sources, brought an orderly analysis of the entire conflict out of this chaos. He accompanies his analysis of the entire battle with excellent movement maps representing important phases and events. These include the charge upon the Colorado Volunteers by Texan Lancers—perhaps the only such charge during the war—actions by Col. Kit Carson's First New Mexico Volunteers in blowing to pieces a mounted charge by the Fifth Texas regiment, and the successful and desperate assault by Confederates on the key Federal artillery battery that ended the fighting.

If this book offered nothing more it would be a highly valued work, but it contains additional useful information, including a helpful order of battle with accompanying unit strengths, with carefully analyzed casualties for both sides. In the better known Eastern campaigns and battles, such statistics are often well and accurately known; in New Mexico they are not. This work corrects that deficiency as well as possible and highlights the large casualty percentages experienced by many units, including the Colorado and New Mexico Volunteers. In doing so, for the last-mentioned troops, Taylor may have exaggerated somewhat in attributing the impressive losses in some of the largely Hispanic units to their having bravely rushed to the defense of the threatened artillery battery. Considerable evidence indicates their casualties may well have resulted from their having broken in the face of the onrushing Texans, and having waited too long to do so. While politically correct, Taylor's conclusion is not historically accurate.

As with any work of this depth, there are a few nits to be picked (although very few). The author's explanation of military organization during the Civil

War is not quite correct. For example, the use of "platoons" and "sections" within infantry or cavalry regiments was seldom if ever encountered. Likewise, especially during the New Mexico Campaign, the term "comrades-in-battle" was never used, to this reviewer's knowledge, the enlisted men being loosely organized into "messes" of a half-dozen to a dozen soldiers whose care, supply, etc., was entrusted to a sergeant, usually a neighbor and friend of the messmates. There is also slight contradiction in the author's analysis of composition of the artillery batteries in action at Valverde and of the subsequent Texan defeat at Glorietta a month later. Any such faults are less than minor, however, and in no way detract from or even influence Taylor's overall study of Valverde.

John Taylor, an engineer for Sandia National Laboratories in Albuquerque, has consulted all the available published and unpublished material that has come to light and has likewise sought the advice and counsel of those historians in New Mexico and Texas who are considered expert in various phases of this most interesting and important campaign. By doing so, and through a clear and direct writing style, he has produced an outstanding study of the Battle of Valverde. The book is a major contribution to the body of literature, well produced by the publisher and can be wholeheartedly recommended to any student of the Civil War—especially any interested in the war in the far west, as well as any reader drawn to the history of the Southwest in general.

Don E. Alberts   Rio Rancho, New Mexico

The Struck Eagle A Biography of Brigadier General Micah Jenkins, by James J. Baldwin, III, (Burd Street Press, P. O. Box 152: Shippensburg, PA 17257), 1996. Charts, maps, appendices, biblio., photos, index. 471pp. HC. $34.95.

Prince of Edisto: Brigadier General Micah Jenkins, C.S.A., by James K. Swisher (Rockbridge Publishing Co., P. O. Box 351, Berryville VA 22611-0351), 1996. Maps, photos, notes, biblio, index. 188pp. HC. $25.00.

Studies of Civil War brigadier generals, as well as field-grade officers, can be most enlightening about the course of the war. These men held the primary responsibility for translating the strategy of the army's commanding officers into the reality of the battlefield. In the absence of modern-day communication devices, they frequently had to make split-second decisions when confronted with factors unknown to their superior officers. Outcomes of battles often rested on these decisions. Thus it is important for historians of this period to understand these men: their training and background, relationships with both superior and subordinate officers, and their actions and decisions as they directed troops in the heat of battle.

Both books under review offer a brief overview of Jenkins' prewar life, beginning with his privileged youth on Edisto Island, South Carolina, his studies at South Carolina Military Academy in Charleston (The Citadel), and his efforts, with a few of his fellow graduates, to open the Kings Mountain Military Academy in Yorkville that would funnel students into their alma mater. Rightly, however, both books focus on Jenkins' military career. He entered the Confederate Army as colonel of the 5th South Carolina Volunteers. Following the Battle of Manassas, in which he saw limited action, Jenkins organized a specialized force, the Palmetto Sharpshooters. Serving under James Longstreet, his conduct during the first year of the war received high praise from his commanding officers and he was promoted to brigadier general on July 22, 1862, shortly after the Seven Days Campaign. In Robert E. Lee's restructured Army of Northern Virginia, Jenkins' Brigade, along with the brigades of James Kemper and George Pickett, formed a division commanded by Kemper under Longstreet.

Wounded at Second Manassas, Jenkins missed the Sharpsburg Campaign, saw scant action at Fredericksburg and missed Chancellorsville when his brigade accompanied Longstreet to North Carolina in the spring of 1863. Jenkins' Brigade also missed Gettysburg, serving instead as part of the force withheld to defend Richmond. Despite his relative lack of battlefield experience, Longstreet requested that Jenkins' Brigade accompany him to north Georgia in September 1863. Bottled up in rail traffic in Atlanta, Jenkins did not arrive on the Chickamauga battlefield until the day after the battle. He remained with Longstreet for the rest of his service, participating in the futile effort to dislodge Ambrose Burnside from Knoxville before returning to Lee's army early in 1864. On May 4-6, 1864, during the Battle of the Wilderness, Jenkins was with Longstreet when a group of Virginia soldiers mistook them for Union cavalry and opened fire. Both men were wounded, Jenkins mortally.

Of these two books, Swisher's is the less satisfactory. The author provides good detail when it is necessary to understand the role of Jenkins and his men, and he also makes an effort to explain the larger context in which Jenkins was involved. For instance, he outlines the poor performance of the army's command structure at Seven Pines and offers a lengthy discussion of the Seven Days

Campaign so the reader will understand the need for Lee's reorganization and the place assumed by Jenkins.

Unfortunately, Swisher depends on a fairly limited number of secondary sources, many of them dated. For example, his account of the Battle of Fort Magruder, when Jenkins first came to the attention of his superiors, rests on Douglas Freeman's *Lee's Lieutenants*, unidentified essays from *Battles and Leaders* and the *Southern Historical Society Papers*, Longstreet's *From Manassas to Appomattox*, Stephen Sears' *George B. McClellan*, and Jenkins's report from the *Official Records*. Swisher ignores many other reports of this battle in the *Official Records* that mention Jenkins, including Longstreet's, all of which provide a good perspective on the importance of Jenkins' role. Swisher constructed his account of the Chickamauga Campaign without a single reference, even in the bibliography, to Peter Cozzens' *This Terrible Sound*, the current standard work on that battle.

Moreover, he has not always used his sources accurately. On page 99 he describes the transporting of Longstreet's troops to north Georgia and states that, "The only serious incident of note was a near-riot in Charlotte when Benning's Georgia brigade determined to exact revenge on an unpopular newspaper editor by burning his establishment." This event occurred in Raleigh, and the Georgians did indeed ransack W. W. Holden's pro-Union Raleigh *Standard*. The source Swisher cites for this account related it correctly. Swisher also claims on page 101 that Jenkins and his men arrived at the Chickamauga battlefield on September 21, when it is clear from the *Official Records* that they arrived on the preceding day.

From a more technical standpoint, Swisher's use of the passive voice and his style of notation are frustrating. The initial reference to a source contains all the essential information; however, subsequent references too often only use one or two words from the title and a page number. In subsequent notes the author's last name should accompany the short title unless, of course, the source does not have a specific author—in which case the reader can readily find the full citation in the bibliography. In any event, the reader should not have to sift back through pages of previous notes just to decipher a citation.

James Baldwin's book, considerably longer than Swisher's, is much the better of the two. The prose flows smoothly, and Baldwin offers more detail about the war in general and the evolution of Jenkins' units than does Swisher. Baldwin also makes much more extensive use of manuscript sources, and his citations are clear. The result is a deeper understanding of both Jenkins and his role in the war. For instance, Baldwin's account of the movement of Longstreet's Corps to north Georgia includes mention of a brief visit that Jenkins made to his home in Yorkville, South Carolina, where he found his pregnant wife caring for their desperately ill two-year-old son. Five days after reaching his destination he learned that his son had died. Baldwin shares with his readers excerpts from Jenkins' letters to his wife, which are located in the South Caroliniana Library and from which he reconstructed the event. Swisher does not include this information. Baldwin also offers a fuller explanation of the controversy that erupted between Jenkins and Evander Law over who would lead John B. Hood's Division while the Texan recovered from his wounds received at Chichramauga. This level of depth throughout distinguishes the two books.

I have one caveat concerning Baldwin's work: he states in the Preface that occasionally he has "'taken the factual event and added certain minor details based on my best estimate of how the event reasonably would have occurred. This has been done solely to make the event come to life for the reader" (p. xiii). When has he embellished events? How often did he embellish them? Occasionally a footnote makes a specific mention of such additions (see p. 147, for example), but the reader is left to wonder if all such instances are duly noted.

One of the most valuable aspects of detailed studies of brigadier generals, as well as of lower-ranked field grade officers, is the understanding of the battle that ensues from a detailed examination of their execution of general orders. The formulators of master strategy almost never knew all of the intricacies of the geography of the area, and could never predict either the movements of the opposing army or the role that fate would play as unit commanders fell in combat. Both of these books recognize the significance of such an understanding and provide insight into Jenkins' battlefield performance. Baldwin's detail and depth of research into primary source material render his the stronger of the two. For the reader primarily interested in an overview of Jenkins' life, either title will suffice. For the serious scholar whose interest extends beyond casual curiosity, Baldwin's *The Struck Eagle* is the only choice.

Nancy Smith Mideette   Elon College

The Civil War Diary of Lt. J. E. Hodgkins, Aug. 1864 to July 1865, edited by Kenneth Turino, (Picton Press, P.O. Box 1111, Camden, ME 04843), 1995. Photos, index. 178pp. HC. $22.50

Joseph E. Hodgkins rendered invaluable service as he soldiered and penned his way through the Civil War. Starting as a raw recruit from Lynn, Massachusetts, he chronicled life at the front, in battle, in the hospital, in prison and in the trenches. Emerging as an officer, he served from start to finish. Few accounts give the wealth of detail, even to the point of creative redundancy, that Hodgkins gives. One can feel the pangs of hunger and crunch of hardtack as Hodgkins marches with the 19th Massachusetts Infantry. A deeply religious Methodist, he committed himself fully to the cause, yet longed for the day when he could return to his home and his girl, Lou, whom he eventually married. Three times he returned home: once after he was wounded, once when he reenlisted with his unit and once after he was released from the notorious rebel prison at Andersonville, Georgia. After each furlough he rejoined his unit, fighting to the very end.

Today's well-fed citizens—even those of us who have served in the armed services—find it hard to image living on such meager rations, sleeping with a rubber blanket and marching with ill-fitting shoes worn out or toeless in freezing weather. On Hodgkins first Thanksgiving he writes: "My dinner is composed of 'salt pork turkey' and hard tack. I have made this my washing day having been to the stream and washed my clothes. Wrote home today" (p. 14).

When Hodgkins encountered the hot war it was at Fredricksburg, and he vividly rendered his account, as he continued to do as the war progresses. Crossing the river and surging forward, Hodgkins' company encountered too much fire and fell back toward the river, where the men were put on picket duty. "Looking behind the fences running parallel with the river," Hodgkins reports, "a horrible sight met our gaze. The Rebs lay thick along the fence just as they had fallen, killed by our round shot and shell. . . " (p. 16). And turning to his own condition: "It is freezing cold tonight. The river is skimmed over, and I have to keep moving to keep from freezing. My toes are on the ground and I need a new pair of boots more than anything else." Coming from the shoe-making town of Lynn, Hodgkins understood the need for shoes properly fitted and in good repair. In the army he learned the price that comes from not having them.

When it comes to the heat of battle, Hodgkins is no less graphic: "We move on the double quick. . .till we reach a steep hill. Here we form in line of battle and advance up the hill and over the crest, when we meet with a very warm reception in the shape of bullets, which fall like rain around us. . . " (p. 17).

Shortly after a ball passes through Hodgkins' haversack, a tin plate, a spoon, a *Lynn Reporter*, and struck "me" in the side first carrying the skin away. Moments later a minie ball went through "my arm like lightening." With his limb powerless to raise his gun, Hodgkins moved off the field with "shells humming and balls whizzing, making music not so pleasant" (p. 18).

Hodgkins finally prevailed on a surgeon to treat his wound after a 30-hour wait (his injury was less severe then many). We learn how the wounded fared and how they passed their time during recuperation. After his furlough and with the advent of spring Hodgkins chronicled not only regular swims in the Potomac, which provided a regenerating exercise for the wounded arm, but assigned duties and the ceremonial activities in Washington.

Returning to the much decimated ranks of the 19th, Hodgkins was promoted to corporal. It is during the winter of 1863-64 that he vividly describes the cold and snow as the troops seemed to march from one end of Virginia to the other. For the reader the detailed daily accounts add a wealth of understanding of the average soldier and his dedication. Even reenlistment proves almost a necessity, but gains him a February furlough.

Back in the trenches before Petersburg, with a spring of fighting behind him, Hodgkins and his unit are taken prisoner. They are stripped of their blankets, their haversacks, their money and their canteens. He was initially dispatched to Richmond, and eventually south to Andersonville and the horrors of that infamous Rebel prison. Boredom, a lack of adequate shelter and minimal rations took their toll on the men. Hodgkins kept recording it all, from the tattered condition of his clothes supplemented by a shirt from a comrade who died, to the meager rations and horrendous weather. Even in his darkest days and with "terrible hunger" Hodgkins could record: "It is a beautiful Sabbath morning" (p. 106). He managed with the cold and wet night after night to walk for warmth and at times find a roof to share with fellow members of his regiment.

A flaring rheumatism plagued him throughout his stay, and it was this rheumatism which led a Rebel doctor to allow him to be exchanged and sent home. Hodgkins rises to the occasion with an inspiring and comprehensive description of his condition, his feelings and his convictions, even to the point of his feelings for the stars and stripes when he first saw it again. Returning after a furlough to his regiment, Hodgkins tells of life before Lee's final retreat. Now an officer, his account turns from that of a man in the ranks to his new status. He comes in contact with various generals, and at one point in his military career meets President Abraham Lincoln (who had received an overwhelming majority among the prisoners when their captors allow them to vote while in Andersonville).

Few accounts give such a wealth of day-to-day information, which makes *The Civil War Diary* an exemplary contribution to the literature of the era. Its editor, Kenneth C. Turino, added significant value with his sensitive and effective handling of the wealth of material which Lieutenant Hodgkins left behind. In the hands of a less dedicated and less competent editor, the reader would have been left mired in redundant detail. A word of commendation also needs to be added for the splendid introduction by Steven C. Fames, who filled in the blank spots in the life of Hodgkins. The rewards are in the reading.

Fred J. Martin, Jr.   San Francisco, California

Joe Brown's Army: The Georgia State Line, 1862-1865, William Bragg, (Mercer University Press, 6316 Peake Road, Macon, Georgia 31210-3960), 1995. Appendix, biblio., index. 175pp. Paper. $16.95.

The military forces that fought for the South during the Civil War consisted of several legally different types of troops. The great majority of units in the Rebel armies were "volunteer" forces raised by the individual states and then transferred to the Confederate government for duty. Readers of Civil War military history, however, soon encounter dozens of other kinds of units—militia, "provisional troops," home guards, junior (and senior) reserves, local defense troops, and so on. We know relatively little about most of these forces.

In *Joe Brown's Army* William Harris Bragg tells us the story of one of these obscure military forces—the Georgia State Line. This unit was one of seven legally different bodies of troops raised by the state for its own defense. (The militia, three separate state armies created in 1861, the Georgia State Guard, and the Georgia Reserve Force were the others.)

The State Line owed its being to Governor Joseph E. Brown's conviction that Georgia could not rely upon the distant Confederate government to protect it from the Yankees. The Confederate War Department, after all, had ordered most Georgia volunteers off to the armies in Virginia and Tennessee and would not return them when Brown picked up rumors of a coming Federal invasion and screamed for help. The governor therefore reasoned that the state needed a military force under its own control.

In 1862 the Yankees captured Fort Pulaski at the mouth of the Savannah River and struck at the crucial (and state-owned) Western & Atlantic Railroad in northwestern Georgia. After these events and in response to Brown's pleas the state legislature authorized creation of a two-regiment force that became the Georgia State Line. From early 1863 until it was surrendered by Brown on May 7, 1865, the State Line performed military duty under the governor's orders. Its tasks included suppression of any slave insurrection that might occur, guarding railroad bridges, chasing deserters, garrison duty, and patrolling areas of the state (especially in North Georgia), where there was much opposition to the Confederacy. The State Line troops also operated with Confederate forces in defense of the Georgia coast and in the Atlanta Campaign of 1864. On several occasions they ventured beyond Georgia's borders to take part in operations that directly affected the state. In November 1864, for example, they were at the Battle of Honey Hill in South Carolina. There they helped win a victory that enabled the Rebels to hold on to Savannah for a few more weeks. In such operations, be it noted, Brown placed the State Line troops under the command of Confederate officers and, in general, the state troops fought well.

Bragg's account originated as a Master's Thesis at Georgia College. It is based on impressive research in both published and unpublished sources. Much of the story Bragg tells revolves around Governor Brown's struggle to secure passage of the legislation necessary to create the State Line and his successful efforts to protect that unit from both his political enemies within the state and from Confederate efforts to place the troops under the permanent control of the War Department in Richmond.

There are relatively few personal accounts from men who served in the State Line, and for that reason the book is essentially an administrative history of the State Line units. Where the sources permit, however, Bragg gives us a look at a few of the individual soldiers and some of their experiences. For example, Lieutenant Colonel John M. Brown, one of the governor's brothers, served in the 1st Regiment, Georgia State Line, until July 22, 1864, when he was mortally wounded during the fighting around Atlanta.

The appendices offer brief coverage of a company of the State Line that was used as cavalry, the State Line hospital, "Military Justice in the Georgia State Line," and short sketches of eight members of the unit (seven officers and one enlisted man). Yet another appendix gives muster rolls listing members of the State Line. These rolls are incomplete (no fault of Bragg's) and none dates from a later period than May 1864.

Joe Brown's Army has several weaknesses. The writing style is somewhat wooden—although this is owing in large part to the sources. The book is grossly overfootnoted with 438 footnotes burdening its 129 pages of text, maps, and illustrations. Many of these footnotes should have been consolidated, and some of them insult the reader's intelligence by repeating information that has been given in the text (p. 38, n. 11, for example).

Bragg has a problem with pronouns. He frequently uses a plural pronoun with a singular antecedent. The State Line, for example, was singular, or the State Line were plural, but it/they could not possibly have been both—although Bragg has it/they as both, sometimes in the same sentence (p. 104, for example). The index does not include the names from the roster, an omission that considerably reduces the roster's value. The work would also have been strengthened if Bragg had made some effort to sketch briefly how other Confederate states tried to deal with the question of state military forces. Was the Georgia experience typical? Was it unique?

Joe Brown's Army is a work that can help readers understand the Civil War and the war's impact on the society that fought it. We can hope that Bragg or other scholars will prepare similar studies of other state and local military forces. Such works will help give us a much more complete idea of how the Confederate states (as well as the Confederate States) met the challenges of the Civil War.

Richard M. McMurry   Americus, Georgia

* * *

BOOKS, BOOKS, BOOKS
A Notice of Recent Publications

This is the first in a series of review/notices of publications on the American Civil War. Previously we have attempted to find reviewers for all books submitted by publishers that bore any pertinence to *Civil War Regiments'* niche. What we intended was in-depth reviews, virtually without word limits, to allow a full discuss of contents as well as the reviewer's opinions and reactions to what was included, or omitted, and how well the book was researched and written. Alas, the flood of books, books, books first produced an accommodation that involved presenting synopses of our reviewer's work. Now we go to this format. We will continue to seek full reviews of some books while presenting others in paragraph-length summaries, some with quite personal observations, that will still provide those interested with the basic facts and pertinent bibliographic information if they wish to order the book.

This new approach commences with this issue of *Civil War Regiments* and will continue as long as the publisher wants or your correspondent holds out. Let us begin. Here are notices of seventeen books that deal with some aspect of our favorite subject. Since this whole thing is arbitrary, I have grouped them thusly: letters, diaries, writings; regimental histories; reprints of venerable studies; and special topics.

Among letters, etc., Elizabeth Whitley Roberson's *In Care of Yellow River: The Complete Civil War Letters of Pvt. Pinson Landers to His Mother, with drawings by Stephen McCall* (Pelican Publishing Company, 1101 Monroe St., Gretna, Louisiana, 70053, $11.95 pb), was published in 1994 by Venture Press in Fort Lauderdale, Florida, and has been reissued by arrangement with the author. As the title indicates, it reproduces the correspondence of Landers, a member of the 16th Regiment, Georgia Volunteers, and specifically of a company known as the Flint Hill Greys. The letters were left on the streets of Atlanta for the trash man to collect, retrieved by a passerby, and given to Robertson twenty years later. The letters begin on August 11, 1861, and continued until shortly before Landers' death in October 1863. They are now in the possession of the Gwinnett County Historical Society in Lawrenceville, Georgia.

Georgia Sharpshooter: The Civil War Diary and Letters of William Rhadamanthus Montgomery, edited by George Montgomery, Jr. (Mercer University Press, 6316 Peake Road, Macon, Georgia 31210-3960, $16.00 pb). Perhaps this story and quote will address the flavor best: in 1891, an auditor inspected records in Marietta, Cobb County, Georgia and asked County Clerk Montgomery why there were no records for the years before 1865. The explanation: ". . .that was the date that General Sherman, the son-of-a-bitch, came through Marietta burning our homes, city buildings, and confiscating our food and stock. He is now dead and in hell and I'm glad of it. (p. vii)." Montgomery (February 15, 1839-November 30, 1906), was a member of the Palmetto Guards, Second South Carolina Volunteers, Bonham's Brigade. He participated in combat at Fairfax Courthouse, First Manassas, Chickahominy, Seven Pines,

Malvern Hill, Second Manassas, Sharpsburg, Fredericksburg, Gettysburg, Chickamauga, Lookout Mountain, the Wilderness, Spotsylvania Court House, and Cold Harbor. Not all his observations are as salty as the above quotation, and the diary entries are quite brief.

Norfolk Blues: The Civil War Diary of the Norfolk Light Artillery Blues, edited by Kenneth Wiley (Burd Street Press, Beidell Printing House, 63 West Burd Street, Shippensburg, Pennsylvania 17257), is the diary of John Walters, an immigrant from Holland to Norfolk. Wiley provides an introduction that is biographical and descriptive of the scene in Norfolk during Walters' time there. The bulk of the book is the diary, naturally, which commences on May 8, 1862, and concludes on April 20, 1865. A concluding narrative chapter addresses "Reconstruction and Resumption" in Norfolk. A roster of the men of the Light Artillery Blues, which lists name and rank only, is followed by biographical sketches of varying lengths on each. A few black-and-white photos are included.

A different kind of writing is presented in *"Right or Wrong, God Judge Thee": The Writings of John Wilkes Booth,* by John Rhodehamel and Louise Taper (University of Illinois Press, 1325 South Oak St., Champaign, Illinois 61820, $24.95 cloth). The press claims that "all the known writings of [Booth] are included in this collection. . .More than one-half of this material has never been published before (jacket)." They claim that the most important item included, discovered at the Player's Club in Manhattan, is a funeral oration "similar to Mark Antony's" that makes clear that Booth's hatred for President Abraham Lincoln was formed early and felt deeply. Also included are love letters to a young girl in Boston in 1864 and a diary kept during his flight following the assassination. Excellent illustrations and annotations enhance the presentation. This is quite a scholarly volume.

Among specific regimental studies, we include *Sabres in the Shenandoah: The 21st New York Cavalry, 1863-1866,* by John C. Bonnell, Jr., and *Bloody Banners And Barefoot Boys: A History of the 27th Regiment Alabama Infantry CSA,* compiled and edited by Noel Crowson and John V. Brogden (both by Burd Street Press, Division of White Mane Publishing, Box 152, Shippensburg, Pennsylvania 17257, $34.95, cloth, for Bonnell, and $19.95, cloth, for Crowson and Brodgen). I suppose the latter volume could have gone in the preceding section, but it seems as appropriate here. It was written by Dr. J. P. Cannon, a private in the ranks of the 27th, and portions of it previously appeared in the *Washington National Tribune.* It is a narrative rather than a diary, but the first-person style lends that flavor. Included are the ever-useful tables of battles in which the unit engaged and a roster of members. Illustrations are in the back and lack adequate resolution. Bonnell's study is a traditional narrative and is dedicated to, among others, the author's ancestor, the Rev. George Byron Simmons, a corporal in the 21st New York. Actions covered are principally in the Shenandoah Valley, including New Market and Jubal Early's raid on Washington. Quite brief biographical sketches of unit members, plus some maps and illustrations, are included.

Among the Golden Oldies are Charles W. Ramsdell, *Behind The Lines in the Southern Confederacy*, edited and with a foreword by Wendell H. Stephenson (Louisiana State University Press, Baton Rouge, Louisiana 70893, $11.95 cloth), and John William De Forest, *A Union Officer in the Reconstruction*, edited with an introduction and notes by James H. Croushore and David Morris Potter (also LSU Press, $12.95 cloth). Ramsdell's venerable book began as his Walter Lynwood Fleming Lectures at LSU and was first printed in 1944, reprinted in 1972, and now again in 1977. The lectures, or chapters, are entitled "The Emergence of Wartime Social and Economic Problems," "Experiments in Political Control," and "Failure and Disintegration." A bibliography of all of Ramsdell's writings conclude the volume. Stephenson himself deserves a generous mention; I met him at what was then the Rice Institute in Houston in 1959 when he came down from Oregon to deliver lectures of his own. Green as grass, I was yet to learn of his central role in the founding of the Southern Historical Association and in editing its journal. It is wonderful that real gold endures. Similarly, De Forest's observations during Reconstruction provide a close-up of life in those troubled times, enhanced by De Forest's literary abilities.

Our special topics section offers a variety indeed, beginning with David B. Freeman, *Carved In Stone: The History of Stone Mountain* (Mercer University Press, 6316 Peake Road, Macon, Georgia 31210-3960, $32.95 cloth), that narrates the development of Stone Mountain, located sixteen miles east of Atlanta, Georgia, in DeKalb County, from its beginning as a natural phenomenon to a modern recreational park. The part that will interest most of us, of course, is the sculpture on the face of the mountain of Robert E. Lee and his corps commanders begun in 1915 by Gutzon Borglum but not completed until 1958. Spectacular photos of this work accompany the narrative. And we cannot forget that the second coming of the KKK was born on this promontory as well.

Moving North, we find Kevin Conley Ruffner's *Maryland's Blue & Gray: A Border State's Union and Confederate Junior Officer Corps* (Louisiana State University Press, Baton Rouge, Louisiana 70893, $34.95 cloth) reminds us anew of the agony of the sons of the border states who were pulled and twisted by loyalties to the Union and to the Southern way. Ruffner says that as many as

60,000 Maryland men fought in blue and 25,000 of them fought in grey. This work focuses on 365 men from Maryland who served either in the Army of the Potomac's Maryland Brigade or the Army of Northern Virginia's Maryland Line as captains or lieutenants. The majority of the text is a narrative of their service, but a lengthy section devoted to biographical data on the 365 featured officers offers valuable information on their lives and military records.

Douglas L. Wilson, *Lincoln Before Washington: New Perspectives On The Illinois Years* (University of Illinois Press, 1325 South Oak St., Champaign, Illinois 61820, $26.95 cloth), says that "selections in this book address topics as disparate as William H. Herndon's informants, Lincoln's favorite poem, his mysterious broken engagement, the text of his debates with Douglas, and a previously unknown assault on Peter Cartwright (jacket)." Since we are never going to exhaust our interest in our famed and magnificent sixteenth president, here is one more log for the fire. Wilson concentrated on the struggles of a younger Lincoln than we remember from the copper penny or the five-dollar bill. Few could withstand such intensive investigations of their lives, much less of their young lives, and remain so venerated.

Southern Thunder: Exploits of the Confederate States Navy, by R. Thomas Campbell (Burd Street Press, 63 West Burd Printing House, Shippensburg, Pennsylvania 17257, $19.95 cloth), follows the author's previously published *Gray Thunder* with more stories of the Confederacy's warships, especially the *Sumter, Arkansas, Cotton, Georgia, Advance,* and *Tennessee*, and the men who sailed them. The book is illustrated heavily with photos, drawings, and maps.

B. Keith Toney's *Battlefield Ghosts* (Rockbridge Publishing Company, Box 351, Berryville, Virginia 22611, $12.00 pb), presents stories appropriate for late-evening camping on or near our battlefields. Toney is a licensed guide at Gettysburg National Military Park and a good story teller. The history is good; the stories are the thing.

Monocacy: The Battle That Saved Washington, by B. Franklin Cooling (White Main Publishing Company, Box 152, Shippensburg, Pennsylvania 17257, $34.95 cloth), addresses the action at Monocacy, Maryland, during Robert E. Lee's offensive against Washington in 1864, or what we call Jubal's Raid. The thesis is that this was a decisive battle because hard fighting there delayed the Confederates and provided time to rally defenders for the nation's capital. Lost time there, it is suggested, cost the Confederacy the opportunity to change history.

Noel C. Fisher, *War At Every Door: Partisan Politics and Guerrilla Violence in East Tennessee, 1860-1869* (University of North Carolina Press, Box

2288, Chapel Hill, North Carolina 27515-2288, $29.95 cloth) discusses the fierce struggles over secession, reluctance to accept Confederate authority, and the partisan warfare that began before and continued after the official Civil War in his troubled area. We are working from an uncorrected proof here, but the photos, few as they are, look excellent.

Comes now finally, Cities And Camps of the Confederate States, by Fitzgerald Ross and edited by Richard Barksdale Harwell (University of Illinois Press, 1325 Oak Street, Champaign, Illinois 61820, $15.95, pb). This book was written in 1865, appeared again in 1958, and now is published once more. It is an English visitor's view of the South, fraught with all the dangers and advantages of travel literature.

In summary, a lot of books pour from the nation's university and public presses. We will continue our efforts to provide reviews or notices of them.

Dr. Archie P. McDonald
Department of History
Stephen F. Austin State University

The Battle of Carthage:

An Interview with Author David C. Hinze

Interviewed by Theodore P. Savas

The following interview with historian David C. Hinze is also printed in his newly-released book, co-authored with his former student Karen Farnham, entitled *The Battle of Carthage: Border War in Southwest Missouri, July 5, 1861* (Campbell, CA 1997). Since it compliments Jeff Patrick's edited article on Guibor's Battery, and is particularly appropriate for this issue of *Civil War Regiments*, we decided to publish it for our readers in its entirety.

* * *

TPS: My initial concern with your original proposal was whether or not a small battle west of the Mississippi River deserved a full-length book. Why does it?

DCH: Because what happened in Missouri in early 1861 set the stage for the remainder of the war in both that state, which was a critical border region, and much of the Trans-Mississippi Theater.

TPS: Fair enough. Give us an overview of the situation in Missouri on the eve of the Civil War.

DCH: Missouri was a state of divided loyalties. By 1860 the eastern counties, primarily centered around St. Louis, were more economically aligned with Northern states than the western or interior regions. St. Louis also had a large immigrant population, primarily German, and far fewer slaves than the inland counties. The Germans were also staunchly abolitionist in their leanings. But, Missouri had a pro-Southern governor in Claiborne Fox Jackson, who was elected on a moderate plank. He publicly steered a moderate course while privately preparing to slip the state into the Confederate fold if and when that time arose. Each side drilled militia units, and each prepared for war. Their focus was the Federal arsenal in St. Louis. Whoever controlled it could effectively equip an army and thus dominate any opponent.

TPS: What were the repercussions of Fort Sumter in Missouri?

DCH: That was the triggering mechanism for war in Missouri. After Fort Sumter, as arsenals and supply depots across the South fell to Southerners, Federal Congressman Frank Blair, with Nathaniel Lyon, launched preemptive strikes against the growing Missouri state militia. The first was at Camp Jackson. That fiasco erupted in bloodshed in the streets of the city and galvanized opposing points of view. Fort Sumter led to Camp Jackson, and the pretense of peace within the state evaporated. Lyon's move solidified Federal control over the arsenal and kept valuable munitions out of the hands of Governor Jackson's private army.

TPS: Describe the events immediately leading up to the July 5, 1861, engagement at Carthage.

DCH: After an attempt to mediate the situation failed, Governor Jackson issued a call to arms and formed the Missouri State Guard. This state militia army (I want to emphasize *state*) coalesced in the interior counties, a pro-Southern area popularly known as "Little Dixie." The State Guard was led by a popular ex-governor and Mexican War hero, Brig. Gen. Sterling Price. Unfortunately for the Southerners, Price got sick and went home, leaving behind a poorly-equipped and untrained army under the command of the governor. Jackson was a crafty politician without an ounce of military sense. [Nathaniel] Lyon moved quickly up the Missouri River and defeated the Rebels at Boonville on June 17. This little skirmish—which was a lot more important that most people realize—forced the state militia to fall back in two separate columns, one from Boonville and the other from Lexington, deep into the southwestern corner of the state. It was Jackson's hope that he could unite his two wings and eventually stop the Federals.

TPS: Essentially he was trading space for time?

DCH: Yes. He really had no other choice.

TPS: How did Lyon respond to Jackson's withdrawal?

DCH: Lyon was aware that a Confederate army—and the distinction is important, because Jackson's men were *state* troops; they did not belong to the Confederacy—was forming in northern Arkansas. Lyon had to keep that army and the Missouri State Guard apart. He was a very aggressive and capable general and he designed an aggressive and pretty bold strategy to deal with Jackson.

TPS: What was his plan?

DCH: His plan was to follow the State Guard and catch it from behind or shepherd it into the corner of the state while a second column under Brig. Gen. Thomas Sweeny marched southwest out of St. Louis to cut off Jackson and possibly destroy him. Lyon's wing was to play the role of the hammer, and Sweeny the anvil. It was a classic pincer strategy.

TPS: For that early in the war, Lyon really demonstrated an offensive streak. . .

DCH: Yes, he was very aggressive. He could have marked time after Boonville and not risked his growing reputation, but he wanted to destroy Jackson. That was his goal and he moved to implement it.

TPS: But the Federal plan ultimately failed. Why?

DCH: In a word, logistics. Primarily it was because Lyon, while a good tactician, was not well schooled in matters of supply. Few generals were that early in the war. He didn't understand how difficult it was to feed and equip an army campaigning in the field far from its base of supplies. His departure south from Boonville was delayed because of too few wagons and bad weather, and Tom Sweeny got mired down for much the same reason in St. Louis and Rolla. Sweeny's column eventually moved southwest through the railhead at Rolla and on to Springfield, but Sweeny remained in the rear dealing with his supply problems. His senior officer stepped in and led about 1,100 men out of Spring-field after the Missouri State Guard. His name was Col. Franz Sigel.

TPS: Was Sterling Price back with the state army at this juncture?

DCH: No, and he was sorely missed. "Old Pap" Price had recovered but was riding south into Arkansas to try and get General Benjamin McCulloch's Confederates to march into Missouri to help the state troops.

TPS: How large was Jackson's command at this time?

DCH: The two state troop columns merged north of Carthage at Lamar on July 3. Jackson's army now numbered about 6,000 men, but only about 4,000 were armed. These are just rough numbers. Organizational records are nonexistent.

TPS: So Sigel marches north and finds Jackson's army. . .

DCH: Much to his discomfiture! (laughter) There was a small skirmish on the night of July 4-5 along Spring River, which tipped off both commanders that their opponent was in the vicinity. Sigel marched his men early the next day, about 1,100 strong and eight field pieces, through Carthage and into the prairie to defeat Jackson. Jackson also had his men on the road early, about 4:00 a.m. The two sides met early on the morning of July 5 about nine or ten miles north of town.

TPS: Describe the initial phase of the battle.

DCH: It was more of a series of engagements, a running battle that covered about twelve hours and more than ten miles before it ended. The Missouri State Guard aligned for battle on a slight ridge across Sigel's axis of advance—across the Lamar-Carthage Road—and waited. The terrain was almost flat prairie land, so they could see Sigel coming for some distance. Jo Shelby gave a good account of himself in front of the state militia, his first engagement of the war. Sigel, even though he was badly outnumbered, marched his men right up to the enemy and deployed. It was all very Napoleonic in form and style. Both sides exchanged artillery fire for about half an hour from a distance of 800 yards. During that time Southern cavalry, which was placed on both wings, separated from the main body and attempted to envelop Sigel, who had no cavalry of his own.

TPS: The realization of what was happening to him must have come as quite a shock!

DCH: (laughing). More than he ever let on. He also had thirty-two baggage wagons a couple miles behind him, and he was miles from any support. His primary concern was to protect his wagons and extricate his men.

TPS: How did he get out of such a tight spot?

DCH: That's an interesting question and we spend a substantial amount of the book discussing the issue. He withdrew from the initial fighting at just about the last moment he could do so. He then deployed a small but powerful rear guard at Dry Fork Creek, a mile or so behind his first position of the morning. Dry Fork is a deep stream with wooded and steep banks and just one ford. It was perfectly suited to a rear guard defense. Christian Essig and his four artillery pieces were directed to hold the ford with the assistance of four companies of infantry. Sigel essentially utilized his superior firepower just long enough and effectively enough to hold the Southerners at bay while he slipped his wagons and the majority of his infantry toward Carthage.

TPS: And even with a large arm of cavalry and relatively open terrain the Southern-ers could not catch him? That is just incredible?

DCH: That is one of the mysteries of the battle. It is indeed incredible, although no one has seriously tried to explain why. The simple answer is that the cavalry was poorly handled—and I am being generous. General James S. Rains, the Eighth Division com-mander of the Missouri State Guard, led his troopers personally, and he did not have a clue as to what he was doing. Walk the terrain with battle reports in hand and it doesn't take long to figure out Rains (and most of the cavalry leaders) were in way, way over their heads. Sigel's artillery had earlier stunned the horsemen more than they let on in their reports and drove both wings further out, allowing him time to disengage south to Dry Fork. The Southern infantry was also disrupted from the artillery fire and had a problem getting started after him.

TPS: What happened at Dry Fork?

DCH: The real pitched fighting of the battle took place there. A classic artillery duel was waged between Hiram Bledsoe and Essig; Bledsoe and his crew took a terrible pounding. When the Southern infantry was relatively well aligned, a strong assault was launched against the creek. The men fought at close range for about half an hour over the wooded banks until Sigel's men finally fell back. The fighting was so fierce that many of the men called the day-long fight the battle of Dry Fork instead of Carthage.

TPS: So Sigel was driven from Dry Fork?

DCH: Well, we're not sure. Sigel says he learned he was flanked by cavalry and withdrew, although that may only be part of the story. I personally believe he was flanked by infantry crossing the creek and decided to withdraw. . .

TPS: But the Federals actually were flanked further south by cavalry?

DCH: Yes, that's true, in what turned out to be the best opportunity for the Rebels to defeat Sigel and capture his entire column.

TPS: So what happened?

DCH: Colonels Benjamin Rives and Ben Brown and some 500-700 troopers had managed to cross Dry Fork, slip around Sigel's right flank deep into his rear and take a position behind a small stream that cut across Sigel's front. Buck's Branch Creek, like Dry Fork, had only one narrow and very muddy ford. If the Southerners could hold the ford for any length of time, their infantry, which was just a couple miles back, could strike Sigel from behind. It was a perfect situation for them and a terrible predicament for

Sigel. The ford was a real logistical bottleneck, and the Southerners were present in sufficient numbers to cause a real problem.

TPS: And yet Sigel managed to escape. . .

DCH: This is a really fascinating part of the story and I don't want to spoil it for the readers. Suffice it to say that he wiggled out of a very tightly-drawn box. The man had lots of luck on retreats!

TPS: . . .and reach Carthage?

DCH: Eventually, yes, but it was a close-run affair.

TPS: Which officers handled themselves with distinction on the Southern side? Obviously not Rains!

DCH: (laughing). No, not Rains, or Ben Rives either, for that matter. I think Colonel Richard Hanson Weightman contributed largely to the victory. He led a brigade in Rains' Division like a veteran and did a great job. I think he was the best infantry commander on the field. He kept it together pretty well and drove his men forward relentlessly. If he hadn't been killed at Wilson's Creek, I think he would have gone on and done great things. Mosby Parsons also performed very well at the head of his division. He went on and carved out a very respectable career. The Confederacy misused Parsons. He was very capable.

TPS: Like Rains, you don't have much good to say about Governor Jackson.

DCH: Well, whatever we wrote we tried to be objective and evenhanded. Jackson is a real enigma. He disappears from the written record as soon as the battle is ready to begin. In fact, not once is he mentioned in any of the nine Southern reports that cover a twelve to seventeen hour span. There is this story that has gained credence over the years, largely local lore, that Jackson turned over command of the army to James Rains just before the fight. Karen [Farnham] and I believed it until we studied all the battle reports and realized that there isn't a single shred of evidence to support that and quite a bit that disproves it. In fact, we went into this project with lot's of preconceived notions because of what others had written, and much of it is simply wrong.

TPS: So Rains did not command the army. That is just a myth?

DCH: We think so, yes. Like all battles, Carthage has a bushel full of them.

TPS: Anyone stand out on the Federal side?

DCH: Francis Hassenduebel, who led a battalion of the Third Missouri, seems to have contributed significantly to the end result. Christian Essig handled his guns very well throughout the day. You know, it is interesting that Sigel chose Essig for the toughest task of the day [holding Dry Fork Creek], and then ignored him in his battle report! Sigel credited instead the head of his artillery, Franz Backoff. We're not sure, but we think Backoff was just "along for the ride," so to speak, at Carthage. He was also a crony of Sigel's from the old country.

TPS: What is your analysis of Sigel's generalship during the campaign?

DCH: Sigel's performance was typical of his pre-Civil War career in Europe, where he fought with the German Revolutionaries in 1848. He was trained at a Prussian academy and Sigel was a text book type of general. Whenever situations became fluid or changed dramatically from his preconceived notions of how the fighting should develop, he usually had no contingent plan other than to withdraw. But, he could keep his head pretty well during retreats. He was a soldier full of contradictions.

TPS: He struck me as being incredibly overconfident.

DCH: Sigel was very overconfident and he badly underestimated the danger posed to his regiments by the Missouri State Guard. I think he knew Jackson's army was a semi-organized rabble, but it was still a dangerous enemy. Sigel thought that training and good artillery would overcome numbers, but in this battle they tended to neutralize each other.

TPS: So Sigel gets a mixed review. . .

DCH: (sigh). His initial blind search out of Springfield was foolhardy. Look, he was out seeking a battle in enemy territory with an enemy that he knew outnumbered him. I think he was counting on sheer discipline to win the day at Carthage, and the terrain was perfect for a European-style battle that he favored. Sigel bashing is a popular sport among Civil War historians, and I will grant you that he demonstrated on several fields that he was not a capable field commander. He bungled the beginning of the fight at Carthage about as badly as you can . . .

TPS: But his retreat was well performed. . .

DCH: Yes it was. He fought the rest of the day as well as anyone could have done under very trying and stressful circumstances. He utilized his strengths and exploited the terrain to extricate his men and wagons.

TPS: What would have happened, in a larger sense, if Sigel had defeated Jackson's men—if it had been another Boonville?

DCH: Well, if either Lyon or Sigel had eliminated Governor Jackson's Missouri State Guard or soundly defeated it in the field again, the war in Missouri would have been radically different. Pro-Southern morale would have sunk like a stone, reinforcements would have been hard to come by and the state would have remained in Federal hands on a far more firm footing than it did. The Battle of Wilson's Creek [August 5, 1861] would not have taken place and Lyon would not have been killed. Many writers overlook Lyon because he was removed from the equation so early in the war, but his passing was a big, big loss to the Union. He demonstrated superior skills as a field commander. He had a lot to learn, but he was willing to fight.

TPS: So why hasn't anyone written a book about the campaign and battle until now?

DCH: This was a difficult project. There are very few firsthand sources on the battle, which is particularly vexing if you want to base your work them and not secondary materials. We have spent years researching this action and little, relatively speaking, has come to light. Almost nothing exists in the Library of Congress, and the National Archives gave up nothing but a few muster rolls and compiled service records. Similarly, letters and diaries and the like are few and far between.

TPS: So the after-action reports were doubly valuable to you.

DCH: Yes, but so many of those are missing. None of the reports prepared by Sigel's subordinates have been found, which means the Federal perspective is largely told through Sigel's very biased pen and a couple of quasi-reliable reminiscences. Half of the Southern reports are missing. It was also very early in the war, just about two weeks prior to the fighting at Bull Run. The battle was fought on the edge of the frontier, removed from large population centers. . .there were not many witnesses.

TPS: In other words it wasn't near Washington or Richmond?

DCH: Exactly. And, no reporters were traveling with either army.

TPS: Did the Battle at First Bull Run steal some of the limelight?

DCH: Compared to Carthage, Bull Run was a immense affair. And it was fought on the doorstep of the North's capital. News of the battle shoved Carthage into undeserved shadows. Wilson's Creek and Lyon's death compounded the situation.

TPS: Was the fight at Carthage the first real Southern victory of the war?

DCH: Actually, yes it was. It was the first real land engagement as well, the South's first true field victory. It went a long way toward buoying the Southern cause in the Trans-Mississippi. . .

TPS: What about Philippi or Big Bethel?

DCH: Well, at Philippi there was no pitched fighting and far fewer men involved. You hear a lot about Big Bethel, and the opposing forces at Bethel outnumbered those on the field at Carthage. What you don't hear is that only a small portion of each side managed to get into the fight [at Big Bethel]. Plus, it was not part of a large land campaign with the possibility of affecting the course of the war in the area in which it was fought.

TPS: What other ramifications came about after Carthage?

DCH: The men of the Missouri State Guard gained valuable experience and went on to form the nucleus of the First and Second Missouri brigades. As you known, these were two of the premier combat units of the war. Franz Sigel's defeat also allowed the linkage of Price's Missourians—and I reemphasize *state* militia—and McCulloch's Confederate army. This combined force defeated Lyon a month later at Wilson's Creek. Carthage also kept the Granby lead mines in Southern hands, and kept Southern morale up, at least for a while.

TPS: You spoke earlier of Sigel's strength in artillery and the Southern advantage in horsemen. I found the battle fascinating from the perspective of mobility versus firepower.

DCH: In many respects that is what this battle was all about. Sigel had two well-drilled and disciplined artillery batteries, eight guns in all, against seven light (primarily 6-pound) Mexican War-vintage Rebel pieces with poorly-trained crews and inferior homemade ammunition. Not much of a match. . .

TPS: The exchange at Dry Fork Creek proved that.

DCH: Yes it did. Sigel also had a powerful infantry component. Most of his soldiers fielded rifled muskets or .69 caliber smooth bores, while the State Guard had a wide assortment of arms, from squirrel rifles and shotguns to pistols and hunting knives. So Sigel had more firepower and discipline. The key ingredient he lacked was cavalry. He did not have any and was burdened with a large train of wagons which slowed him down even more. The State Guard, on the other hand, had about 1,000 horsemen positioned on each wing of the army and generally open or partially wooded terrain over which to maneuver.

TPS: And mobility won the day?

DCH: It is not as clear cut as that. The mobility and speed of the State Guard cavalry turned Sigel's flanks and forced his retreat several times, but decisive victory eluded the Southerners. . .

TPS: Defined as the capture or destruction of Sigel's small force?

DCH: Yes. Federal artillery—especially Essig's pieces—preserved Sigel's career and allowed him to survive. Complete or near-complete destruction was well within Southern reach on two or three occasions. Sigel was literally sitting in Governor Jackson's palm and he was unable to close more than one finger at a time. And Sigel kept wriggling out of each situation. That he was able to do so was largely attributable to inexperienced Southern cavalry leadership and well-applied Federal firepower.

TPS: The Missouri State Guard was really a colorful organization. How effective as a fighting force was it at Carthage?

DCH: We really need more firsthand accounts to make that judgment, and we don't have them. So much of what happened is speculation and logic. It's important to remember that the State Guard, at this early stage, was barely organized. It was a militia body of inexperienced troops led by inexperienced, and in many cases inept, leaders. The rank and file endured significant hardships and still fought remarkably well. This is especially true when you realize that they were untrained, poorly-equipped and haphazardly armed. Certainly the State Guard gave a good account of itself.

TPS: So whatever weaknesses it had started at the top?

DCH: Yes. The rank and file went on to prove themselves as superb soldiers. Jackson, by virtue of his gubernatorial capacity, was the army's leader at Carthage. What most people ignore is that he failed to take any role in the fighting. Some of the writing produced on this battle, Thomas Snead's [Jackson's aide-de-camp] in particular, is often little more than a thin attempt to cover up for Jackson's negligent handling of the army. I think the answer is pretty clear. He left his four division commanders to fight on their own hooks, and three of the four did a pretty good job. Don't forget, they were also inexperienced.

TPS: Anything else you would like to add about either the battle or your book?

DCH: [Pause] Yes, a couple things. First, readers should keep in mind that the situation here, I believe, was unique. You have Federal troops under Nathaniel Lyon and Franz Sigel engaging state troops—militia—under a state governor. The Missouri State Guard was not part of the Confederate army. That fact alone makes this engagement significant. I mean, imagine one of today's governor's leading armed men against our army. It was an amazing situation.

TPS: Yes, it was. And second?

DCH: I have studied this battle for years and Karen and I have walked the ground many, many times. We started this project believing certain things because we had read or heard about them for so long. After studying the battle reports and other firsthand accounts, we realized much of it was either simply wrong or open to serious debate. . . .

TPS: For example?

DCH: Well, the Southern divisional alignment was different than we had been led to believe, and several dramatic stories about the battle turned out to be impossible and largely myth.

TPS: In other words, your interpretation of the fighting differs substantially from conventional accounts?

DCH: Yes. But in all matters we strove to be objective and thoughtful in our interpretations and conclusions. Ultimately whether we agree or disagree with another writer or historian is irrelevant. Our goal is to focus attention on the early war in Missouri. If we can successfully do so, everyone benefits, and more scholars will pay attention to the war in the Trans-Mississippi Theater.

TPS: I am going to set you up here. This is your first book. How are you going to handle readers who take you to task for your conclusions?

DCH: Everyone is entitled to their own opinions, of course. We tried to base all of our conclusions on the best available documentary evidence. Some of it is admittedly very sketchy. Assuming they read the book and *then* disagree about something, I would only ask that they explain their positions and show me manuscript sources that support their contentions. This is still a labor of love under construction, and if anyone has anything to share, we would appreciate hearing from them.

INDEX

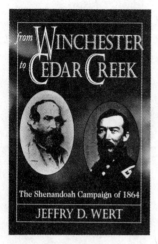

The Death of General Sedgwick, *by Julian Scott, courtesy of the Historical Society of Plainfield/Drake House Museum*

The Battles for Spotsylvania Court House and the Road to Yellow Tavern May 7–12, 1864

Gordon C. Rhea

A riveting sequel to Rhea's highly acclaimed *The Battle of the Wilderness, May 5–6, 1864*

"Gordon Rhea's *Spotsylvania* is a splendid piece of historical research and writing. It unquestionably will be the definitive word for decades to come on that pivotal confrontation between Lee and Grant, and is destined for recognition as one of the great military classics on the Civil War in Virginia."—Robert K. Krick, author of *Stonewall Jackson at Cedar Mountain*

A Dual Main Selection of the History Book Club
Illustrated • $34.95

Brothers in Gray
The Civil War Letters of the Pierson Family
Edited by Thomas W. Cutrer and T. Michael Parrish

"This is an outstanding collection of contemporary Civil War letters written by a set of brothers from Louisiana who served in the Confederate Army. Splendidly edited, the work is highly recommended to all who are interested in the vicissitudes of life among the soldiers of the great conflict."—Charles P. Roland, author of *Albert Sidney Johnston: Soldier of Three Republics*

Illustrated • $34.95

Maryland's Blue and Gray
A Border State's Union and Confederate Junior Officer Corps
Kevin Conley Ruffner

"Ruffner's astute analysis of the junior officers from Maryland illuminates two societies on a collision course, in this case within the boundaries of a single state. With remarkable mastery of the extensive archival sources as well as skillful use of the printed evidence, Ruffner demonstrates in detail how the sectional struggle transformed the lives of his hundreds of subjects. [This] is an invaluable tool for all scholars and students of the Civil War who wish to understand a pivotal population in this pivotal state."—Michael P. Musick, National Archives and Records Administration

Illustrated • $34.95

LOUISIANA STATE UNIVERSITY PRESS
P.O. Box 25053 • Baton Rouge, LA 70894-5053 • Credit card orders: 800-861-3477